I0824158

TRUMP 2.0

TRUMP 2.0

The Revolution That Will Permanently Transform America

SEAN SPICER

Regnery books may be purchased in bulk at special discounts for sales promotion, corporate gifts, fund-raising, or educational purposes. Special editions can also be created to specifications. For details, contact the Special Sales Department, Regnery, 307 Fifth Avenue, 4th Floor, New York, NY 10016 or info@skyhorsepublishing.com.

Regnery® is an imprint of Skyhorse Publishing, Inc.®, a Delaware corporation.
Visit our website at www.regnery.com.
Please follow our publisher Tony Lyons on Instagram @tonylyonsisuncertain.

10 9 8 7 6 5 4 3 2 1

Library of Congress Cataloging-in-Publication Data is available on file.

Cover design by Brian Peterson
Cover image by Getty Images

Print ISBN: 978-1-5107-8620-2
Ebook ISBN: 978-1-5107-8621-9

Printed in the United States of America

Contents

Foreword

In November 2024, we won the most important election victory in the history of our country, and we saved America from destruction. With the help of incredible hardworking patriots all across our land, we won all seven swing states by millions of votes, we won the Electoral College by 312 to 226, we won the popular vote for the first time of any Republican in decades, and we won 86 percent of all counties in America, 2,700 to 525. It was a sweeping mandate to Make America Great Again—and that is exactly what we are doing.

When I took office on January 20, 2025, I inherited a nation in crisis. Joe Biden gave us a stagnant economy, inflation at record levels, a wide-open border, horrendous recruitment for military and police, rampant crime at home, and wars and chaos abroad. Our country was being laughed at all over the world.

But since that glorious day, we have seen the most dramatic turnaround of any country in history. Today, our economy is booming, incomes are rising, investment is soaring, inflation is plummeting, our border is closed and totally secured, and America is respected again all over the world—all because we have a president who puts America First.

In our first year, we passed the largest tax cuts in history, the largest regulatory cuts in history, and the largest spending cuts in history. Economic growth has exploded to numbers unheard of in recent times, and in twelve months, I secured a record-breaking $18 trillion dollars of investment into the United States. A short time ago, we were a DEAD country—now, we are the hottest country anywhere in the world.

We are rapidly rebuilding the greatest economy in history with big wage gains, and falling prices for energy, mortgages, and other pillars of the American Dream. In 2025, the murder rate saw its single largest decline in recorded history, reaching the lowest level in 125 years. I secured Most Favored Nation Agreements to achieve the largest reduction in drug prices in history—with price differences of 300, 400, 500, and even 600 percent. We got Critical Race Theory and Transgender insanity out of our schools—and we got men out of women's sports. We made eight peace deals in ten months, including ending the war in Gaza. In January, we captured the outlaw terrorist Nicolas Maduro and brought him back to face American Justice. And with a historic operation in Iran, we are ensuring that the world's number-one state sponsor of terror never obtains a nuclear weapon. For decades, presidents have been trying to solve these problems. I actually solved them.

In everything we do, we are fighting for the law-abiding, hard-working people of our country. This is the essence of "Trump 2.0," and there are few people who understand it better than my friend and former White House Press Secretary Sean Spicer. Sean has been with us since the beginning. He played a central role in helping us defeat Crooked Hillary Clinton in 2016—and he has been a warrior for our cause ever since.

If you want to understand the people, the policies, and the process of my second term in office, read this book. I hope you enjoy it, and always remember—the best is yet to come.

President Donald J. Trump
Washington, DC
March 2026

Introduction

One of the difficulties of writing a book titled *Trump 2.0: The Revolution That Will Permanently Transform America* is that the president is constantly making America great again.

By the time this book goes into production, there will be new people, policies, and processes that are making the United States once again work for the American people.

While I will continue to cover those victories on *The Sean Spicer Show*, it's important to take a moment to reflect how far we have come since Trump took office on January 20, 2025.

Most presidents hope for a signature win during their four years in office, but think about what less than a single year has meant for the Make America Great Again movement.

The White House website has an extensive list of President Trump's accomplishments in just the first twelve months back in office.

Has there been a more consequential president in United States history?

I doubt it.

As the president himself forecasted:

"We're going to win. We're going to win so much. We're going to win at trade, we're going to win at the border. We're going to win so much, you're going to be so sick and tired of winning, you're going to come to me and go, 'Please, please, we can't win anymore.' You've heard this one. You'll say, 'Please, Mr. President, we beg you sir, we don't want to win anymore. It's too much. It's not fair to everybody else.' And I'm going to say, 'I'm sorry, but we're going to keep winning, winning, winning.' We're going to make America great again."

What we're witnessing isn't just the beginning of a new administration.

What we're witnessing is the beginning of a new direction for the United States of America.

It's not just one area or one thing that is being reformed.

It's the entire United States government that is being massively transformed.

Just think about President Biden's administration. I would bet that Americans couldn't even name a single member of his cabinet. It was truly a cabinet of forgettables. The Trump 2.0 cabinet, on the other hand, is a cabinet of absolute winners. Just watch the televised cabinet meetings. It's like a monthly accountability report. Trump goes person by person around the table, asking each cabinet member to list their achievements in the previous month, and it's streaming live so there is no hiding. Honestly, I cannot even remember if Biden held a single cabinet meeting. I am sure he did, but clearly there was nothing noteworthy.

Trump 2.0 isn't just the president's second term in office.

It really is the beginning of a new age of American greatness.

As I said at the outset, what makes this term so uniquely different and, in my opinion, consequential in the long run, is that President Trump's second term in office is not sequential.

With the exception of one other president in American history, every two-term president has been back-to-back. While we've had it once before in our history, this is the first time in modern history that it has happened.

The importance of this cannot be overstated.

When you have time to think and plan, you come back more determined, more aware, more focused, and that is what President Trump and his team did in their four years out of office.

For example, look at the role the America First Policy Institute (AFPI) played in launching Trump 2.0.

It is an entire think tank that was established by senior Trump staffers in all areas.

I'm talking about Chad Wolf, Trump's acting secretary of homeland security; Brooke Rollins, who was his Director of Domestic Policy in the White House; and Linda McMahon, who had not only been the Administrator of the Small Business Administration, but also the head of the America First Action PAC during his first term. These are people who are not only loyal to President Trump's vision for America; they are people who carefully plotted his return to office; they are people who understand the policies, the processes, and the people needed to get the job done.

In between the administrations, these were the people who were able to stop, think, and ask the right questions: What would we do if we got back into office? How would we get the staffing right? Who were the right people to serve in a second term? Equally important, who were the people to keep out of a second term? After all, one the great lessons from Trump 1.0 was not just getting the right people in, it was keeping the wrong people out.

Moreover, these were the America First experts who asked: What policies would we implement this time around? How would we get them done? What stopped us during the first administration? What were the obstacles? What were the challenges? How do we overcome them the next time around? AFPI laid out the plans. They not only articulated the outcomes they wanted, but the people, policies, and processes they needed to realize them.

AFPI and the Heritage Foundation became the MAGA brain trust during the four years of the Biden administration.

I met with AFPI to think through the press and communications office at the beginning of the Biden administration. If Trump, or for that matter any Republican, won back the White House, what should be done differently? What would we want this office to look like? How should the staffing be changed or adapted to address the new media landscape? What would our priorities be? How would we restructure this office so it reflects the interests of the American people who voted President Trump back into office? How would we communicate more effectively overall? The time between Trump 1.0 and Trump 2.0 was well spent. It was like a team that plays another at the beginning and end of a season. After the first game, you reflect on what you did well and how you would change at the next encounter.

When you look at the actual policies that AFPI and Heritage both laid out, those policies have or are in the process of becoming realities.

For everything from agriculture, to public health, to how to take care of our veterans, to border security, we had a plan—and that plan started paying off on day one of Trump 2.0.

The *Mandate for Leadership: The Conservative Promise*—also known as Project 2025—was treated as a boogeyman during the campaign. But the dirty secret about Project 2025 is that every four years since President Reagan, the Heritage Foundation has laid out a series of issues that would be helpful to the next administration, the next Republican administration.

What made Project 2025 unique was its scope and its reach. For the first time, they brought in countless additional conservative groups beyond the Heritage Foundation to be part of this project. The list of contributing organizations really is a "who's who" of conservative politics:

Alabama Policy Institute
Alliance Defending Freedom
American Compass
The American Conservative
America First Legal Foundation
American Accountability Foundation
American Center for Law and Justice
American Cornerstone Institute

American Council of Trustees and Alumni
American Legislative Exchange Council
The American Main Street Initiative
American Moment
American Principles Project
Center for Equal Opportunity
Center for Family and Human Rights
Center for Immigration Studies
Center for Renewing America
Claremont Institute
Coalition for a Prosperous America
Competitive Enterprise Institute
Conservative Partnership Institute
Concerned Women for America
Defense of Freedom Institute
Ethics and Public Policy Center
Family Policy Alliance
Family Research Council
First Liberty Institute
Forge Leadership Network
Foundation for Defense of Democracies
Foundation for Government Accountability
FreedomWorks
Hillsdale College
Honest Elections Project
Independent Women's Forum
Institute for the American Worker
Institute for Energy Research
Institute for Women's Health
Intercollegiate Studies Institute
James Madison Institute
Keystone Policy
The Leadership Institute

Liberty University
National Association of Scholars
National Center for Public Policy Research
Pacific Research Institute
Patrick Henry College
Personnel Policy Operations
Recovery for America Now Foundation
1792 Exchange
Susan B. Anthony Pro-Life America
Texas Public Policy Foundation
Teneo Network
Young America's Foundation

If you're familiar with these organizations and the important work that they do, it's really hard not to be impressed. The Heritage Foundation led a super team of conservative thinkers—one that looks like the Republican version of the Avengers—to produce this mandate for leadership.

The Heritage Foundation usually does this on their own. But in this cycle, they brought in outside conservative groups that helped them brainstorm the issues that were important to the next administration.

And it wasn't just these groups; it was the people who led those policy blueprints. They were not just a bunch of think-tank academics (no offense, think-tank academics) but America First policy champions, many from Trump's first term, who led the effort in drafting the policy chapters. People who had played in that first game, who saw the opposition forces inside and outside of government, and thought strategically about how game two could be more successful.

Ken Cuccinelli wrote about the Department of Homeland Security. Kiron K. Skinner wrote about the Department of State. Dustin J. Carmack wrote about the intelligence community. Daren Bakst wrote about the Department of Agriculture. Ben Carson wrote about the Department of Housing and Urban Development. Mike Gonzalez wrote about the Corporation for Public Broadcasting. Paul Winfree wrote about the Federal Reserve. Peter Navarro wrote about the case for fair trade. Russ Vought, who had been Director of the Office of Management and Budget, and is back again, wrote about the federal workforce and budget.

As I said, this was the America First Avengers.

And they were uniting to produce a new vision for the United States—a vision that puts the American people first.

At the same time that AFPI was working on its blueprint for the next administration, Newt Gingrich had another group, America's New Majority Project, led by Joe DeSantis, that was testing and polling issues. He noted, "What you have here, that people have not really dug into enough, is that when Trump was forced into the wilderness for four years, the entire team at America First Policy Institute . . . had four years to sit down and think." As he explains, "they had decided early on that you're only going to get the scale of change they want if you're very tough and very determined and every chance you get, you take the opportunity."

The policy planners had serious help on the ground. America First Works, a relative of AFPI, was led by former Trump campaign staffer Ashley Hayek that banked 606,733 votes from no and low propensity voters (the folks that do not come out to vote often) in key presidential counties through what Ashley said was their "aggressive ground game."

Separately, the Sentinel Action Fund, run by Jessica Anderson, was birthed as a Senate-focused operation to ensure President Trump would have strong partners in Congress. While President Trump was winning big in key states and building his operation, Sentinel Action Fund was working to support conservative candidates who would contribute to a strong Senate majority and help get President Trump's nominations though and his agenda passed. To do this, they used tools like absentee and early voting to target the key low propensity voters in Pennsylvania, Montana, and Ohio who could help make these Senate elections "too big to rig." With ground game outreach tools like door knocking and relational organizing, Sentinel Action Fund helped turn out over 550,000 low propensity voters across these three target states.

Many commentators in the left-wing media, and even some in the right-wing media, thought that Trump was down for the count, sitting on the sidelines, and retired for good. Not by a long shot.

Sure, he was in the wilderness—as Newt puts it.

But this wasn't idle time.

He and the team of leaders across the country, who had remained committed to the America First version, were getting ready for the next battle. As the results of the 2025 election showed, this was the battle they won by a landslide.

More to the point of this book, they weren't just preparing to win.

They were preparing to govern.

Having served in the president's administration, I understand the stakes.

I also understand how Monday turns into Tuesday, and then Wednesday, and before you know it your first term in office is over.

For the presidents who have back-to-back terms, that first term quickly turns into the second term.

The staff that you had on January 20 of your first term in office is the same staff you have on January 21 of your second term in office.

Just look at previous two-term administrations. The people, the policies, and the processes of the second term look like a mirror image of the first term.

Of course, there's some shuffling that happens. There are some minor adjustments. But big picture, these don't look like two different terms in office. They look like one long term in office.

There is no downtime to take a step back, to pause, and to ask the right questions—the questions that need to be asked by those in power. Are we fulfilling our promise to the American people? What's holding us back? The people who are with us today, should they be with us tomorrow?

Again, I was in the first administration.

I know that there wasn't any downtime.

You don't get downtime when you're running the most powerful country in the world.

That's a problem.

It's been a problem for every president who has served back-to-back terms.

That, fundamentally, is why this administration will be so consequential.

All of those questions over four years. All those discussions about the people, the policies, and the process. All those debates about what we need to do better this time around to ensure that we have the right agenda from day one. All those strategic discussions about how we can prevent the Democratic Party from stopping that agenda. All of these discussions and debates happened before President Trump took office on January 20, 2025.

This is what makes Trump 2.0 different.

From day one, there has been no learning curve. There have been no delays. There has been no confusion about what the agenda is and how it will be implemented. There has been no hesitation through deliberation. The deliberation took place from 2020 through 2024. And now the American people are seeing the results.

This administration started off ready to go on day one.

Just look at the super team that entered power when Donald Trump was sworn into office on January 20, 2025.

Vice President JD Vance, Secretary of State Marco Rubio, Secretary of War Pete Hegseth, Attorney General Pam Bondi, Secretary of Interior Doug Burgum, Secretary of Veterans Affairs Doug Collins, Secretary of Transportation Sean Duffy, Secretary of Commerce Howard Lutnick, Secretary of Education Linda McMahon, Secretary of Energy Chris Wright, Secretary of Treasury Scott Bessent, Secretary of Labor Lori Chavez-DeRemer, Secretary of Housing and Urban Development Scott Turner, Secretary of Agriculture Brooke Rollins, Secretary of Health and Human Services Robert F. Kennedy

Jr., Administrator of the Environmental Protection Agency Lee Zeldin, Director of the Office of Management and Budget Russell Vought, Director of National Intelligence Tulsi Gabbard. Director of the Central Intelligence Agency John Ratcliffe, Trade Representative Jamieson Greer, Ambassador to the United Nations Mike Waltz, Administrator of the Small Business Administration Kelly Loeffler, and Chief of Staff Susie Wiles.

A story published by *Vanity Fair* in December 2025 made it clear why somebody like Susie is so effective. "As the crises of Trump 2.0 pile up—from Signalgate to revenge and retribution to the Epstein files to alleged war crimes on the high seas—Wiles has worked at the center of the storm, the Trump whisperer who sees it all. 'I am entering my ninth year altogether, my fifth year day-to-day,' she says of working with Trump. 'So it's hard to surprise me.'"

This is cabinet full of disruptors, visionaries, and America First loyalists.

This is a cabinet of consequence.

And it is a cabinet that has been supported by other leaders, including Richard Grenell, who is Special Presidential Envoy for Special Missions and President of the Kennedy Center, Border Czar Tom Homan, and Elon Musk, who valiantly led the Department of Government Efficiency—a department that didn't even exist in the previous administration.

In Trump 1.0, many of his senior staff and cabinet officials met each other late in the transition or even in the first couple weeks of the new administration. Not so this time. In many cases they have known Trump for years, if not decades. Pam Bondi and Trump go back decades, Hegseth and the president have known each other at least ten years, and Howard Lutnick and Trump go back even further. Karoline Leavitt served in the first Trump White House, as did fellow communications staffer and social media guru Margo Martin. Communications Director Steven Cheung goes back to the first campaign, and he was part of my communications team in Trump 1.0. The list of long-time relationships in Trump 2.0 goes on, but suffice it to say the getting-to-know-you phase that we had in Trump 1.0 just simply is not there this time.

These leaders getting the job done; they weren't appointed by accident.

All of the change they're implementing—none of it is happening by accident.

It's happening because Donald Trump and his supporters assembled the people, the policies, and the processes for his second administration. They were working while the Left was fighting over the correct pronouns to use, feeling secure in their 2020 win, and wrongfully believing that the America First movement had come to an end.

That was a serious miscalculation.

The Democrats are now facing the painful realization that it couldn't have been further from the truth.

As the *Mandate for Leadership: The Conservative Promise* explains, "To execute requires a well-conceived, coordinated, unified plan and a trained and committed cadre of personnel to implement it. In recent election cycles, presidential candidates normally began transition planning in the late spring of election year or even after the party's nomination was secured. That is too late. The federal government's complexity and growth advance at a seemingly logarithmic rate every four years. For conservatives to have a fighting chance to take on the Administrative State and reform our federal government, the work must start now." As these conservative leaders note, this "is the conservative movement's unified effort to be ready for the next conservative administration to govern at 12:00 noon, January 20, 2025."

We were ready.

We were also lucky that President Biden gave us a new legal precedent to instill our agenda.

I wrote in the *New York Post* in November 2024: "Early in his term, President Biden made history: He fired, en masse, his predecessor's appointees to presidential boards and commissions before their terms ended. On Monday, when President Trump is sworn in for his second term, he should not hesitate to follow the precedent that Biden established. Like every president before him, Trump appointed thousands of people to boards and commissions during his first term. In order to make the Biden administration answer for these unprecedented dismissals, America First Legal, led [by] former Trump aide Stephen Miller, decided to take action. I signed on to the case they filed, which became known as *Spicer v. Biden*."

This was a crucial case, one that would shape the direction of Trump's second administration.

As I explained, "The lawsuit was filed right before my term would have expired—I had no expectation of being reappointed to the board by a Democrat President. The goal was to get the Biden administration to argue affirmatively in court that it had the absolute authority to remove and replace any appointee. As our lead attorney Gene Hamilton [who has since served as Deputy White House Counsel to the president during this second administration] stated: 'Even if the Biden administration prevails in its arguments, President Biden has perhaps unwittingly created a precedent that will be followed by all future administrations.' Gene was right: The Biden arguments, which a court affirmed, will now benefit President Trump."

It wasn't an easy fight.

It's never an easy fight.

"Our case was dismissed by the district court—and while our appeal was pending, the US Court of Appeals for the DC Circuit ruled, in the parallel case of *Severino v. Biden et al.*, that a presidential appointee in a similar position to mine is removable at will by the president. In the end, the DC Circuit clarified the extent of the president's removal authority for such positions, which will be helpful for all future administrations to understand. If President Trump dismisses Biden board and commission appointees on Jan. 20, he will be on firm legal ground—and will simply be following the precedent established, and fought for, by Joe Biden."

Imagine my surprise in February 2025 when a reporter from the *Washington Post* called to ask my response to Trump dismissing the entire board of the then John F. Kennedy Center for the Performing Arts. Taken by surprise, I asked him why he cared about what I thought of the change. "Oh, you haven't seen the statement of the Kennedy Center?" he asked. "They cited your case," he informed me. Apparently they would not fight back, citing *Spicer v. Biden* as the guiding authority for President Trump's actions.

Because of President Biden's actions and the decision of the courts to uphold them in *Spicer v. Biden*, President Trump has now been given more power to put the people in place who will enact his agenda. Equally important, the president now has the power to remove the people who are going to thwart his agenda to make America great again.

A month before the *Post* reached out to me, I encouraged President Trump to take advantage of the power that this case had given him.

On January 16, 2025, I tweeted: "on Monday, when President Trump is sworn in for his second term, he should not hesitate to follow the precedent that Biden established."

On February 14, 2025, the *Washington Post* ran the headline, "How did Trump so easily take over the Kennedy Center? Ask Sean Spicer."

As the *Post* (regretfully) concluded: "An obscure court decision involving Joe Biden's presidential board appointments and Trump's former press secretary was the key to seizing one of America's premier arts institutions."

Not only were Trump and AFPI planning the next administration; under Biden's leadership, they were being given more power to enact their agenda during that next administration.

If you hear any Democrat complaining about what is happening now, please tell them to thank Joe Biden and his team.

You have to love it when the chickens come home to roost.

Politics is obviously a unique terrain of society. The personalities, the legal ups and downs, the intersections with the media, the different branches of power, and the stakes of the game make it a truly unique beast.

At the same time, politics shares similarities with other corners of life. If you think about the months leading up to your first marathon, putting your first college lesson plan together, or preparing for the opening of your first restaurant, you're always going to think about how you would do things differently the second time around.

Many people aren't given that gift of a second chance.

Donald Trump was.

This is unlike any other term that's occurred in the past.

Given the reality that nonconsecutive presidential terms have only happened one other time since 1789, it's possible that we may never have a term like this again in the future—at least in our lifetime.

The Heritage Foundation and the dozens of organizations it collaborated with understood the stakes of all of this when they worked on their report. In many ways, the stakes were as high as they have always been. But, so too, in many ways they were different.

"In the winter of 1980, the fledging Heritage Foundation handed to President-elect Ronald Reagan the inaugural *Mandate for Leadership*. This collective work by conservative thought leaders and former government hands—most of whom were not part of Heritage—set out policy prescriptions, agency by agency for the incoming President. The book literally put the conservative movement and Reagan on the same page, and the revolution that followed might never have been, save for this band of committed and volunteer activists. With this volume, we have gone back to the future—and then some.

"It's not 1980. In 2023, the game has changed. The long march of cultural Marxism through our institutions has come to pass. The federal government is a behemoth, weaponized against American citizens and conservative values, with freedom and liberty under siege as never before. The task at hand to reverse this tide and restore our Republic to its original moorings is too great for any one conservative policy shop to spearhead. It requires the collective action of our movement. With the quickening approach of January 2025, we have two years and one chance to get it right."

They got it right.

We got it right.

Donald Trump's election win is the payoff of years of hard work by conservative thinkers, strategists, and everyday Americans across the country who knocked on doors and showed up at the polls in record numbers to put our president back in office.

Trump 2.0 isn't the end of that hard work.

And it's not the end of the wins.

It's really just the beginning.

My friend and current Deputy Chief of Staff Dan Scavino noted to *Vanity Fair* why this term would be so different than the first. "When we came into office in Trump 1.0," he says, "the Russia hoax kicked in right away, and it was nothing but investigation after investigation after investigation. This go-around, we came in, we won. There's no investigations. We control the House, the Senate, and the White House, and the president can focus on his policies." Scavino says Trump is relentless. "My toughest challenge is honestly keeping up with the president, because he is literally nonstop, he's always go, go, go."

A story in *The New Yorker* in December 2025 noted how the personnel this go-round was critical to its success. "During Trump's first term, his agenda was frequently stymied by what MAGA acolytes consider disloyal political appointees and deep-state bureaucrats. 'Trump One was a disappointment in a lot of ways,' a strategist with close ties to the administration told me. 'People got let in that were not aligned. Everybody is super psycho afraid of being screwed over again.' This time, rooting out perceived internal enemies has become an obsession. Cabinet secretaries have required staff members to take random polygraph tests. A high-level administration official told me that, during one of the interviews for her position, her interlocutor opened his mouth to reveal that he had a MAGA tattoo on the underside of his lower lip. 'It's over the top, but it's the currency of the realm,' the high-level official said. As the strategist put it, 'We've fought too hard to get here—that's just the feeling that permeates everything.' At dinner one night, a lawyer with ties to the administration told me, 'We took power, but we're in a cold war, and we may not win.'"

At the end of year one of Trump 2.0 all the planning is paying off, getting results for the America First agenda. Even the *Washington Post* was forced to admit in a story that "President Donald Trump has signed more executive orders in less than a year of his presidency than he did in his entire first term—repeatedly bypassing Congress and forcing the courts to grapple with the constitutional bounds of his power."

And here is the real kicker, despite the prevailing narrative in the left-wing legacy media, the American people are giving Trump credit. As Open Source Zone tweeted, "Trump is the most popular president of the 21st century at this point in his presidency per RCP." That data from Real Clear Politics shows that Trump's December 14, 2025 job approval is 43.7 percent. In 2013, Obama's was 42.6 percent. In 2005, Bush's was 42.5 percent.

That's what progress looks like.

Chapter 1

Securing the Border

In March 2024, the United States border had all but ceased to exist. On average, there were 4,488 border encounters per day. After President Trump took office for the second time in January 2025, that number plummeted. In March 2025, there were just 264 border encounters per day. On February 1, 2026, the White House noted it had been eight months without a single illegal crossing. Is anyone who has been paying attention for the past four years surprised?

During an interview with two senior officials from the US Customs and Border Patrol on my podcast later that spring, I asked them what changed. And they said there are two things that mattered. Number one, under the four years of Joe Biden, the Border Patrol was not allowed to do their job. They were supposed to stop people from coming into the country illegally and they were directed not to do so. When people came into this country illegally, they were allowed to continue on. They were given a notice to appear for a hearing, knowing full well that they would never show up. They were given the ability to stay in the country legally, and in many cases they were given a hotel room, a phone, and sometimes even a gift card. That stopped day one in Trump 2.0. The Border Patrol was once again allowed to do their job.

But more important is the signal that was sent. The Biden administration made it clear that if you come to our border, you will be welcome. Conversely, when Donald Trump came back into office, he made it very clear the door to illegal crossings was closed. We have a lawful way of entering this country—that's back to being the only way in. The cartels promised vulnerable populations that they could get you into America for a price. That option is gone. The message went out loud and clear: you are not getting in, and if you do, we are sending you back. The actions and message made a big difference.

Just think about the lengths that people take to travel from South America to come to the United States. If you know that the door is closed, you're not going to risk that dangerous trek. But if you believed it was open, you might be willing. Making it very clear that we will not let you in—and that if you do get in, we will send you back—has deterred a ton of people.

What Trump is doing isn't political. This isn't a Republican policy or a Democratic policy. It's not conservative policy or liberal policy. It's just common sense. If you want to have a country, you need to have borders. Borders are what distinguish one country from the next. If you do not have borders, you do not have a country. And if you treat your borders as little more than a line in the sand, then people are going to cross that line.

This is not some kind of esoteric political theory. You don't need to read John Locke, Thomas Hobbes, and Immanuel Kant to grasp it. You don't need a JD from Harvard or a PhD in philosophy from Princeton to understand what happens when millions of people cross your border illegally. You cease to have a country.

People who have worked with me know I often repeat the mantra: data doesn't lie. And the data shows that the Biden administration and various states under his leadership incentivized illegal immigration. The Department of Government Efficiency, which hadn't even been in operation for a year, discovered that the Federal Emergency

Management Agency, FEMA, sent $59 million to luxury hotels in New York City. Why? To house illegal immigrants.

FEMA's primary role is to provide emergency disaster assistance; this is money that should be dedicated for American citizens who have survived disasters. Back in September 2024, Hurricane Helene devastated North Carolina. There were two thousand landslides. WLOS NEWS 13, reporting from Henderson County, described the scene as "a living nightmare." Mark Oliver, a co-owner of Foundation Woodworks, saw his business drowned in sixteen feet of water. The front of the building fell off. He did not have the proper insurance to cover the $500,000 in damages. "If you'd ask me what I was doing, I was going to quit and go work for a friend," he said. "Bankruptcy was something we were looking at, which was scary." Fortunately, his church and other volunteer organizations helped him. Do you think he would have benefited from a portion of that $59 million?

The wildfires at the beginning of 2025 destroyed much of California. In January of that year, Democratic Mayor of Los Angeles Karen Bass was traveling in Africa as her city burned. Her incompetence was on full display when she told Californians to get help "at URL." "If you need help, emergency information, resources, and shelter is available. All of this can be found at URL," the blundering mayor explained as she read from a script. Californians are right to be angry at the governmental incompetence that was both a prelude and a response to the wildfires. As David R. Henderson of the Hoover Institution noted, "The extent of destruction from the Southern California wildfires is due, in part, to government ownership of water distribution and government's failure to take care of tinderbox forests. That's not the end of it. In highly regulated California, I predict, local governments will continue to put roadblocks in the way of rebuilding." Don't you think these Californians should have had access to that $59 million?

This just illustrates that the crisis at the border isn't just a crisis at the border. It's a crisis that affects many corners of our government, even corners like FEMA—which, by any reasonable measure, should not be involved in funding illegal immigrants, and it most certainly should not be funding them at the expense of the American people. So when President Trump talks about stopping criminal illegal immigrants quite literally in their tracks, he's also talking about putting an end to this era of widespread government malfeasance and malpractice.

Again, this shouldn't be anything other than common sense. And to be frank, outside of the liberal media, this is common sense. A public opinion research poll that was published by the Pew Research Center on February 15, 2024, asked many Americans it they thought "the US government is doing a bad job handling the migrant influx." According to the data, 80 percent said yes. Of those surveyed across the political spectrum, 84 percent of US adults who were polled believe that "US immigration policies will make it easy to stay in the country once they arrive." Seventy-seven percent of Americans polled also believe the border situation is a "crisis" or a "major problem." A mere 17 percent believe it's a "minor problem," and just 4 percent believe it's "not a problem."

Among liberals, the concern dissipates. Just 15 percent believe "the large number of migrants seeking to enter the US at the border with Mexico" is a "crisis." But these partisans on the Left are the outliers. Even Democrats and those who lean left were fed up with that was going on. 22 percent believed there was a crisis, and another 44 percent believed this influx of immigrants under the Biden administration was a "major problem." As Pew concludes, "only about a quarter of Democrats and even fewer Republicans say the government has done a good job dealing with large number of migrants at the border."

As a reminder, this analysis comes from the Pew Research Center—not from a conservative think tank like the American Enterprise Institute or the Heritage Foundation.

Outside the left-wing echo chambers—where liberals contend that we should give "legal status" and a pathway to citizenship to anyone who makes the trek, that we should have open borders, that every city in the US should be a sanctuary city, that we shouldn't deport people, even people who have committed violent crime against native-born citizens—most Americans, including many traditional Democrats, share these concerns on immigration policy. The border dissolved under Biden. His policies exacerbated crime, the flow of drugs, lower employment rates, and they even cost us critical funding from government agencies like FEMA. This single issue was a major reason why the American people re-elected Donald Trump.

I can somewhat understand why affluent liberals who live in cities like San Francisco, Boston, and New York City support sanctuary cities. I can somewhat understand why they don't want a wall at our southern border. I can even somewhat understand why they supported President Joe Biden's global invitation to anyone anywhere who wanted to come to the United States, legally or not. I can understand it because I know that they know that they don't believe it really affects them (although I would argue they might think it, but it's not true). It's not their jobs that are going to be taken. Peter Stern, the CEO of Peloton, doesn't have to worry about an undocumented immigrant undercutting him for lower wages. Sheryl Sandberg, the ex-COO of Meta (formerly Facebook), won't ever lose her job to an illegal immigrant. They are, in more ways than one, isolated from many of the most detrimental effects of the Democrats' border policies.

Those effects include crime. Just read the headlines. "An illegal alien MS-13 gang member, convicted of raping and murdering 37-year-old Rachel Morin—a mother of five children—in April, was sentenced to life in prison without the possibility of parole on Monday." "3 Venezuelan Illegal Aliens Released by Biden into US Charged in Texas Capital Murder Case." "Illegal Alien Accused of Attempted Murder for Throwing Molotov Cocktail at Officers During L.A. Riots." You don't have to search far and wide to come across these stories. If you spend more than thirty seconds outside of the paywall of the *New York Times*, you'll come across them. These are the stories that the American people are sharing on X, Facebook, Rumble, Truth Social, and other platforms.

And some of these stories are really, really awful. As reported by journalist John Binder, "a judge sentenced Martinez-Hernandez to life in prison without the possibility of parole, a second life sentence, and another 40 years in prison for raping and bludgeoning Rachel [Morin] to death in what has become known as the most horrific crime in Harford County, Maryland, history." Who is Martinez-Hernandez? He's a criminal illegal immigrant from El Salvador with ties to the MS-13 gang. He shouldn't have even been in this country, let alone on the trail where Rachel was going for a jog. This was a man who had already been accused of murder in his home country.

Because of Joe Biden's border policies, America lost a daughter, a sister, a mother, and a friend.

These headlines are changing under Trump 2.0. Just read the headlines since Trump took office last November. "ICE Arrests Illegal Alien with 38 Arrests, 15 Convictions, Including Sexual Assault." "Illegal Alien, Alleged Accomplice Arrested in Kansas for Oklahoma Kidnapping, Rape Case." "ICE Arrests Illegal Alien Accused of Killing High School Sweethearts in WI." All three of those headlines are from *one* week at the end of August 2025. It's clear that the change that the American people voted for is happening. The Americans who have had to confront these violent criminals on the streets of their neighborhood are starting to feel safe again.

The American people have gotten the message. In poll, after poll, after poll, President Trump is seeing the majority of Americans approve of how he is handling immigration. According to a poll conducted by The Economist/YouGov, the majority of Americans approve of how he is doing. The same is true in a poll conducted by CBS/YouGov, and another by CNN.

The Department of Homeland Security's top public affairs official, Tricia McLaughlin, spoke for the majority of American people when she said, "Under the Biden administration, serial criminal illegal aliens were allowed to terrorize Americans. We are restoring law and order and putting the safety of Americans first. No longer is America a safe haven for the world's criminals."

When the *San Francisco Standard* reported that California Governor Gavin Newsom bought a nine-million-dollar mansion in the town of Kentfield, it made me wonder if he would be moving among the people he so openly welcomed into his state. Let's just say, I don't think you are going to find a large group of MS-13 gang members in his new neighborhood. Can you imagine how differently officials like Newsom might view their own policies if they lived in the neighborhoods full of the people who they supported illegally entering the country? The same is true of Nancy Pelosi. She owns a sprawling vineyard sixty-five miles north of her San Francisco district. Do you think she has to confront members of Barrio 18, also known as the 18th Street Gang, on her street? Of course not. It's the poor and working-class people in California who do. The Left loves to support policies they will never have to deal with—it's always good for thee, just not me.

White House Deputy Chief of Staff Stephen Miller reflected the perspective shared by many Americans when he sat down with CNN. "The people that you don't connect with and understand, the people whose manufacturing jobs have left, who have been besieged by high-crime communities, and who've been affected by a policy of uncontrolled immigration—those voices, those experiences don't get covered on this network."

Karen Bass, the mayor of Los Angeles, tweeted on August 19, 2025, that ICE needs to stand down. "The targeting of Angelenos working at fruit stands and car washes must end. This is un-American." Apparently, it's un-American to remove people who aren't Americans. In Bass's worldview, it's un-American to put Americans first. This is the sort of doublespeak that George Orwell warned us about in *1984*. War is peace. Freedom is slavery. Ignorance is strength. That's the Party's slogan in Orwell's masterpiece. These days, it sounds a lot like the slogan of the Democratic Party.

Rob Henderson, a psychologist trained at the University of Cambridge, didn't come from an affluent background. He came from poverty, and he grew up in a foster home. The military was his path to a better life, and eventually a doctorate at Cambridge. Reflecting on the deluge of erroneous beliefs he has seen among the affluent class of liberal elites, he coined the term *luxury beliefs*. "In the past, upper-class Americans used to display their social status with luxury goods," he wrote, "today, they do it with luxury beliefs." It's a luxury to believe in open borders when you live in a posh neighborhood with zero criminal illegal immigrants. It's a luxury to say San Francisco should be a sanctuary city, when you yourself live in a mansion outside the city. It's a luxury to not have to deal with all the consequences produced by the policies you support.

Remember that study from the Pew Research Center? "A majority of US Hispanics (75 percent) describe the recent increase in the number of migrants seeking to enter the United States at its border with Mexico as a major problem or a crisis." Furthermore, "most say the government is doing a bad job dealing with it." While most people are concerned about the border, affluent liberals are concerned about what pronoun you're using. Even on that issue, the Democrats have missed the mark of the very people they purport to represent. When Pew polled Hispanic adults about the term "Latinx," more than 75 percent had never even heard of it. Just 3 percent use it to describe themselves. In other words, affluent leftists made up a term for Hispanics that made them feel better.

That 3 percent is overrepresented among the highly educated, highly affluent cadre of liberals who control media outlets like the *Washington Post*. They are incredibly overrepresented among the cadre of liberals who control institutions like Harvard, Yale, and Princeton. At Harvard, you can complete a secondary field in "Latinx Studies." If you're a professor, you can be part of the Association of Harvard Latinx Faculty and Staff. Inside Yale's library, you can do research within the "Latinx Studies collection," or study with professors like Albert Laguna, who specializes in "transnational Latinx literatures and cultures." Princeton, for its part, celebrates "Latinx Heritage Month," seemingly unaware of the fact that virtually no one who is part of that community uses that bizarre term. That's just what is happening inside the HYP schools—Harvard, Yale, Princeton, the elite of the elite, the trendsetters in American education. At most other colleges and universities across the country, it's much the same. The professors, administrators, and other campus leaders are utterly divorced from the Hispanic constituencies they purport to represent.

It's the Democrats' distance from real Americans—not the professors who are teaching "Latinx studies" at Yale—that has pushed Hispanic voters toward Donald Trump. As sociologist Musa al-Gharbi reported in *The Guardian*, Trump increased his share of the Hispanic vote between 2016 and 2020. And no, "toxic masculinity" isn't the explanation for that shift. "In 2016, Democrats won Hispanic and Latina women by 44 percentage points; in 2020 they won by 39." Think about that, Trump actually gained votes as the liberal media decried him as a racist and misogynist who only wanted to help white Americans. Hispanics and other groups saw through the lies.

As the data shows, "in 2020, Joe Biden won Hispanic voters by 25 percentage points, and Hispanic voters supported Hillary Clinton by an even wider margin in 2016. But Trump drew nearly even with Kamala Harris among Hispanic voters, losing among them by only 3 points." Who would have guessed? Certainly not the professors at Harvard, Yale, and Princeton, who were occupied writing books about how Trump hates the "Latinx community." And certainly not the legacy media outlets, who thought all his talk about illegal immigration, and deportation, and the border—buttressed by a big beautiful wall—was going to cripple his chances of securing votes from the Latino community.

Yet, here we are.

It's Trump 2.0.

President Trump now has historic levels of support among Hispanic voters.

And as he continues to deport criminal illegal immigrants, secure the southern border, and make our cities safe again—cities that have been plagued by violent gang members who didn't even come here legally—his support among Hispanic voters is likely to continue to grow.

As the Democrats continue to play pronoun games, and downplay the crime in the cities they control, I imagine that their constituencies are slowly going to turn on them.

It's one thing to have the luxury to prattle about open borders from within the safety of your gated suburban neighborhood or, in Congresswoman Pelosi's case, a vineyard; it's quite another when your daughters walk home in a Los Angeles neighborhood controlled by the 18th Street Gang.

One of the unintended blessings of the Biden administration, especially following Trump's successful first term in office, is that it allowed the American people to see just how bad the immigration crisis is under Democratic leadership—and just how effectively it can be dealt with under Republican leadership. The difference between Biden and Trump isn't a superficial difference in decorum, manners, and press releases. It's quite literally about the Americans who have to live in neighborhoods directly impacted by violent immigrant crime: a life-or-death difference.

Those Americans who came here legally, who are putting in the work day in and day out, they actually have a fighting chance under President Trump to create a better life for themselves and their children. Under Trump's leadership, they don't have to worry about their jobs being sold out under the table to the illegal migrant who will work for less money. As the organization Latinos for Trump proclaims, "Latino Americans for Trump is founded on the fact that with President Trump, the Latino Community in this country has a president who is committed to removing the obstacles that keep minorities from achieving the American Dream."

What makes the most recent election results so interesting, in which Trump secured almost half the Hispanic vote, is that it's the Democrats who have been pandering to Hispanics (or as they would say, "the Latinx community") for decades. But Trump 2.0 is proving that policy, not pandering, is what wins the hearts and minds of the Hispanics who came here legally.

As Latinos for Trump contends, "President Trump did more for Latino Americans than any administration in history!" And they have the facts to back it up.

- √ President Trump's pro-growth agenda delivered an economic boom, which drove down unemployment and expanded opportunity for Hispanic Americans.
- √ Under President Trump's leadership, the Hispanic community saw a record low unemployment rate, record high Hispanic homeownership, and record low poverty.
- √ Under President Trump, median real income for Hispanic households surpassed $50,000 for the first time in history.
- √ Nearly 350,000 Hispanic Americans were lifted out of poverty and the Hispanic poverty rate reached a historic low of 18.3 percent in 2017.
- √ Real wages for Hispanic males rose 3.9 percent while President Trump was in the White House.
- √ Under the Trump administration Hispanic household wealth rose by 65 percent.
- √ President Trump delivered the biggest tax cut in history and freed business from stifling regulations, allowing Americans of all demographics to prosper.
- √ President Trump reversed the Obama administration's disastrous policy of easing restrictions on Cuba that allowed more funds to flow to the repressive Castro regime.

- √ The Trump Administration imposed sanctions on the Cuban military and intelligence officials who undermine democracy and repress the Cuban people.
- √ In November 2018, President Trump signed an executive order authorizing sanctions against the corrupt Ortega regime in Nicaragua.
- √ On January 23, 2019, President Trump recognized Venezuelan National Assembly President, Juan Guaidó, as the Interim President of Venezuela.
- √ After taking office, President Trump issued five executive orders that hindered the Maduro regime's ability to sustain its control over the country's economy and state-owned assets.
- √ As of June 2020, the Trump Administration had sanctioned at least 144 Venezuelan individuals or Venezuela-connected individuals, and the State Department had revoked more than 700 visas, including 107 of former diplomatic personnel.

Unfortunately, the Hispanics who voted Trump into office in 2016 have had to deal with backlash from radical progressives who have accused them of betraying their own people.

"Betty Rivas and her husband spent 20 years building up their business from a small lunch wagon to a full-blown restaurant," reported Fox News in 2016, "but now all that hard work is being threatened because she attended a Donald Trump rally. Rivas, who owns Sammy's Mexican Grill in Arizona, said that she has received threats and menacing phone calls after Trump pulled her up on stage during a rally over the weekend while she was holding up a sign that read 'Latinos Support D. Trump.'

"The restaurant owner thought that her encounter with the billionaire businessman would simply be a good story to tell friends, but word of her appearance with Trump—and her sign—spread over Facebook and the comments soon followed. There were calls to boycott Sammy's Mexican Grill, along with other more threatening notes, and then people started haranguing her over the phone. . . . Rivas, who is from Mexico, said that she doesn't want to be viewed as racist and that she supports the Latino community.

"'I want to tell the Latino community that I'm not a racist. I love Mexico. I'm a Mexican,' Rivas said. 'I never thought Donald Trump would have called me up to say hello.'"

That first term in office, many Hispanics risked their lives and their businesses to support Donald Trump, and it paid off.

It's going to pay off again during this second administration.

Believe me: that first term in office, that was just the beginning.

Trump 2.0 is going to initiate even bigger wins for Hispanic Americans.

Since taking office again, Trump is already getting the job done. In spectacular fashion, he launched one of the most impressive joint military operations in history that ended in the arrest of Venezuela's illegitimate leader, Nicolás Maduro, an authoritarian and a drug trafficker who has flooded the United States with fentanyl-laced cocaine. As Pam Bondi so eloquently put it, "Under President Trump's leadership, Maduro will not escape justice and he will be held accountable for his despicable crimes."

His removal wasn't just a service to the Venezuelan people who have been celebrating night and day. It wasn't just a service to the American people who have been plagued by the long shadow of Maduro's drug empire. It was a service to everyone around the world who is impacted by the cartels.

When I sat down with Mark Hall, the Senior Advisor to US Border Czar Thomas Homan, to discuss how President Trump's war on the cartels is impacting their ability to push drugs, traffic people, and otherwise turn a profit from human suffering, he made it clear that they understand the importance of this fight.

"We are adversely impacting the cartels. There is absolutely no doubt about it. . . . They are not going to go quietly into the night, throw up their hands, 'Well, you know, President Trump won.'"

While the cartels refuse to retreat easily, the resolve of our president is strong. He clearly understands the stakes and will fight to stop crime in its tracks.

And he has a built a team with incredible leaders like Mark Hall and Tom Homan who not only have the leadership to do what President Biden said couldn't be done, they also have the willpower.

As I've said before, and as I will no doubt say again, leadership matters—so does willpower.

These men, who both have the tactical knowledge that can only be gained in the trenches, are part of the unprecedented team that Donald Trump has assembled to secure our border and make America great again.

Last year, I was invited on Sky News Australia to discuss President Trump's appointment of former Acting ICE director Tom Homan as the new border czar. "It tells me something very clear," I explained, "that when Donald Trump talked about taking the border seriously, about border security, he meant it."

I've known Tom a long time. This guy means business. President Trump's decision to bring him on board in this new role of "Border Czar" to fulfill this monumentally important role in his administration sent a very strong signal not only to those who are in this country illegally, but those thinking about coming to this country illegally.

Stop right now—you are not getting in.

Tom Homan will not stop. Tom Homan does not yield. If you have ever heard Tom speak, you know this mission is personal to him.

When AOC questioned him during the House Oversight Committee hearing in 2019, he did not pander or falter. He did not mince his words. He was the same Tom Homan I have always known: a man who is not just principled, but unwavering in his commitment to his principles.

Here is part of the exchange during that hearing:

Representative Ocasio-Cortez: So you provided the official recommendation to Secretary Nielsen on family—for the United States to pursue family separation?

Mr. Homan: I gave Secretary Nielsen numerous recommendations on how to secure the border and save lives.

Representative Ocasio-Cortez: But it says here that you—you gave her numerous options, but the recommendation was option three, family separation.

Mr. Homan: What I'm saying, this is not the only paper where we had given the secretary numerous options to secure the border and save lives.

Representative Ocasio-Cortez: And so the recommendation—of the many that you recommended—you recommended family separation.

Mr. Homan: I recommended zero tolerance.

Representative Ocasio-Cortez: Which includes family separation.

Mr. Homan: The same as it is with every US citizen parent that gets arrested when they're with a child.

Representative Ocasio-Cortez: Zero tolerance was interpreted as the policy that separated children from their parents?

Mr. Homan: If I get arrested for DUI and I have a young child in the car, I'm going to be separated. When I was a police officer in New York and I arrested a father for domestic violence, I separated that father from—

Representative Ocasio-Cortez: Mr. Homan, with all due respect, legal asylees are not charged with any crime.

Mr. Homan: When you're in the country illegally, it's a violation of 8 United States Code 1325.

Representative Ocasio-Cortez: Seeking asylum is legal.

Mr. Homan: If you want to seek asylum, go through the port of entry, do it the legal way. The Attorney General of the United States has made that clear.

Watching that exchange, we all knew that this is the man who is going to put the country and the safety of the American people first.

This is the man who didn't need another position in the government—he has retired multiple times from the government. But this is a personal mission for him. He isn't a career politician. He's a patriot. And this work that he does is his life's work.

On the day that President Trump was inaugurated, Tom executed a plan to help make the border secure and deport criminals from our country—criminals that are here illegally. He didn't just randomly pick cities. He didn't just randomly take action—or, even worse, simply consider taking action. He had a plan and he executed it. He was ready for action on *day one.*

This is why Trump 2.0 is so different. They had time to plan, time to think it through, and it shows. Four years out of office may have been the greatest blessing for our side.

When he spoke at the Turning Point USA conference in July 2025, he had a message to anti-ICE protestors: "You want some? Come get some."

Since he became the Border Czar, he has been utilizing all the tools in the law enforcement agency toolbox—from Immigration and Customs Enforcement, to Customs and Border Protection, as well as all the other assets throughout the Department of Homeland Security—to target known criminals who are in this country illegally and deport them.

He knew where to start, he knew how to start, and he knew what levers of government he had to pull—the roles of these various agencies, and how they fit into the overall plan he had crafted. Tom hit the ground running. None of this happened by accident.

Like the rest of Trump's team, Tom Homan is a doer.

A US Customs and Border Protection report from June 2025 noted, "Illegal crossings in June dropped to the lowest level ever recorded—just a fraction of what they were under the previous administration." There were just 25,228 total encounters nationwide, which is the lowest monthly total in CBP history. There were also *zero* parole releases—compare that to the 27,766 who were released in June 2024.

Tom Homan is doing what Biden said couldn't be done. Leadership matters. So does willpower.

As I have said a million times, this is not just a rule of law issue. It's an issue of national safety.

Women and children are being trafficked across our borders. That should outrage every single American. That should have been the focus of the House Oversight Committee hearing where Homan was a witness. AOC should have asked: "How do we use every resource we have to stop this?"

Stephen Miller, who led America First Legal during the four years Trump was out of office, has focused on using every resource we have to stop this. As he proclaimed in a campaign speech for President Trump, "vote for the right to have a secure sovereign border and for the right to have a government that puts American citizens ahead of illegal aliens." As the president's homeland security advisor, he refuses to trade safety for political correctness. "America," reflects Miller, "is for Americans and Americans only."

Trump understands that enforcement can happen without new laws—you just need new leadership. Tom Homan, Stephen Miller, and other people working to keep this nation safe and secure have let ICE and our border patrol agents know that their work will not only be protected, but vigorously supported by this administration. The days of lax immigration enforcement and the Biden caravans are over. Around the world, immigrants looking to enter this country illegally have been put on notice.

All the while, this administration is facing a media that supports and encourages illegal immigration. They often lie by claiming that Trump is at war with immigrants, or he is trying to deport immigrants—notice the sleight of hand? Unless you are a Native American, we are all descendants of immigrants. Trump isn't deporting us. He is deporting illegal aliens (that is the legal term). The key word is *illegal*.

Just look at how the lefties at *Axios* try to frame the issue. "President Trump's plan to deport 'millions' of immigrants has reached a critical point: Its success likely will depend not on removing criminals, but on telling people who are in the US legally they're no longer welcome," Brittany Gibson and Russell Contreras wrote.

This isn't journalism.

This is fearmongering. And to use a phrase they love, it's spreading misinformation.

Notwithstanding the liberal narrative to the contrary, not everyone who is crossing the border is coming here to build a better life for themselves and their children. Gang members, drug dealers, and criminals fleeing the authorities in their home countries all flow in when the border is open.

The drug trade, in particular, is an ongoing threat to American safety that our brave border control agents have to wage war against on a regular basis.

In June 2025, CBP seized a whopping 742 pounds of fentanyl. This is the fentanyl that is sending our sons and daughters, our parents and grandparents, to their graves. While the Democrats are advocating open-air drug markets in cities like San Francisco, it's our border patrol agents who are preventing these drugs from getting into our country.

Ironically, they are getting threatened, doxed, and physically assaulted by progressives for enforcing the law.

Indeed, anyone who cares about stopping the opioid crisis—I'm talking to you Representative Ocasio-Cortez—should be rushing to thank someone like Tom Homan.

It's not an exaggeration that we now have the most secure border in American history.

And it's not just our southern border. President Trump imposed a 25 percent tariff on Canada because Canada has failed to stop the export of chemicals used in the production of fentanyl. In response to the president's tariff, Canada is now dedicating more resources—from manpower to money—to help secure our northern border. It's that kind of security that is going to keep the American people safe. Mark Hall summarized the situation on my show: "The Canadians are our partners in this. They're invested. And they understand." They understand that this is what real change means. They understand that this is what real justice looks like.

This isn't the so-called "justice" of sanctuary cities.

This is the justice that Americans want.

When you look at that list produced by Latinos for Trump, which is by no means an exhaustive list, it really is just accomplishment after accomplishment. To say that Donald Trump is the most consequential president for Hispanic Americans isn't hyperbole. It's what many Hispanics themselves are saying.

If the past three elections taught us anything, it's that Hispanics are sick and tired of the Democrats' pandering. They don't care about "white fragility." They're not interested in "Latinx." They don't want to suffer through mandatory HR trainings about "unconscious racism." They want immigration enforcement. They want the rule of law upheld.

Trump 2.0 is giving them what they want.

Above all, it is giving Americans what they want.

Notwithstanding the racially divisive rhetoric of the Democrats—which they refuse to let go of—the differences between different racial and ethnic communities in the United States are not more important than what we have in common.

At the end of the day, we all want to live in safe neighborhoods. We all want to have good-paying jobs. We all want to feel hopeful about our own futures as well as the futures of our children, and our grandchildren, and their children. We all want to feel pride in our country. We all want to feel like we are part of this country.

Stephen Miller summed up why Trump 2.0 will be so consequential in an interview with *Vanity Fair*. "We came into the second term fully, completely ready and prepared to contend with that bureaucracy and ultimately to impose democratic will onto that bureaucracy."

In November 2025, the White House issued the updated National Security Strategy for the country that stated: "The Era of Mass Migration Is Over—Who a country admits into its borders—in what numbers and from where—will inevitably define the future of that nation. Any country that considers itself sovereign has the right and duty to define its future. Throughout history, sovereign nations prohibited uncontrolled migration and granted citizenship only rarely to foreigners, who also had to meet demanding criteria."

Barack Obama promised "hope" and "change," with all those propagandistic posters, but it's the Republican Party that is now delivering on that decades-old promise. President Biden didn't deliver. There is no way Hillary Clinton or Kamala Harris could have delivered.

There is only one president who can—and will—deliver.

President Donald J. Trump.

Chapter 2

Trade, Tariffs, and Fairness

If you tuned into any mainstream or social media recently, you've probably gotten the impression that America is going through an unprecedented economic apocalypse.

On my podcast, I talked about the rationale behind Trump's tariffs—returning manufacturing to America and leveling the global economic playing field.

On April 2, 2025, what Trump called "Liberation Day," these reciprocal tariffs went into effect, putting other countries on notice that the US is no longer going to be walked over.

In the wake of these tariffs, the stock market took a dive—a predictable result and something that Trump warned would happen in the short term.

While the talk of restoring American greatness is easy to swallow, the process of getting there is a lot harder. It's not going to be easy. After years of allowing other countries basically unfettered access to our country while US companies face high tariff and non-tariff barriers, the return to an America-first economy is going to come with some growing pains and not going to happen overnight.

While we might not get the kind of instant fix that we want, it is definitely worth it in the long run.

Trump's trade policies are about leverage—not ideology.

These tariffs aren't a Band-Aid solution. They address the very heart of the problem.

When you get to the core of things, there will be growing pains.

But do they warrant the kind of reaction we've seen on the Left?

Democrats and the mainstream media have both univocally condemned Trump's use of tariffs, and in some cases cheered for failure.

You may be wondering: When did Democrats become such staunch defenders of companies and workers in other countries?

A quick look back in time reveals many of these Democrats supported the very same policies. But this isn't the first policy they have done a U-turn on.

First there was the turn against electric vehicles. The liberals who had once championed Elon Musk now hurl bricks through Tesla windows. Elon was the environmental hero of the century until he aligned himself with President Trump.

Oddly, the Left is also suddenly deeply concerned about the stock market. Now they're grieving when Wall Street firms struggle. What happened to all that rage from Occupy Wall Street? Weren't these the same people smashing Starbucks windows and posting selfies of themselves flipping off the Wall Street bull? Didn't they want to see The Street burned to the ground? Thirteen years ago, even CBS News had to acknowledge the truth. They published a terrifying segment titled, "Vandalism/violence breaks out during Occupy protests." In it, the glass window of a Nike store is shattered. American Apparel also got hit. So did the banks.

It was that anger—and that momentum—that catapulted Bernie Sanders, then a relatively unknown socialist from the state of Vermont, into the forefront of the Democratic primaries in 2016.

It's a wonder they don't have whiplash from the switch-up.

Take this tweet from Andrew Yang, former Democratic presidential candidate, condemning the Trump administration for deliberately destroying value: "I have never seen so much value destroyed deliberately. This is the worst leadership ever." X users were quick to point out, however, that during his candidacy in 2019, he tweeted that "anyone who pays attention to stock prices as a barometer of how Americans are doing is missing how most people live."

Maybe he changed his opinion between now and then.

Or maybe, like many of his fellow leftists, he's grasping at anything he can to attack Trump—even if it means reneging on his own position.

Because Trump is delivering on so many of his promises, Democrats are forced to resort to these types of criticisms in an effort to manufacture panic and outrage.

This is the same party that has long been advocating the very changes that Trump has initiated—changes that they themselves have been unable to initiate. White House press secretary Karoline Levitt, in a press briefing, pointed out the hypocrisy.

"Democrats have long said that America has been ripped off by countries around the world. They just don't want to admit it now—because it's President Trump who is saying that. In June of 1996, Nancy Pelosi spoke on the House floor. She urged her colleagues at the time to fight against the status quo trade policies that had contributed to America's trade deficit with China."

Pelosi, of all people, should be cheering for President Trump. She should be singing, dancing, and waving red, white, and blue pompoms as Trump addresses the very concerns that she expressed twenty-nine years ago.

She's the one who originally asked, "How far does China have to go? How much more repression? How big a trade deficit? How many jobs have to be lost for the American workers? How much dangerous proliferation has to exist before members of this House of Representatives will say, 'I will not endorse the status quo.'"

"I will not endorse the status quo."

So after years, decades, President Trump takes on the status quo and instead of applause, she helps lead the attacks.

While Trump often refers to Pelosi as Crazy Nancy, a better nickname might be Hypocrite Nancy. After all, it takes an astonishing amount of cognitive dissonance to go from decrying America's deficit with China to decrying Trump's attempt to address it head on as "senseless." Thank goodness she is finally retiring, although I have to admit I am not sure who I will follow to base my stock trades off anymore.

"The Trump administration's flagrant ineptitude," Pelosi claims, "is tanking our economy in a self-inflicted disaster that leaves hardworking American families bearing the brunt of the pain." In a last-ditch appeal, Pelosi actually quoted Ronald Reagan: "We should beware of the demagogues who are ready to declare a trade war against our friends."

Has something changed since her remarks on the House floor in 1996? Am I missing something? Is Xi Jinping no longer in power? Is democracy thriving in Beijing? Does the People's Republic of China now belong to the people? Has China become "our friend"?

To be sure, Hypocrite Pelosi was right twenty-nine years ago. Even a broken clock is right twice a day.

But her public condemnation of Trump's tariffs, her fear-mongering about the next Great Recession, and even her out-of-context appeal to President Ronald Reagan, a man who understood the need to secure America's future in the global order as well as anyone—and who probably just rolled over in his grave listening to his words come out of Pelosi's mouth—it really is a new low.

As President Reagan also said, "You and I have a rendezvous with destiny. We'll preserve for our children this, the last best hope of man on earth, or we'll sentence them to take the last step into a thousand years of darkness."

Representative Pelosi had a moment of clarity about America's future back in 1996. She understood that a dark period in American history could be on the horizon if the problem of China was not addressed. It's a shame that her clear vision of the future has been obscured by the #NeverTrump goggles that she and the Democratic Party refuse to take off.

At this point, the Democrats' hypocrisy is frankly astounding; but it isn't just limited to talking points.

This happened before . . .

In 2022, there was a very similar dip in the stock market, just with one small difference—the man in the White House.

When the market fell on Biden's watch, the media insisted that there was no cause for panic. Biden's surrogates even changed the definition of recession to minimize the appearance of any economic harm, and the media all too gladly repeated the talking points.

But now?

Leftist media is actively stoking panic, making a situation—a short-term dip—markedly worse.

For example, CNBC's Jim Cramer forecasted a "Black Monday," as he predicted a 1987-style market crash.

It never came.

In reality, the market remained relatively unchanged, with the Nasdaq actually closing higher on Monday following the announcement.

Short-term concern about the market is understandable, but the kind of fearmongering we've seen on the Left is totally ridiculous.

The bottom line: restoring American trade is not going to be easy or quick.

If it was going to be a walk in the park, leaders long before Trump would have tried it.

The way I see it, we have two options:

A) We continue down the path we've been on for the last thirty years, dying a slow death as we siphon off our last remnants of economic independence. This is the thousand years of darkness that Reagan warned us about. Other countries charge US companies huge tariffs to do business in their countries while they have almost tariff-free access to our market.

B) We deal with the growing pains of rebuilding an America-first economy to reestablish our independence both financially and in manufacturing. Make America Great Again—it isn't just a campaign slogan. It's an achievable goal.

Trump's all in on option B, and the tide is already turning.

Countries are lining up to make deals to tear down their tariffs, and companies are eyeing US locations to invest in.

The market? As of the publication of this book, we are hitting record highs in the stock market.

To quote the great philosopher Charlie Sheen, "Winning!"

During Trump's first term in office, the country gained ten thousand manufacturing jobs. In the final year of the Biden administration, America was losing an average of nine thousand jobs per month. When the *New York Times* proclaims, as they did in June 2025, "manufacturing jobs are never coming back," it's clear these journalists are not interested in a mindset that doesn't fit inside their Overton window.

As John Carney of *Breitbart* reflects, Trump's actions reflect "a strategic goal: encouraging the reshoring of manufacturing and rebuilding domestic supply chains." Moreover, we're once again attracting foreign capital. Carney sums it up best: "President Donald Trump's tariff policy is about a lot more than raising import duties. They're a lever, and the fulcrum is foreign investment. From chip plants in Arizona to battery factories in the Southeast, foreign companies are pledging billions in exchange for access to the world's largest consumer market. This is the new 'deal economy'—less about rates, more about commitments."

Importantly, we're getting these commitments on our terms.

For too long, America hasn't been getting the deal it deserves. For too long, we've been involved in deals so lopsided that a third grader could tell you they are unfair.

In this day and age, why do we allow other countries to have almost unfettered access to the US market, while facing high tariff and non-tariff barriers from other countries?

One of the things that's so interesting to me about our role in global trade is that it's very similar to our role in the North Atlantic Treaty Organization (NATO).

On both fronts, America brings a tremendous amount of value. In trade, it's the value we bring to the global economy. In NATO, it's the value we bring to defense. On both fronts, we are the ones making enormous contributions—economically, militarily, and otherwise—while it's often other countries who reap the most benefits from those contributions.

Let's just be honest: Do you think it's the United States who benefits from having countries like Luxembourg, Slovenia, and Montenegro in NATO? Or do you think its these countries who benefit from having the United States in NATO?

According to the World Bank, the United States had a Gross Domestic Product of $29.185 trillion in 2024. We contribute 3.4 percent of our GDP to our national defense, which is well above the 2 percent alliance countries had agreed to prior to 2025. Can you guess the GDP of Luxembourg? It's about $93 billion. They contribute 1.3 percent of their gross national income to their national defense; that's just 0.9 percent of their GDP. What about Slovenia? They have a GDP of $72,485,010,000. They contribute just 1.3 percent of their GDP. Montenegro has a GDP of just $8.27 billion. At 2 percent, they're contributing pennies compared to what the United States contributes. If you just look at the raw data, how is this a "good deal" for America? A child could look at those numbers and tell you that there is a glaring problem.

And, by the way, do you know the deal every country made? Every country agreed to spend 2 percent of their GDP on their own defense. The idea is simple: if everyone is individually strong, we are collectively unbeatable. But along the way, most countries got in on the joke. The US will spend well beyond the required 2 percent, so why bother? That's right, they chose to spend their money on roads, bridges, and social services for their own people, while they let the Americans bear the burden. We, the United States, spend by far the largest amount on national defense in dollar terms, which accounts for roughly two-thirds of all NATO countries' combined annual defense spending

With trade, it's the same imbalance. The US not only has one of the largest and strongest markets in the world, it also has one of the lowest barriers to access. That's why other countries love to do business with us. They can come here and face almost no tariffs. Meanwhile, they face almost no non-tariff barriers. What does that mean? A non-tariff barrier, to give you the SparkNotes explanation, is like an automobile emissions standard. If you look at the barrier to entry to a lot of markets in other countries, it's not that they necessarily have a high tariff for automobiles, it's that they have standards that you have to meet for automobiles to get them into the country. Often, it's incredibly expensive for automobile manufacturers to meet these standards. Intentionally or not, it makes these countries less hospitable to Americans companies. In some cases, these countries establish a standard that an American company would likely never meet.

By way of another example, I say: "You can come stay at my house anytime you want, but in order to stay here, you have to learn five foreign languages, count backward from five million, and you have to dance on your head for twenty-five minutes, all while juggling half a dozen bowling pins." Undoubtedly, you would say: "That's crazy. I'll never be able to do that." "Well," I could respond, "that's your decision. I'm giving you an open invitation to stay at my house, but you're choosing not to follow the rules. That's your problem, not my problem." That's what we've allowed to happen in trade. For the longest time, we've allowed countries to have access to our market, while they haven't allowed us the same kind of access to theirs. We've rolled out the red carpet for them, while they have asked us to dance on our heads. At the end of day, all President Trump is asking for is fairness and common sense.

This isn't President Franklin D. Roosevelt's New Deal.

This is President Donald J. Trump's Art of the Deal.

It's Trump's leadership—sharpened by decades of experience as a world leader in business—that will allow America to retain her vaunted position as leader of the global economy.

"If you change the rules," reflects Carney, "you change the incentives. And if you change the incentives, you can change the structure of the US economy—who builds, who works, and what gets made."

You don't just change the American economy; you change the world economy.

In the process, we're isolating one of our greatest adversaries: China.

Remember when Trump announced global reciprocal tariffs?

Those tariffs came with some conditions: namely, that the nations shouldn't retaliate in kind.

This is what liberals don't understand. Even if Trump isn't "liked" by a lot of global leaders, they respect him.

Which is why after the tariffs were announced, most nations jumped to negotiate a resolution with the administration.

Except for one: China.

Instead of heeding Trump's warning, China hiked its tariffs on the US from 34 percent to 84 percent.

They must have forgotten who they were dealing with.

On Wednesday—a week after the "Liberation Day" when reciprocal tariffs went into effect—Trump announced a new policy.

This new policy paused all reciprocal tariffs for ninety days, honoring the nations who chose not to retaliate.

But what about China?

Under this new policy, tariffs on China were raised to 125 percent (from a previous 84 percent).

That's going to hurt.

It's going to make American businesses who rely on cheap factories in this communist country wonder if it makes more sense to invest and manufacture here in the United States. "Honest to God, no exaggeration," remarked Rick Woldenberg, the CEO of Learning Resources, which has been manufacturing its products in China for four decades, "It feels like the end of days."

But for the business leaders who put America first, the tariffs are an unbridled win.

Even business leaders in other countries have applauded Trump for standing up to China. What Canadian entrepreneur, investor, and *Shark Tank* host Kevin O'Leary told a CNN panel is what business leaders around the world are saying. "Nobody has taken on China yet, not the Europeans, no administration for decades."

O'Leary is someone who has done business in China. "I speak for millions of Americans who have IP that have been stolen by the Chinese. I have nothing against the Chinese people. They brought great literacy, art, and tech to the world. The government cheats and steals."

As O'Leary explained, you may not like Trump. You may not like his style. You may not like his rhetoric. But finally, we have a president of the United States of America saying, "enough is enough." O'Leary, never one to mince his words, expressed a sentiment that many Americans share: "I want Xi on an airplane to Washington to level the playing field."

They don't call Trump the master of the deal for nothing.

This latest development shows a shrewd plan that economically isolates China—one of our biggest adversaries—from the rest of the world. While Joe Biden was asleep at the wheel of foreign policy for four years, President Trump is back directing traffic.

Once again, the United States is in control.

The most beautiful thing about what is happening to China right now is that they brought it all upon themselves. They did not listen to the president, and now both their country and their people are paying the cost—literally.

At the end of the day, this is about more than tariffs.

Secretary of the Treasury Scott Bessent hit the nail on the head during a press conference at the White House back on April 9, 2025. "We saw the successful negotiating strategy that President Trump implemented a week ago today. It has brought more than seventy-five countries forward to negotiate. It took great courage for him to stay the course until this moment. What we have ended up with here as I told everyone a week ago in this very spot: do not retaliate and you will be rewarded. So every country in the world who wants to come and negotiate, we are willing to hear you, we're going to go down to a ten percent baseline tariff for them. And China will be raised to 125 due to their insistence on escalation."

Bessent understands economics. He's been in the global investment management business for forty years, doing his work in sixty countries. He's taught economic history at Yale University. But, above all, he understands—and he is passionately committed to realizing—Donald Trump's agenda. This is the agenda that, once again, puts the American economy *first*.

And he's not the only member of this second administration who has the policies and the understanding of the process to get things done. Reprising his role from the first term is Peter Navarro. He is overseeing the president's efforts to bring back manufacturing. Take the deal that he struck with Nippon Steel and US Steel in Pennsylvania; this wasn't an either/or situation where we gave up US Steel. He found a way to make sure that we saved the company through critical investments from Nippon steel—while the US retained a key ownership aspect of it. As Navarro put it, "Nippon Steel is going to have *some* involvement, but no control of the company."

For his part, Navarro has been equally supportive of the tariffs that President Trump initiated to make the world economy once again work for Americans. "The end of the United States," that's how Navarro described what would happen if the Supreme Court struck down the president's global tariffs. Like the rest of the team that the president has assembled, Peter Navarro is here to put an end to the America Last status quo.

Trump's initial policy of reciprocal tariffs gave countries two choices: come to the table and negotiate with the administration for better terms or retaliate and face the consequences.

China chose the latter.

Trump knows China well and he likely expected this outcome.

And when they played into his hand, he implemented this new policy that pits China against the rest of the world.

A China vs. US trade war could be dangerously contentious and economically devastating for Americans.

But China vs. the world? Through his carefully executed plan, Trump harnessed the economic power of the world to keep China in check.

In the process, he's raised the stakes for Xi Jinping. "Xi can only stay the supreme leader if people are employed. If we wipe out any business—because we are still 39 percent of all consumables on Earth and 25 percent of the world's GDP—America is the number one economy on Earth with all the cards."

O'Leary and other business leaders who want to see America retain its rightful place as the global economic leader know that we will not retain this role forever—unless we deal with China. In O'Leary's words, "It's time to squeeze Chinese heads into the wall now."

I agree with Kevin O'Leary. The time for inaction is over. It should have been over a long time ago. For years, we have been steering this country in the wrong direction. Without Trump's leadership, we would have continued to steer it in the wrong direction for decades.

Can you imagine Kamala Harris taking on the People's Republic of China? It's easier to imagine her making bad TikTok videos than going toe-to-toe with one of our most powerful adversaries.

The Biden-Harris era of acquiescence is over. The Trump-Vance era of global leadership is here.

It's time to put Xi Jinping's feet to the fire. It's time to put the American people first.

Trump knows who he's dealing with, and he knows what it takes to beat them.

Before he ever stepped foot in the Oval Office, the president established himself as the master of the art of the deal. Like a chess grandmaster, Trump understands all the moves on the chessboard of international relations. And like a grandmaster, he is always one step ahead of his opponents.

It's the president's mastery over the art of the deal, his vision for the future, and his commitment to not backing down—from challenges abroad and from challenges at home, even within his own party—that is now making the United States great again.

But you still wouldn't know that from the media coverage.

Rather than recognizing the win, the media is insistent on predicting an American recession.

Take this article from CNN that paints the reciprocal tariff pause as a frantic attempt to stave off a recession, rather than a brilliant negotiating tool. They write that "economists significantly increased forecasts for a recession after Trump proceeded with the reciprocal tariff package, which called for tariffs as high as 50% impacting dozens of countries." Joe Brusuelas, chief economist of RSM US, told CNN that the ninety-day pause is "unlikely to stave off a recession."

One year in, the quotes from the self proclaimed economic experts have not aged well.

Even when Trump wins, the left-wing legacy media paints it as a loss.

NPR published a piece titled "US stocks slump again as euphoria over Trump's tariff pause fades." According to the folks at NPR, "Prior to Trump's U-turn, the policies had caused significant upheaval and wiped trillions of dollars of value from global stock markets. The White House's actions had also seen US government bond yields soar—concerning investors and economists alike."

The *New York Times*, for its part, seems more concerned with the welfare of people living in other countries than the welfare of people living in this country. At the end of August 2025, they ran an article titled, "Trump's Tariffs Will Crush India's Exporters, Threatening Livelihoods." He literally cannot win. Another article they ran was titled, "Taiwan Strained by 20% Tariffs." The *New York Times* is reflexively for the opposite of what Trump does.

If you were only getting your news from CNN, NPR, and the *New York Times*, you would think the global economy is in shambles and Americans are going to be eating crow tomorrow.

That couldn't be further from the truth.

While the liberal ideologues continue to push their prewritten narrative—that no matter what Trump accomplishes, the end of the world is on the horizon—actual experts, who are more interested in the truth than partisan politics, are trying to inform the public with facts. Kevin Hassett, the director of the National Economic Council at the White House, is someone who has been critical in all these negotiations.

"The president decided that he was going to charge tariffs on countries that were equal to either their tariffs or their non-tariff barriers so that we would basically be treating them like they treat us. And of course, they've been mistreating American workers for a long, long time. After he made that announcement, then countries from all over the world, more than seventy countries called us up and said, 'Look, we got to talk. We got to talk.'"

"And up to ten or fifteen countries," continued Hassett, "even made specific offers of, 'Hey, we'll do this. We'll treat you better in the future if you reduce your tariffs.'" As Hassett points out, the momentum was so positive that the administration considered closing a couple of the offered deals. In the end, the administration chose to initiate a pause.

Imagine that, treating them as they treat us.

This wasn't a political stunt.

It certainly wasn't a flash in the pan.

It's all part of the plan.

It's all part of the Trump 2.0. agenda.

Nothing is happening by chance. Nothing is happening by accident. In his book *The Drift: Stopping America's Slide to Socialism*, Hassett describes what President Trump told him about negotiating deals. "If I was having some trouble closing a real estate deal, I would sue the guy if he didn't give me what I wanted. A threat to sue would have no effect. But if I sued him the day before closing and then offered to withdraw the lawsuit as part of the deal, they almost always signed. They knew you meant it." This is the strategy that President Trump had talked to him about. As he concludes, and I could not agree with him more, "we're really serious about making America great again."

President Trump's policies, as I know with as much certainty as I know that the sun will set in the evening and rise in the morning, are going to be a success. We are not only ensuring security and prosperity for Americans today, we are ensuring security and prosperity for our children, and their children, and their children's children.

This isn't about passing a bill here or there. It's not about correcting the course of a sinking ship. It's about rebuilding that ship—our great nation—so that it not only survives the coming storms, but thrives.

Of course, these recent developments certainly don't mean we're out of the economic woods yet—they aren't a magic fix. In the real world—not the make-believe world of politicians like New York's new mayor, top socialist Zohran Mamdani—there are no magic fixes. The are no magic wands. There are only hard-won victories.

Isn't that all the more reason to celebrate victories like these when they do come?

When the liberal media relishes—and exaggerates—the growing pains we are experiencing, and when it attempts to portray those growing pains as permanent losses, it's almost like they *want* America to lose.

But the partisanship of the mainstream media is nothing new. What is an interesting new development, however, is seeing a similar response from many so-called conservatives.

Tariffs are a historically polarizing issue, even within parties, and it was eye-opening to see how many people purportedly on the Right jumped to attack the president's approach.

In his speech to the House Republican Conference, Trump rebutted his critics. "The shrill voices that you're hearing this week about tariffs are the same scoundrels and frauds who never thought twice about when the United States lost 90,000 factories and plants. Think of that. 90,000. How do you do 90? If you had a map, a big map, the size of that wall, and you had a pin for each factory, you wouldn't have enough room. You think of it, 90,000 factories since NAFTA. The worst trade deal in history, by the way. And we had it terminated. Everybody said you'd never be able to."

The president won on renegotiating NAFTA and he's winning on tariffs.

He went on, "I respect Mexico, I respect Canada, but they cheat like hell. Canada charges for our dairy products, 270 percent. Nobody knows that. They charge you 2 percent for the first two cartons of milk. And after that, you go up to 270 and the press says they've only charged 2 percent. No, that's for the first two cartons. You know, we can't have that and we have to be wise to it and get along with everybody, but we have to call people out."

Rebalancing trade with Canada, China, Mexico, and other countries—those are real wins.

And it's Donald Trump—not the swamp in DC—who is getting them.

In the president's words, "the same people now telling me about how to deal with China are the ones who sold out America for decades to China."

I love that line. It's another reminder who the so-called experts are.

What's even more interesting to observe is how many Republicans, after it was clear Trump was getting results, snapped back to hailing the president's economic genius, touting the fact that there was a plan all along.

Constructive criticism is always good.

But flip-flopping, knee-jerk reactions to policies for clout? Not a great look.

It's been a long time since we've had a president who is serious about putting America first like Trump.

The American people voted for radical change in 2024. Millions of votes—millions of voices—said "enough is enough."

If Trump 2.0 has taught us anything, it's the value of patience and trusting the process.

Remember when the experts—the so-called experts—announced that inflation was going to be the worst it has ever been? They said that Trump was going to blow the lid off the economy.

Quite the opposite has happened.

In June 2025, the US Treasury ran a surplus for the first time in over a decade, stock markets have reached all-time highs, and inflation projections have come in below what the experts predicted.

"US stocks hit record high," announced the *Financial Times* on August 12, 2025.

Tariffs are tools. Trump knows how to use them. Workers are winning again.

The so-called experts all predicted an economic catastrophe on par with the Great Depression—quite the opposite has happened.

But, again, that doesn't mean there won't be challenges.

When you're restructuring the way international business has been done for decades, instead of just passing another milquetoast policy that people will forget in twenty-four hours, you need patience—and you need to trust the process.

As I say throughout this book, this is the team of people who understand the process. This is the process of producing real, lasting change that benefits America.

In our world of instant gratification, I know it's not easy to be patient. It's not easy to trust a process, especially as the naysayers continue to cast their doom-and-gloom predictions.

But remember this: we've got the architect of the art of the deal in the White House, and what we're seeing as these tariffs continue to play out has only solidified the president's reputation.

In August 2025, the Associated Press reported that "US inflation was unchanged" and that we are witnessing "falling gas and grocery prices."

In other words, the so-called experts got it wrong—yet again.

Leftist media and shaky conservatives will continue to gripe, and many of them will try to exploit whatever growing pains may arise for their own advantage, but the results speak for themselves. Companies are coming to America, billions in investments are headed our way, manufacturing is on the rise, and the markets are sure to follow.

It's not a surprise that this is happening.

Whether it's Administrator of the Environmental Protection Agency Lee Zeldin talking about getting rid of regulations that are stifling businesses, or Secretary of Energy Chris Wright's commitment to the agenda that is "getting rid of nonsense and bringing back common sense," it's all part of the Trump 2.0 plan to make the American economy first again.

The plan is working and greatness is ahead.

In an old *Inc.* magazine article published before Trump was first elected to the Oval Office, the master of the deal is quoted as saying:

"Get going. Move forward. Aim High. Plan a takeoff. Don't just sit on the runway and hope someone will come along and push the airplane. It simply won't happen. Change your attitude and gain some altitude. Believe me, you'll love it up here."

Buckle up America—the best is yet to come.

Chapter 3

NATO Finally Pays Up

Back in August 2025, NATO Secretary General Mark Rutte was on Laura Ingraham's show on Fox News. Rutte was there to discuss the meeting that had occurred that day between European leaders at the White House. Ingraham brought Rutte on to give his assessment against the backdrop of what Trump's critics have been saying about him: "He wants to ruin NATO, he wants to break up NATO, he's a great disruptor, he doesn't know what he's doing." Ingraham, who has built her reputation on cutting through the rhetoric, wanted to know what Trump was actually like behind closed doors.

"Well," explained Rutte, "he was amazing, and he is amazing. And let me tell you this, that his criticism of NATO was right. What he was saying is that the US is spending so much more on its defense, and therefore spending on the collective defense of NATO territory than the Europeans." The bottom line isn't that Trump "wants to ruin NATO." He certainly doesn't want to "break up NATO," as the liberal media has accused. At the end of the day, the president wants to make sure that NATO is a fair deal for the American people. At the NATO summit, America finally got the deal it deserves.

"The great thing is," explains Rutte, "and I hope the Americans see this, probably one of his biggest foreign policy successes of his presidency, of his, of Trump 47, is that during the NATO summit, we committed collectively to this 5 percent spending, including 3.5 percent on the core defense spending. That's the same the US is spending. So now we are equalizing what the US is spending, what the Europeans are spending. And he has therefore taken a different view. He always said that he supported NATO, but he also expected the Europeans to pay up, to spend more. He has been successful in doing this."

The updated National Security Strategy of the United States made it clear: "President Trump has set a new global standard with the Hague Commitment, which pledges NATO countries to spend 5 percent of GDP on defense and which our NATO allies have endorsed and must now meet."

This is the path Trump had begun carving out in the summer of 2025. In June, he flew out to the Netherlands for the NATO summit to put the American people first. Even NPR, which has Trump derangement syndrome as bad as any liberal media outlet, couldn't help but acknowledge that it was "the Trump-dominated NATO summit." When it's a Trump-dominated NATO summit, it's an America-dominated NATO summit. The America First movement isn't just about doing what we need to do inside our own border; it's also about making sure other countries are playing the role we need them to play in the global order—because when America leads, everybody wins.

At the summit, there were thirty-two countries. These member states include Belgium, Canada, Denmark, France, Iceland, Italy, Luxembourg, Netherlands, Norway, Portugal, United Kingdom, United States, Greece, Turkey, Germany, Spain, Czech Republic, Hungary, Poland, Bulgaria, Estonia, Latvia, Lithuania, Romania, Slovakia, Slovenia, Albania, Croatia, Montenegro, North Macedonia, Finland, and Sweden. These are countries with different politics, cultures, and languages. At times, these are countries that have had contentious relationships with both the United States and each other.

Yet, President Trump was able to unite them all. Not only was he able to unite them, he was also able to unite them in a way that serves

American interests. At the summit in the Netherlands, all thirty-two leaders endorsed a final summit statement that said: "Allies commit to invest 5 percent of GDP annually on core defense requirements as well as defense- and security-related spending by 2035 to ensure our individual and collective obligations." When America's allies are paying their fair share, everyone wins. Each of them having a strong national defense isn't just good for us, it's good for them and for Europe as a whole.

"It's a historic moment that we will be ramping up defense expenditure to five percent. I strongly, and Estonia strongly, support it," announced Estonian Prime Minister Kristen Michal.

"Without the support and without the leadership of Donald Trump, it would be impossible," added Polish President Andrzej Duda.

Even the Associated Press couldn't help but conclude: "After less than 24 hours on the ground in the Netherlands, Trump headed back to Washington having secured a major policy change he's pushed for since 2017: a significant boost in defense spending by other NATO countries."

CNN analysts Joseph Ataman and Clare Sebastian called it "a diplomatic masterstroke."

The *Wall Street Journal*, hardly Trump's biggest supporters, were left with no option but to call a spade a spade: "Trump Wins the Battle of NATO."

This is the future that Trump envisioned years ago, even before he had been elected to the Oval Office in 2016. As he told CNN's Wolf Blitzer almost a decade ago, "It's costing us too much money, and frankly, they have to put up more money. They're going to have to put some up also. We're paying disproportionately, it's too much, and frankly, it's a different world than it was when we originally conceived of the idea and everybody got together."

This is the same Donald Trump who went to work to solve this problem when he took office. In 2018, he tweeted: "The United States is spending far more on NATO than any other Country. This is not fair, nor is it acceptable. While these countries have been increasing their contributions since I took office, they must do much more. Germany is at 1%."

Another way to think about this: Let's say we all agree to go out to lunch every Wednesday. And let's say we all agree to split the tab—because that's fair. What happens if I'm the one who pays most of the tab every Wednesday for weeks straight? At some point, it would be preposterous for me not to remind my friends that I never agreed to that. If I never reminded them, I would look like a dupe. We have gone decades with everybody just assuming that the US would pick up the collective tab for the defense of Europe.

And here's the ironic part: The liberal college student who backpacks abroad for a summer, and who comes back prattling about how beautiful the bridges, roads, and public parks are in Europe, and why can't America be like that—guess how Europe is paying for that? While Europe is building these bridges, roads, and public parks, America is paying to defend them.

Not anymore.

The most recent NATO Summit was the realization of Trump's vision, his hard work, and his unbridled global leadership. What he has done—everyone, even people on the Right, said it couldn't be done. Imagine if President Joe Biden had brokered this deal? The *New York Times* would declare him the hero of the century. He would be on *Time*'s list of the 100 most influential people in 2025. He'd be given the keys to every city in America.

Many European leaders even mocked Trump when he said they were going to be paying more. They mocked him. Now they're paying billions more for defense. Trump doesn't bluff.

For any other president, this would have been the biggest win of their presidency. This would be the bulk of their chapter in America's history books.

For President Trump, it was just par for the course of his first year in office. In the Trump administration, business as usual is unprecedented—and, frankly, inconceivable—wins for the American people.

What many people don't understand is that this isn't just a win for global peace. The fact of the matter is that any US president who is not demanding fairness in these types of agreements is hurting US taxpayers. It's not their job to finance a bad deal brokered by Barack Obama, Joe Biden, and other presidents who put Americans last. I mean, can you even imagine what NATO would have looked like under Kamala Harris? The American people would almost certainly have been funding it even more.

That isn't an exaggeration. When Biden took office, he proclaimed that "America is back." Amanda Sloat, the former senior director for Europe on Biden's National Security Council, said that "one of President Biden's top priorities when he came into office was rebuilding and revitalizing the trans-Atlantic relationship." We all saw how successful that was. After watching him flub during his debate with Trump, it's reasonable to ask: Could Joe Biden even point to Russia, China, and Iran on a map?

Of course, if a successful trans-Atlantic relationship is one in which the American taxpayers bear the brunt of foreign nations not paying their fair share—and relying on the United States to keep them safe—then Biden delivered on his promise. America was back. It was back to being the country that gets taken advantage of by other countries.

It's funny, the only people who think it's ludicrous for Trump to call out these other nations are the folks in Davos—the elites, the foreign policy snobs, the people who don't have to worry about where their tax money is going.

The American people aren't stupid. They voted for change in 2016. They voted for change again in 2020 and 2024. They know what the right leadership in the Oval Office can do. They also know that there is only one man who can use that office effectively. While Biden's term was marked by the art of the coverup, Trump's second term in office has been marked by the art of the deal.

"My style of deal-making," wrote Trump in *The Art of the Deal*, "is quite simple and straightforward. I aim very high, and then I just keep pushing and pushing and pushing to get what I'm after." "More than anything else," he adds, "I think deal-making is an ability you're born with. It's in the genes. I don't say that egotistically. It's not about being brilliant. It does take a certain intelligence, but mostly it's about instincts."

This is how an outsider—one who didn't cut his teeth as a state senator, or a representative, or a governor, or an even elected member of his local city council—was able to broker one of the most important international relations deals in history.

The monumental importance of this most recent deal with NATO cannot be overstated.

But since Donald Trump is who he is, even legacy outlets that acknowledged that this unprecedented victory—both for the United States and for global peace— still treated it as some kind of fortuitous accident, a lucky turn of events for a president who doesn't understand how to negotiate effectively with other world leaders. Reading their articles and watching their talking heads prattle on television, you would think that Trump just happened to stumble into a new, historically unprecedented relationship with NATO.

Their narrative is always that the emperor has no clothes.

In reality, these seismic shifts in international relations don't happen by accident. They happen when you have a plan. They happen when you have the leaders who will get to work implementing that plan. Trump 2.0 is illustrating what is possible when all the pieces on the chessboard fall into place. Trump's knights, and his rooks, his bishops, and all of his other allies playing their part in this game—Secretary of War Pete Hegseth, Director of National Intelligence Tulsi Gabbard, Treasury Secretary Scott Bessent, Commerce Secretary Howard Lutnick, and the list goes on—are not only highly qualified people for their jobs, they are fiercely loyal to President Trump and his agenda.

"Nobody has done more . . . than President Trump to restore NATO as an alliance," announced Secretary Hegseth as he stood beside NATO's chief. "The reason I'm here is to make sure every country in NATO understands every shoulder has to be to the plow, every country has to contribute at that level of 5 percent."

That NATO summit shows what is possible when President Trump has the team he needs to bring his vision of the future to fruition.

It shows that *anything* is possible when the United States is leading the way.

Right now, there are real threats in the world. Both militarily and economically, Russia is a threat. Both militarily and economically, China is a threat. Iran, a country where radicals can be heard chanting "Death to America!" is a threat. North Korea is a country that produced a propaganda video that showed the White House in the crosshairs of a sniper and the US Capitol building exploding in a ball of fire. They are a threat.

The innumerable number of terrorist cells around the world who want to destroy the United States and her allies—many of whom are aided and abetted by foreign governments—they are threats.

This isn't the kumbaya world that many liberals believe we live in. In the world of realpolitik, America and her allies have real enemies. These are enemies who have enormous resources at their disposal: weapons, technology, manpower, and economic power. We must be prepared.

As President Ronald Reagan declared in his speech at the Republican National Convention on July 17, 1980, "We know only too well that war comes not when the forces of freedom are strong, but when they are weak. It is then that tyrants are tempted."

Can you imagine the boots of another country's military on US soil? Can you imagine Russia doing to the US what it has done to Ukraine? Can you imagine Hamas turning their attention to the greatest country on planet Earth? None of this should be that hard to imagine.

Similar turns in history have happened before. We should not just be prepared to defend ourselves. We need to be so prepared that we never need to defend ourselves.

The historically unprecedented deal that Trump brokered at the NATO summit in the Netherlands helps to ensure that America and her allies are prepared.

As President Reagan put it in his 1983 radio address to the nation on the observance of Armed Forces Day, "I know that the paradox of peace through a credible military posture may be difficult for some people to accept. Some even argue that if we really wanted to reduce nuclear weapons we should simply stop building them ourselves. That argument makes about as much sense as saying that the way to prevent fires is to close down the fire department. It ignores one of the most basic lessons of history, a lesson that was learned by bitter experience and passed down to us by previous generations."

What is that lesson?

"Tyrants are tempted by weakness," said Reagan, "and peace and freedom can only be preserved by strength. So, let us resolve today, as we honor the brave men and women who serve in our Armed Forces, to give them the support they need to protect our cherished liberties and preserve the peace for ourselves and our children."

In his keynote at the NATO Summit, Secretary General Mark Rutte reiterated just how high the stakes are. "There's an ancient Roman saying, 'If you want peace, prepare for war.' It's a simple idea. Make your defenses so strong, that no one dares to attack you. Today, NATO's military edge is being aggressively challenged. By a rapidly rearming Russia. Backed by Chinese technology. And armed with Iranian and North Korean weapons. We need to unite, innovate and deliver. That's exactly what this forum is all about."

"We're witnessing the birth of a new NATO," said Finland's President Alexander Stubb.

The days of Europe telling the US how to spend our money defending them—those days are over.

If a US president does not demand fairness, it is a disservice to the American taxpayer.

NATO was formed as a collective response to the existential threat posed by the Soviet Union. At the time, the Communist Party of Czechoslovakia, with backing from Joseph Stalin, had just overthrown the country's democratically elected government. The Soviets had also blockaded Allied-controlled West Berlin. It was clear that what President Reagan would later call the "evil empire" wasn't just evil; it was an empire that wanted to expand. The US, with aid provided by the Marshall Plan, ended its approach of diplomatic isolationism. On April 4, 1949, the North Atlantic Treaty was signed.

As President Dwight Eisenhower noted, "We do not keep security establishments merely to defend property or territory or rights abroad or at sea. We keep the security forces to defend a way of life." Back then, that way of life was threatened by the Soviet Union. And it was the US who for years carried the financial burden of their defense against the Soviet Union.

Today, the world is threatened—once again—by communist countries like China, autocracies like Russia, and radical Islamic states like Iran.

The threats are real.

According to the Stockholm Peace Research Institute database, "since 2000, Russian defense spending grew by 227% while China's expanded by 566%. Defense spending remained quite flat over the same period (up by only 22% including the latest increases) in NATO Europe and Canada."

As NATO itself acknowledges: "Since its founding in 1949, the transatlantic Alliance's flexibility, embedded in its original Treaty, has allowed it to suit the different requirements of different times. In the 1950s, the Alliance was a purely defensive organization. In the 1960s, NATO became a political instrument for détente. In the 1990s, the Alliance was a tool for the stabilization of Eastern Europe and Central Asia through the incorporation of new partners and Allies. In the first half of the 21st century, NATO faces an ever-growing number of new threats. As the foundation stone of transatlantic peace and freedom, NATO must be ready to meet these challenges."

While the world's geopolitical landscape has changed since the Cold War and the fall of the evil empire, so too have the technologies of war. Cyberattacks. Drones. The list goes on. But what hasn't changed is the power of deterrence. It is deterrence that has kept America and her allies abroad safe from maniacal dictators who want to recreate the world in their image. It's also deterrence that is keeping America and her allies safe today. Global peace is always precarious. Old threats retreat into the background, as new threats—and new powers of unfreedom—emerge. The United States must remain strong. Peace through strength isn't a political slogan. It's a position that history has demonstrated, time and time again, works.

As United States Secretary of War Pete Hegseth noted in his April 23, 2025, speech at the Army War College: "That is exactly what I have set about to do all 100 days. Fighting for you is the privilege of a lifetime, a deployment of a lifetime. And from day one, and each 100 of those days, our overriding objectives have been clear: restoring the warrior ethos, rebuilding our military, and reestablishing deterrence."

"Restoring the warrior ethos," he explains, "is the most fundamental of those three. Everything starts and ends with warriors in training and on the battlefield. We are leaving wokeness and weakness behind. And refocusing on lethality, meritocracy, accountability, standards, and readiness."

The ongoing war between Russia and Ukraine has demonstrated that NATO is not ready for a battle, much less a war. As they themselves admit, "the war in Ukraine has publicly shown that many Allies were struggling to find available ammunition stockpiles to donate to Ukraine, or to reequip their own forces, and could only deploy limited combat-ready forces at short notice." That's not what the warrior ethos looks like. That's not what a strong military looks like. That's most certainly not what deterrence looks like. That's an open invitation to get dominated by a more powerful country.

As President Reagan put it in his 1983 Address to the Nation on Defense and National Security: "Since the dawn of the atomic age, we've sought to reduce the risk of war by maintaining a strong deterrent and by seeking genuine arms control. 'Deterrence' means simply this: making sure any adversary who thinks about attacking the United States, or our allies, or our vital interests, concludes that the risks to him outweigh any potential gains. Once he understands that, he won't attack. We maintain the peace through our strength; weakness only invites aggression. This strategy of deterrence has not changed. It still works."

More than four decades later, it still works.

President Reagan understood that even though peace comes through strength, you have to adapt that strategy to each new set of challenges. As he put it in that same Cold War address to the American people, "It took one kind of military force to deter an attack when we had far more nuclear weapons than any other power; it takes another kind now that the Soviets, for example, have enough accurate and powerful nuclear weapons to destroy virtually all of our missiles on the ground." In the same vein, President Trump understands that it takes another kind of military force to deter countries like Russia, China, and Iran.

This is what his magisterial move in response to the Iranian nuclear threat was all about. On Sunday June 22, 2025, the President successfully completed Operation Midnight Hammer. The United States military forces conducted a highly complex and coordinated strike against three nuclear sites in Iran. The largest B-2 strike in history delivered twelve GBU-57 30,000-pound bunker buster bombs. Simultaneously, the Navy sent more than thirty Tomahawk missiles from over four hundred miles away. It was an incredibly complex coordinated attack from joint military forces. In future history books, it will go down as one of the most exquisitely performed military operations the world has ever seen.

The day after the strike, former Secretary of the Navy Ken Braithwaite broke it down on my show. "I believe very strongly, as I've shared with you before, that Iran is the most dangerous nation in the world. And the most dangerous nation, as the president said, should never have the most dangerous weapons. So unfortunately, this was something that we were compelled to do. And the Israelis led the way in, and we have now delivered on our commitment to eliminate those sites. It's never a good thing to lose any lives on either side. But, again, to deny this Iranian regime—this theocratic regime—of nuclear weapons was something that the United States had to do."

Absolutely.

It's this decisiveness—always in the interest of the American people—that distinguishes President Trump from our previous president.

Operation Midnight Hammer was the end of TACO night. Trump Always Chickens Out? You couldn't have imagined a better way to shut down the naysayers who erroneously tried to say Trump doesn't follow through on his threats, who said Trump is quick to back off. Anyone who thought the president didn't act with decisive action learned a lesson that weekend. If the president gives you an off ramp, and you don't take it, he will act in America's interests. Iran learned that the hard way.

Everyone else also learned. It's not incidental that NATO's leaders have continued to respond the way they have. It's not a mystery why they are showing President Trump the respect that President Biden could only dream about. President Trump's decisive attack on Iran wasn't just an attack in the interest of the American people. It was an attack that sent a very clear message to leaders watching around the world. If you back the president into a corner, if you play him for a fool, if you think you're going to pull the wool over his eyes, and if you treat him like Sleepy Joe Biden—by building nuclear weapons facilities, by not paying your fair share to a global alliance, and by otherwise disrespecting him and the American people—you're going to learn the hard way that he means business.

While his critics accused him of provoking World War III when he authorized this series of strikes against three Iranian nuclear facilities, he understood—as President Reagan did—that peace is secured through strength. This is the same mindset he brings to his negotiations with NATO allies. When America is weak, as we saw under the Biden administration, the world is unlikely to see peace. But with President Trump at the helm of the most powerful military in history, leaders around the world understand that there will be consequences for their actions.

As the President put it in a post on Truth Social, "We have completed our very successful attack on the three Nuclear sites in Iran, including Fordow, Natanz, and Esfahan. All planes are now outside of Iran air space. A full payload of BOMBS was dropped on the primary site, Fordow. All planes are safely on their way home. Congratulations to our great American Warriors. There is not another military in the World that could have done this. NOW IS THE TIME FOR PEACE!"

He's right.

There is not another military in the world that could have done this. He knows this. Iran's supreme leader knows this. The leaders of countries around the world know this. Now is the time for peace. But peace, as the president knows, comes through strength.

"Mr. President," Mark Rutte texted,"Congratulations and thank you for your decisive action in Iran, that was truly extraordinary, and something no one else dared to do. It makes us all safer."

That's exactly right—it was something no one else dared to do, not any European leader, not the United Nations, and not the United States president before him.

NATO Secretary General Rutte continued, "You are flying into another big success in The Hague this evening. It was not easy but we've got them all signed on to 5 percent!"

Can you believe it?

NATO members are raising defense budgets after decades of not upholding their end of their commitments.

That's the art of the deal. That's the art of America First leadership. That's the art of global peace.

And it's just the beginning.

As President Trump pronounced in a campaign speech back in 2016, "We're gonna win so much, you may even get tired of winning. And you'll say, 'Please, please. It's too much winning. We can't take it anymore, Mr. President, it's too much.' And I'll say, 'No it isn't. We have to keep winning. We have to win more!'"

He is right. We're going to win with every new obstacle, challenge and threat that emerges.

Above all, we're going to continue to think big.

As Trump put it in *The Art of the Deal*, "I like thinking big. I always have. To me it's very simple: if you're going to be thinking anyway, you might as well think big. Most people think small, because most people are afraid of success, afraid of making decisions, afraid of winning. And that gives people like me a great advantage."

In other words, Joe Biden is out the door and there is a new sheriff in town.

Just as Wyatt Earp brought law and order to the Wild West, President Trump has brought law and order back to the world of international relations. A world in which President Donald J. Trump leads is a world in which the United States and her allies win. It's a world in which America continues to lead with big ideas and even bigger achievements.

That is the world I want to live in.

Even after all of what has been done to make NATO countries live up to their own commitments, if some are still wondering why this matters, Tulsi Gabbard dropped a massive bombshell on December 20, 2025, at the Turning Point USA AMFest that almost went entirely unreported.

"As you know, President Trump has been persistently and relentlessly pursuing a peace deal to finally end the war between Russia and Ukraine. He talks frequently about the need to end the killing and the bloodshed, and his teams are negotiating now as we gather here. But what I've seen over these months is that every time they make progress and they move closer and closer to that hope for peace, the warmongers in the Deep State step up and try to do everything they can to stop them. Predictably, they use the same old tactics that they've always used. The Deep State within the intelligence community weaponizes intelligence to try to undermine progress. They leak it to their friends in the mainstream propaganda media to try to spread this and push a false narrative. They foment fear and hysteria as a way to justify the continuing of the war and their efforts to undermine President Trump's efforts towards peace, and do so specifically in this case in order to try to pull the US military into a direct conflict with Russia, which is ultimately what the EU and NATO want. We cannot allow this to happen. We have to see clearly what's happening before our very eyes and stand united in this cause of peace."

Wow! The European Union and NATO are trying to drag the United States into a war with Russia, and deep state staffers are actually thwarting peace negotiations, and the media is spreading a false narrative.

Let that sink in.

Chapter 4

Smarter Defense, Cleaner Intelligence

On July 23, 2025, National Intelligence Director Tulsi Gabbard spoke to the American people. From the White House briefing room, she revealed the extent to which President Barack Obama and his administration had tried to delegitimize Donald Trump's 2016 presidency.

"At President Trump's direction and with the support and coordination of the House Intelligence Committee Chairman Rick Crawford, today we've released a declassified oversight majority staff report that was produced in September of 2020.

"The stunning revelations that we are releasing today should be of concern to every American. This is not about Democrats or Republicans. This has to do with the integrity of our democratic republic and American voters having faith that the votes cast will count.

"There is irrefutable evidence that detail how President Obama and his national security team directed the creation of an intelligence community assessment that they knew was false. They knew it would promote this contrived narrative that Russia interfered in the 2016 election to help President Trump win, selling it to the American people as though it were true. It wasn't.

"The report that we released today shows in great detail how they carried this out. They manufactured findings from shoddy sources.

They suppressed evidence and credible intelligence that disproved their false claims. They disobeyed traditional tradecraft intelligence community standards and withheld the truth from the American people.

"In doing so, they conspired to subvert the will of the American people who elected Donald Trump in that election in November of 2016. They worked with their partners in the media to promote this lie, ultimately to undermine the legitimacy of President Trump and launching what would be a years-long coup against him and his administration."

This was the Russia Hoax.

This was the Great Hoax uncovered by Trump 2.0.

What separates Trump's second administration from his first is leaders like Tulsi Gabbard. Not only does Tulsi, a decorated veteran, have all the credentials to lead our intelligence efforts, she has the character we need to drain the swamp.

It's hard to imagine any appointee, much less a career politician, unearthing what she discovered. The American people had been misled. They had been duped. They had been provoked into confusion not by a foreign government—but by their own president.

Because of Tulsi's diligent work and her commitment to seeking the truth—wherever she may find it—all of this is coming to light.

The deep state's falsehoods are like mold in a basement. They not only survive, but thrive out of the public's eye. Sunlight kills mold. The truth kills falsehoods.

It's the truth about the 2016 election—and the ignominious Russia Hoax—that the American people want.

Here's the gist of it.

The first narrative was that Trump colluded with the Russians to cast out Hillary Clinton, to dump opposition research—what political strategists call oppo—on her. The Mueller Report basically threw cold water on that. After ruining countless lives and bankrupting people, the report confirmed there was no evidence. I did not need a report to tell me this. I was there. This was a Democrat-created hoax to make up for how embarrassing Hillary was as a candidate. Quite literally, it said that "the investigation did not establish that members of the Trump Campaign conspired or coordinated with the Russian government in its election interference activities."

We didn't need to waste taxpayer money to find this out.

Of course the Trump Campaign wasn't holding hands with the Russian government.

For many of us, there was never a reason to have a report in the first place. The narrative leading up to the election was that we couldn't collude with ourselves. It was "Trump and his team are a bunch of incompetent numb nuts." We were treated as political outsiders who were too incompetent to organize a voter registration drive, much less one of the greatest presidential elections heists the world has ever seen.

Suddenly, after the Democrats lost the election, we were treated as political masterminds on par with the evil geniuses depicted in James Bond films. All of a sudden, Democratic politicians across the country, and their loyal mouthpieces in the liberal media, were saying, "Trump colluded with Russia. He's an evil genius. He's assembled a team of evil geniuses. And they have not only stolen our election, but they have also done all this other evil stuff."

It seemed like every week a new accusation was leveled against our democratically elected president. It seemed like every week the liberal media was purporting to be on the verge of blowing the lid off the next Watergate. "The case for Trump-Russia collusion: we're getting very, very close," announced the *Washington Post.* "Democrats press the case for Trump-Russia 'collusion,'" announced *Politico.* "Senate panel finds Russia interfered in the 2016 US election," boasted PBS.

To any thinking person with an IQ above 3, these accusations were not only untrue; they were absolutely preposterous. The whole thing seemed as farcical as a *Babylon Bee* article. But the accusations and the investigations gained political momentum. In the ashes of political defeat, the Democrats' disinformation campaigns thrive. And this disinformation campaign thrived like no other.

In hindsight, it looks insane. For those of us who had functioning brains, it looked insane at the time. But here's what you have to understand: The Democratic Party is a unified front. Their modem operandi is to discredit, to silence, and to destroy their opponents. Look at what they did to Bernie Sanders, a member of their own party. More to the point, they also have these "journalists" in their pockets. That's why they were all speaking the same Democratic Party talking points at the same time.

The *Washington Post*, *Politico*, PBS—these outlets are as interested in truth as Ellen DeGeneres is in men.

While the truth did come to light, and President Trump did retain his position in the Oval Office, this disinformation campaign did a tremendous amount of damage. It cost a lot of people time and money. Above all, it misled the American public into believing that this was a stolen election—one that had been stolen not only by their own president, but by the archvillain who leads the former Soviet Union. It also robbed Trump 1.0 of critical time to pursue the agenda he had been elected on. Too many hours, days, and weeks were spent away from the agenda, casting doubt—truly robbing him of a real first term.

Again, it reads like a James Bond script. But in the world of the *New York Times* and the *Washington Post*, it was presented as the truth.

After the Mueller Report, even Democratic hardliners had to acknowledge there was no conspiratorial connection between President Trump and Russia. But while Trump and his team were absolved, the report still contended that Russia interfered in the US election to help Trump win. The investigation established "that Russia interfered in the 2016 presidential election principally through two operations. First, a Russian entity carried out a social media campaign that favored presidential candidate Donald J. Trump and disparaged presidential candidate Hillary Clinton. Second, a Russian intelligence service conducted computer-intrusion operations against entities, employees, and volunteers working on the Clinton Campaign and then released stolen documents." Why? According to the Mueller Report, which reads like a thriller novel rather than a serious attempt to uncover the truth, "the Russian government perceived it would benefit from a Trump presidency."

The Democrats couldn't prove anything illegal had taken place between Trump and Russia, but they could still try to paint Trump as Vladimir Putin's man.

Once again, the purpose wasn't to get to the bottom of anything—nothing had ever taken place. The purpose was to discredit the results of the 2016 election and to turn the American people against the sitting president of the United States of America. In many ways, the Mueller Report was the Bible of an internal coup. It granted legitimacy to the Democrats' otherwise indefensible claims. It gave a veneer of intellectual substance—and, ultimately, authority—to accusations that were as thin as a blade of grass.

This fantastical story—in which Russia effectively put a Manchurian candidate in the Oval Office—never went into the dustbin of history. It continues to be circulated to this day. Leading up to the 2024 election, it was part of the broader disinformation campaign waged by the Democratic Party and the liberal media to confuse the American public, to turn the public against the Republican Party, and to ensure that Trump would never be back in the Oval Office.

It's not hard to imagine a war room, where Democratic donors, politicians, and pundits have worked together to take down this populist leader through coordinated attacks. In addition to the Russia Hoax, there was the lawfare waged against Trump. Just take the kangaroo court in New York, where Trump faced thirty-four counts of falsifying business records. "Alvin Bragg, the Manhattan District Attorney, pursued this case not in the 'interest of justice,' as required by the US Supreme Court, but in a politically charged atmosphere that undermines public trust," writes Fox News contributor Brett Tolman, a former United States Attorney. As he reflected in January 2025, "Lawfare doesn't begin to describe the legal circus we're witnessing this week as a state judge and prosecutor thumb their noses at our US Supreme Court.

Despite the Justices' easy-to-understand immunity ruling months ago, Judge Juan Merchan's petulant ego threatens to undermine our entire constitution by refusing to concede that *People v. Trump* is legally and procedurally flawed and should be dismissed." Tolman rightly believes that New York's kangaroo court is a real "constitutional threat."

And what about that Trump conviction in New York back in 2024? As Trump himself noted the day after the conviction, "They missed the statute of limitations by a lot because this was very old," he said. "They could have brought this seven years ago instead of bringing it right in the middle of the election. So they missed the statute of limitations." As even *USA Today* had to acknowledge, "Trump's case was tried in New York, where the statute of limitations is five years for all but the most serious felonies and two years for misdemeanors. The charge against Trump, falsifying business records in the first degree, is a Class E felony. That means the statute of limitations is five years."

Pause for one moment and reflect on that fact. For all the Left's professed concern about democracy (e.g. the *Washington Post*'s slogan "Democracy Dies in Darkness") and the Constitution being under attack, New York charged Trump with a crime *years* after that statute of limitations had passed. They charged him for an internal bookkeeping issue. There was no victim. Additionally, beyond the statute of limitations expiring, the underlying "crime" was a misdemeanor—except in this case, it would be a felony.

Seth Barrett Tillman, an associate professor in the Maynooth University School of Law and Criminology, also noted the strange jury instructions. "There is some good reason to believe Merchan's jury instructions are flawed, that is, the jury instructions violate Trump's constitutional right to a unanimous verdict." But that doesn't matter in a kangaroo court. All that matters is getting the result you want. And what the liberal establishment wants is Donald Trump to be gone.

That's why they raided Mar-a-Lago.

When his home was raided, Trump said, "These are dark times for our Nation, as my beautiful home, Mar-A-Lago in Palm Beach, Florida, is currently under siege, raided, and occupied by a large group of FBI agents. Nothing like this has ever happened to a President of the United States before."

Hoaxes, court cases, raids—and, ultimately, assassination attempts.

There is nothing the Left won't do to get rid of Donald J. Trump.

It wasn't until December 2025 that we also learned the FBI did not believe there was probable cause for the raid of President Trump's Florida home. They only acted under pressure from the Biden Department of Justice. See, democracy is only under attack when the agenda of the Left is under attack.

But guess what? He's back.

The American people voted him back.

While not the original plan, watching the difference of four years of Biden policies made it crystal clear how much more desirable Trump's policies were. Voters could clearly see the difference between the policies of two presidents in a way they never have in modern history.

This time, he and his team are putting an end to the falsehoods that have circulated for far too long.

These falsehoods, as we're learning, didn't arise from the American people. They arose from those who were in power. They arose from the administration led by Barack Obama. They arose because the Democratic Party knew their days in office were numbered. They knew the American people were going to vote them out of office—in favor of a political outsider—unless they could drastically shift the tide of public opinion.

The Russia Hoax was like a Hail Mary in the fourth quarter of the Super Bowl.

Fortunately for the American people, it didn't land.

Right now, Trump, Tulsi, and the rest of the administration—these erudite intelligence officers who bring decades of experience to the White House—are doing masterful work. I say *masterful* because their work is frankly without precedent.

Through declassified documents, they have uncovered a truth that is much different than the narrative that the Democratic Party and the liberal media has been pushing since the 2016 election. Thanks to Tulsi, and other members of the phenomenal intelligence team that President Trump has assembled, we now have proof that President Putin, in fact, did quite the opposite of what the American people were told he did.

Putin thought Hillary was going to win the 2016 election.

Accordingly, he held back a lot of the opposition research they had on her. That is a fact. Why did Russia hold back on distributing damaging information on Hillary if they really wanted Trump to win? Unless that was not the case. They held it back because they thought she was going to win and they wanted additional leverage when she was president.

Russia stopped interfering in the US in September 2016, months before the election, because—like much of our own country—they assumed she was going to win the election. They assumed she was going to be the next President of the United States of America.

They can hardly be blamed for assuming that.

Remember all the polls that showed Trump had absolutely no chance of defeating the successor to the Clinton dynasty?

The day after the election, journalist Nick Bilton accurately summarized the scene. "Both online polls and live-call polls showed Trump's numbers puttering. And then, this week, on the eve of the most important presidential election in recent history, sites like FiveThirtyEight had Clinton with a 71 percent chance of winning, predicting that she would take Florida, Wisconsin, Michigan, and Pennsylvania. Yet she lost them all, and in turn, the presidency."

Interestingly, the results of those polls were part of the broader rebellion against the liberal elite.

Republican consultant Frank Luntz hit the nail on the head a few days after the election in an article for *Time*.

"While many Americans are surprised by the result," he wrote, "the people who populate the punditry class are truly shocked by it. I'm one of them. Many of us relied on a set of polls that were structurally off by two or three points in favor of Clinton, and exit polls that were simply wrong. Trump voters weren't lying to the pollsters or afraid to be counted. On Election Day and before, they simply refused to be polled. They refused to participate in a political exercise they saw as rigged against them."

This rebellion not only misled the Democratic Party, who believed they had the election in the bag, it misled our greatest adversary: Russia.

As we know, many voters now vote well before election day. Most Americans vote and make up their mind on who to vote for in between Labor Day and Election Day. If you're not a hardcore Democrat or a hardcore Republican, you make up your mind in the last sixty days. If Putin really wanted to influence this election—if he wanted someone to win or if he wanted to screw someone over—he would have dumped all of his oppo in that last sixty days.

But what all of these new reports unearthed by the second Trump administration show is that President Putin didn't do that. Instead, he chose to hold back. Like the chattering class in DC, he assumed Hillary Clinton was going to win on November 8, 2016.

He assumed wrong.

From his perspective, it made all the sense in the world to withhold that oppo. If Hillary was going to be the next president, it made no sense to release it before she took office. It made all the sense in the world to dump it after she took office. Why? Putin wanted to undermine her presidency. He wanted to turn the American people not against a presidential candidate, but against their own president.

It would have been a magisterial strategic move on Russia's part, but there one was major problem: The American people voted for Donald Trump.

The bottom line of what Tulsi has discovered, and what she and her team continue to discover, is that President Obama was aware of all of this. He knew the game that was being played, and he knew the stakes of this game for the 2016 election.

Fortunately for him, the Supreme Court has ruled granting presidential immunity to President Trump, which also grants it to President Obama.

As Trump himself said on July 25, 2025: "It probably helps him a lot. He's done criminal acts, there's no question about it, but he has immunity. He owes me big. Obama owes me big."

He's right.

His administration had all the information that revealed the truth: Russia wasn't backing Donald Trump. No, they were backing the candidate Obama endorsed. They too wanted Hillary Clinton to succeed him. They wanted Hillary to be the next president.

Whereas the narrative said Trump and Putin were in cahoots—conspiring against the American people to squash the heroine Hillary Clinton—the reality couldn't be more different. Obama and Putin were on the same page: A Clinton presidency is what these two leaders wanted.

The Great Hoax, as it would later be called, was an attempt to ensure this happened.

Hillary herself was working to perpetuate this false narrative via the Christopher Steele dossier, also known as the infamous Trump-Russia dossier. Compiled by counterintelligence specialist Christopher Steele, a British intelligence officer, it was presented as the revelation of the century. Described as "probably the most foundational piece of the entire Russiagate scandal," the dossier contained "salacious allegations of purported coordination between Trump and the Russian government."

The dossier claimed that the Republican campaign team was "happy to have Russia as media bogeyman to mask more extensive corrupt business ties to China and other emerging countries." Purporting to illuminate "a well-developed conspiracy of co-operation between them and Russian leadership," the dossier was something straight out of a John Grisham novel.

Putin, the evil genius, was motivated by fear and hatred of Hillary Clinton, who is the undisputed hero of Russiagate, the only one who stands in the way of Russia's takeover of the American government, and the one who this dictator fears the most. It's Clinton, a kind of Wonder Woman, who carries the torch of truth and justice in the face of Trump's lies and deception.

All of this might be a great read if it was inside a Grisham novel, rather than an opposition research hit piece that went on to destroy countless lives and shape the narrative around the 2016 "stolen election" for close to a decade. And who is to blame for that?

Embarrassingly, the Associated Press had to report that "Hillary Clinton's 2016 presidential campaign and the Democratic National Committee have agreed to pay $113,000 to settle a Federal Election Commission investigation into whether they violated campaign finance law by misreporting spending on research that eventually became the infamous Steele dossier."

What the liberal media hailed as some kind of revelatory, objective, and serendipitous report into the truth of the 2016 election was essentially a Democratic Party psy-op.

What the second Trump administration is showing is that the very person who should have been dispelling these falsehoods, the very person who had the insider information to know these were falsehoods, was actually perpetuating them. President Barack Obama wasn't the gatekeeper of truth—he was the architect of mass deception.

Of course, if Russia actually wanted Trump to win the election, they would have dumped all their oppo on Clinton right before the election. They didn't. That wasn't their plan. It was never their plan. And President Obama and his intelligence officers knew that.

Because of Tulsi's diligent work, and because the Office of the Director of National Intelligence is now operating how it should be, we now know the longstanding narrative about Russia and President Trump has as much truth in it as Elizabeth Warren's claim that she is Native American.

Tulsi, the first female combat veteran to run for US president, was once the vice chair of the Democratic National Committee. But in 2022, her commitment to seeking the truth, and to defending the United States from enemies both foreign and domestic, pushed her to leave the Democratic Party.

Given her undeterred willingness to get to the bottom of things, even when it produces backlash, it is one of the many reasons she has been a great addition to President Trump's team. Like the president, Tulsi is not afraid. It's her desire to seek the truth that has made her the most important Director of National Intelligence in American history.

"My job," Tulsi has explained, "as I said when I came into this role, was to make sure that we are telling the truth to the American people and that we're ensuring that the intelligence community is not being politicized."

This former Democrat, who doesn't play by the rules of partisan politics, is doing exactly that.

She is disrupting the status quo—and she is doing so without apology.

A few days after Tulsi's press conference at the White House, the Office of the Director of National Intelligence (ODNI) published a news release: "The ODNI records released on Friday, Senator Chuck Grassley's release on Monday of the appendix to the DOJ OIG's June 2018 report known as the 'Clinton annex,' and the HPSCI oversight report released today confirm a treasonous conspiracy led by President Obama and his national security team, including James Clapper, John Brennan, and James Comey, to manipulate and manufacture intelligence that promoted a contrived false narrative falsely claiming: 'Putin aspired to help President-elect Trump's election chances, when possible, by discrediting Secretary Clinton.'"

As ODNI revealed, "President Obama directed the creation of this January 2017 Intelligence Community Assessment after President Trump defeated Hillary Clinton in the 2016 election, and it served as the basis for what was essentially a years-long coup against the duly elected President of the United States, subverting the will of the American people and attempting to delegitimize Donald Trump's presidency."

These are the key findings of the House Permanent Select Committee in Intelligence oversight report:

- On December 5, 2016, the FBI and ODNI gave HPSCI its first post-election classified briefing, in which there was "no mention of Putin 'aspiring' to elect Trump" by either agency.
- The President's Daily Brief (PDB) drafted on December 8, 2016 stated that no Russian or criminal actors impacted vote counts. This document was pulled hours before it was to be published due to "new guidance." If it had been published, it would have been briefed to both President Obama and President-elect Donald Trump.
- On December 9, 2016, a National Security Council meeting was called with President Obama's senior national security officials, which included CIA Director John Brennan, DNI James Clapper, Susan Rice, Andrew McCabe and others.
- After the December 9, 2016 secret meeting of Obama national security officials, DNI Clapper's assistant sent an email to leaders in the IC with the subject line "POTUS tasking on Russia Election Meddling," and tasking to create a new "assessment per the President's request."
- The HPSCI oversight report reveals that, "unlike routine IC analysis, the ICA was a high-profile product ordered by the President, directed by senior IC agency heads, and created by just five analysts, using one principal drafter. Production of the ICA was subject to unusual directives from the President and senior political appointees, and particularly DCIA."
- Later that same day, Brennan ordered the inclusion of "substandard reporting" on Russian activities, which had previously been withheld from publication because the information was judged "to have not met longstanding publication standards." Some of the information was, later used in the ICA, over the objections of veteran CIA officers, because it was "unclear, or from unknown subsources."

- CIA Director Brennan overruled senior CIA officers who challenged the ICA's claims, stating "we don't have direct information that Putin wanted to get Trump elected."
- Yet, the Obama-directed ICA published on January 6, 2017 explicitly stated: "We assess Putin and the Russian government aspired to help President-elect Trump's election chances when possible by discrediting Secretary Clinton and publicly contrasting her unfavorably to him." The CIA and FBI expressed high confidence in this judgment, while the NSA held moderate confidence.
- However, the HPSCI report reveals "the ICA did not cite any report where Putin directly indicated helping Trump win was the objective."

The ODNI has also explained the role of the widely discredited Steele dossier in this hoax. The dossier was used to create the January 2017 ICA. The takeaways should alarm every American:

"We now know one of the source documents the Obama administration officials used in the creation of the January 2017 ICA was the discredited, unverified Steele Dossier," they explain. Indeed, the HPSCI report states: "Contradicting public claims by the DCIA [Brennan] that the dossier 'was not in any way 'incorporated into the ICA, the dossier was referenced in the ICA main body text and further detailed in a two-page ICA annex." Moreover, they conclude that "John Brennan lied and denied using the dossier in the ICA because he knew it was a discredited, politically motivated manufactured document. He told senior CIA officials to use it anyway." In the words of one of the CIA officers to HPSCI staff: "DCIA [Brennan] refused to remove it, and when confronted with the dossier's main flaws, [Brennan] responded, 'Yes, but doesn't it ring true?'"

Moreover, as ODNI explains, "the bipartisan Senate Select Committee on Intelligence (SSCI) report (Volume 5, 2020) also criticized the FBI's handling of the Steele Dossier, noting its completely unverified nature and purposeful sidestepping of IC procedure in its use. . . . President Obama, Hillary Clinton, John Brennan, James Clapper, James Comey and others, along with their mouthpieces in the media, knowingly lied as they repeated the contrived false narrative they created in the January 2017 ICA with 'high confidence' as though it were fact." Indeed, "Obama's CIA Director, Brennan stated in a memo to agency staff in December 2016, 'There is strong consensus among us on the scope, nature, and intent of Russian interference in our presidential election.'"

In a 2018 interview with the *Harvard Gazette*, Obama's Director of National Intelligence, James Clapper, who oversaw the creation of the January 2017 ICA, concurred that they "provided Trump the same classified assessment that President Obama received," and that included "the high-confidence judgment" that "Putin directly ordered the hacking and election interference." As Clapper concluded, "I think they [Russians] actually influenced the outcome."

For what it is worth, I was actually one of the handful of transition staffers in the room at Trump Tower when the intelligence briefing to Trump took place, and that statement is categorically false.

This isn't an esoteric conspiracy theory like "Bush did 9/11" or "we never landed on the moon."

This is a matter of fact.

Under the direction of President Barack Obama, the US intelligence community manufactured a widespread hoax to subvert Donald Trump.

And, of course, the liberal media ate it up.

The *New York Times* has a whole section of its website devoted to "Trump and Russia."

As they brag, "The *New York Times* revealed the Trump team's connections with the Russians and attempts to sway the F.B.I. director, James Comey. The articles, which won the 2018 Pulitzer Prize for National Reporting, triggered the appointment of Robert Mueller as special counsel."

My favorite part about the *NYT* "reporting" is how resistant it is to facts. Within a few weeks of acknowledging the truth in one article ("How Did So Much of the Media Get the Steele Dossier So Wrong?") by conceding that "many of the dossier's allegations have turned out to be fictitious or, at best, unprovable," they declared in a subsequent article that, ultimately, this doesn't really matter ("Why the Discredited Dossier Does Not Undercut the Russia Investigation").

As Roland Barthes put it in his 1957 book *Mythologies*, "a little 'confessed' evil saves one from acknowledging a lot of hidden evil."

Remember: this wasn't an attempt to undermine faith in the results of an election in Iraq, Afghanistan, Iran, Venezuela, Colombia, or the Congo. This was an attempt by the United States government to undermine faith in the results of an American election.

As John Solomon, from *Just The News*, explained on my show on July 23, 2025: "If this was in any other time in American journalism history, this would be the front line news . . . it is a complete misuse of the intelligence community."

Is it any wonder Americans have such low trust in the media?

Is it any wonder they have such low trust in their elected officials?

"When the National Election Study began asking about trust in government in 1958," reflects the Pew Research Center, "about three-quarters of Americans trusted the federal government to do the right thing almost always or most of the time."

According to that study, "Since 2007, the shares saying they can trust the government always or most of the time have not been higher than 30%."

The Pew data is hardly an outlier.

In the spring of 2024, the Partnership for Public Service conducted a national representative sample of Americans. What they found couldn't be more disheartening: "only 23% of Americans trust the federal government, down from 35% in 2022."

As they reflect, "Recent years have seen distrust in both government and politicians reach near record levels. These trends have serious consequences for the country and for the health of our democracy."

They're right.

As the Organization for Economic Co-Operation and Development (OECD) has written, "Continued low trust environments not only damage social cohesion and political participation, but also limit governments' ability to function effectively and respond to complex domestic and global challenges. Public trust is a pillar of democracy."

America cannot be a trusted leader in the world—from the North Atlantic Treaty Organization to the United Nations and beyond—when it doesn't even have the trust of its own citizens.

In many ways, what the second Trump administration is doing is restoring the public trust that was further eroded under the Biden administration—but, to be perfectly frank, had been eroding for decades.

When you look at the data, there's a partisan disjunction among Americans.

"Today, 35% of Democrats and Democratic-leaning independents say they trust the federal government just about always or most of the time, compared with 11% of Republicans and Republican leaners. . . . Republicans have often been more reactive than Democrats to changes in political leadership, with Republicans expressing much lower levels of trust during Democratic presidencies," concludes the Pew Research Center.

To understand the American people's distrust of their own government, especially Republicans' distrust, one needs to look no further than the paper trail unearthed by Tulsi Gabbard and the Office of the Director of National Intelligence.

Tulsi is not alone in her search for the truth.

Kash Patel is a leader in the national security space: he was a public defender at the federal and state levels, who tried cases from murder to narco-trafficking and complex financial crimes, before joining the Obama administration where he oversaw the successful prosecution of Al-Qaeda and ISIS.

But, more importantly, we have someone in office who is here to serve the President of the United States of America and the American people who voted him into office—first.

He is also absolutely committed to upholding the rule of law as outlined in the US Constitution.

The new Director of the FBI is the person who found the "burn bags." These are where thousands of Russia-related documents that were scheduled to be destroyed were unearthed. In true Trump fashion, Kash announced what he had found on X so everyone was privy to it.

"In 2017/18, I proved the Steele Dossier was fictitious intelligence, weaponized by corrupt FBI officials to deceive a federal judge and unlawfully spy on then presidential candidate Trump's campaign—all paid for by his opponent. The media called me a liar. Now I'm the FBI Director: We just uncovered burn bags/room filled with hidden Russia Gate files, including the Durham annex, and declassified them. Once again, I released the prior FBI's own documents and exposed the truth. The same media is calling me a liar again. Maybe this FBI will release more docs directly, from FBI HQ . . . so we can see who is lying—wouldn't want to deprive the fake news of more bogus Pulitzers."

In other words, Kash doesn't just have the experience, he has the will to help our president enact a regime that, as the progressives often say but never do, speaks truth to power. Kash Patel is only concerned with uncovering the truth for the American people, and he's unafraid of confrontation from within or from outside of the United States government.

He isn't just the FBI Director we have; he is the FBI Director we need. For the first year of Trump 2.0 he was flanked by Deputy Director Dan Bongino, a man of absolute credibility who is committed to the America First agenda. As Trump described this former member of the NYPD and highly respected member of the Secret Service, he is "a man of incredible love and passion for our Country." I can't think of a better man to support the amazing work that Kash Patel is doing.

And what about John Ratcliffe, Director of the Central Intelligence Agency?

He too is a man of incredible love and passion for our country.

He is a man who has arrived in this second administration ready to serve.

He was Director of National Intelligence in the first term, and he understands, especially in light of these revelations, how intelligence can be weaponized.

As we all know, it's not just the Obama administration and Democratic politicians throughout the country who have aided and abetted the Russia Hoax. The Silicon Valley elites have worked hard to discredit Trump and his closest allies.

For example, YouTube and Google banned Dan Bongino from their platforms.

And don't forget what happened after the 2020 election.

Twitter banned the forty-fifth president. Facebook banned the former president. Google pulled Parler from its app store. Twitch disabled the president's channel. Even Shopify worked hard to help the Democrats. They took down two online stores affiliated with Trump.

Imagine if this happened in another country like Egypt or Saudi Arabia? Outlets like the *New York Times* would be running stories about an internal coup, a rigged election, and a concerted effort to remove the former president not just from the Oval Office, but from public life entirely.

Instead, many cheered for the total censorship of a former president who tens of millions of Americans voted into office.

These so-called journalists who collect their income—often a lucrative one—from peddling sensationalized disinformation to the American public, especially as it is related to the Russia Hoax.

Fortunately, many journalists on the Right have been holding the liberal media establishment responsible for its false reporting.

Their diligence has paid off.

As the *New York Post* reflects, "Sally Buzbee, the executive editor for the *Washington Post*, revealed the newspaper was unable to stand by the accuracy of their reporting regarding source Sergei Millian—former president of the Russian-American Chamber of Commerce—noting the recent indictment filed by Special Counsel John Durham this month. . . . Among the many debunked claims Millian alleged was that Russian security services possessed a tape of Donald Trump in a Moscow hotel room with prostitutes who were urinating on a bed where then-President Barack Obama and first lady Michelle Obama had previously stayed."

You can't make this stuff up.

Actually, you can—and both the Democrats and their mouthpieces at outlets like the *Washington Post* have been doing it for decades.

In fact, this is how you win the biggest awards in journalism.

United States Secretary of War Pete Hegseth, an absolutely crucial addition to the Trump administration, asked a question that a number of Americans have asked since the Steele Dossier proved to be a ruse funded by the Clinton campaign.

Shouldn't they give back their Pulitzer Prizes?

"What a big surprise," he said, "a bunch of hit pieces come out from the same media that peddled the Russia hoax. Won't give back their Pulitzers. They got Pulitzers for a bunch of lies."

Secretary Hegseth, a Minnesota native who was commissioned as an infantry officer in the US Army National Guard, has served in Guantánamo Bay, Cuba, Iraq, and Afghanistan, and he has earned several military commendations, including two Bronze Stars, the Joint Commendation Medal, two Army Commendation Medals, the Combat Infantryman Badge, and the Expert Infantryman Badge. He is absolutely qualified to lead our Department of War, and he is focusing on the priorities needed as we face legitimate military threats from Russia, China, Iran, and other nations.

But he's also a leader who understands how the liberal ideological apparatuses operate by misrepresenting and distorting the truth, often to great fanfare from institutions like Columbia University, which awards the Pulitzer Prize. With degrees from both Princeton University and Harvard University, Secretary Hegseth has had an insider's experience of how the liberal elite operate, and how they create the frames that distort the truth.

As he would no doubt agree, there's a reason trust in the mainstream media—especially the liberal media—has eroded alongside trust in the American government.

As Gallup reported at the end of 2024, "Americans continue to register record-low trust in the mass media, with 31% expressing a 'great deal' or 'fair amount' of confidence in the media to report the news 'fully, accurately and fairly,' similar to last year's 32%."

After years of getting bombarded with stories like the Russia Hoax, while real stories like Hunter Biden's laptop get outright censored, who can blame the American people for having record-low trust in the left-wing legacy media institutions?

There is a reason Joe Rogan has the number-one podcast in the world, a podcast that Kamala Harris—unlike President Trump—refused to go on.

And that reason has everything to do with the cataclysmic failure of institutions like MSNOW (formerly MSNBC), the *Washington Post*, PBS, and the *New York Times*.

It also has everything to do with the near total loss of trust in the American government that peaked under Biden's administration.

As the report from the US House of Representatives concluded, "in the final weeks before the 2020 presidential election, 51 former intelligence officials coordinated with the Biden campaign to discredit serious allegations about Biden family influence peddling. In issuing a public statement using their official titles, these former intelligence officials sought to cast an explosive *New York Post* story and Hunter Biden's abandoned laptop as 'Russian disinformation.'" I hate to make the same analogy twice, but the title of their report truly reads like it came straight out of a John Grisham novel: "The Intelligence Community 51: How CIA Contractors Colluded with the Biden Campaign to Mislead American Voters."

It is a sad day in American history when the House publishes a report titled, "How CIA Contractors Colluded with the Biden Campaign to Mislead American Voters."

But it's also a hopeful day, much like the day Director of National Intelligence announced what President Barack Obama and his administration had done to thwart President Trump.

There are going to be many more days of hope—and lasting change—under this second Trump administration.

The intel community needs warriors, not weathermen. Trump 2.0 knows it.

In the end, it's the truth that the American people want.

It's the truth that the American people deserve.

Under Trump 2.0, it's the truth that the American people will get.

Chapter 5

Law and Order

In his 2016 speech at the Republican National Convention, where he accepted the Grand Old Party's nomination for President of the United States of America, Donald J. Trump made a promise to the American people: "When I take the oath of office next year, I will restore law and order to our country."

With the American flag behind him, the Republican nominee reminded his fellow Americans—and the rest of the world—what the United States had devolved into under President Obama's failed leadership.

"Our convention occurs at a moment of crisis for our nation. The attacks on our police, and the terrorism in our cities, threaten our very way of life. Any politician who does not grasp this danger is not fit to lead our country. Americans watching this address tonight have seen the recent images of violence in our streets and the chaos in our communities. Many have witnessed this violence personally, some have even been its victims. I have a message for all of you: the crime and violence that today afflicts our nation will soon come to an end. Beginning on January 20th, 2017, safety will be restored."

On that day in 2016, Donald Trump made a promise to the American people: "we will lead our party back to the White House, and we will lead our country back to safety, prosperity, and peace."

When President Trump took office in 2017, he delivered on that promise.

To fully grasp the importance of the president's first term in office, you have to understand what America had turned into under the Obama administration.

"Homicides last year increased by 17% in America's fifty largest cities," Trump explained at the RNC. "That's the largest increase in 25 years. In our nation's capital, killings have risen by 50 percent. They are up nearly 60% in nearby Baltimore."

The presidential nominee continued, "In the President's hometown of Chicago, more than 2,000 have been the victims of shootings this year alone. And more than 3,600 have been killed in the Chicago area since he took office."

Chicago, the city where Obama cut his teeth as a community organizer in the Developing Communities Project, where he was later hired as an associate at the law firm of Davis Miner Barnhill & Galland, and where he eventually became a US Senator, had become a war zone. By the end of his second term in office, Illinoisans were referring to their flagship city as "ChIraq," a portmanteau of Chicago and Iraq.

Even *Time* magazine—hardly a beacon of conservative thought, their December 29, 2008 "Person of the Year" cover was the Obama "Hope" poster—had to reluctantly acknowledge the grim truth as Obama was leaving office. "The year-end crime statistics showed there were 468 murders in Chicago in 2015 compared with 416 the year before, a 12.5% increase, as well as 2,900 shootings—13% more than the year prior, and up 29% since 2013. Chicago had more homicides than any other city in 2015." This wasn't a random city in a third world country. This was an American city. This was the president's city. It's the city where he married the first lady. Under his leadership, even *Time* had to acknowledge that Chicago was an embarrassment not just to the rest of the country, but to the world.

If Obama had no discernible interest in retaining any semblance of law and order in Chicago, a place that he called home, then you can imagine what other cities in the United States looked like. From the east coast to the west coast, and every state in between, the failures of Democratic leadership were on full display by the time Trump stepped on the RNC stage in 2016. They were on full display by the time he took the stage, promising to restore law and order in the United States.

And yet, the erosion of law and order was constantly being excused—even justified—by the Democrats. "As police cars burned and businesses were ransacked," reflected journalist Rich Lowry, "progressives declared nonviolence 'a ruse' (Ta-Nehisi Coates); hailed looting as 'a legitimate political strategy' (*Salon*); and called the senseless rampage part of a series of, sententiously all-caps, 'UPRISINGS' (Marc Lamont Hill)." This isn't the America that any clear-thinking, law-abiding person would want to live in. This is the dystopian future of *A Clockwork Orange*.

In the most progressive cities, the disaster is particularly bad.

San Francisco now looks like the world's biggest homeless encampment. From 2005 on, reports the *San Francisco Bay Times* in 2015, "the number of homeless San Franciscans has actually gone up." Since then, it's only gotten worse under Democratic leadership. In his 2021 book *San Fran-Sicko: Why Progressives Ruin Cities*, Michael Shellenberger chronicles the devastating effects of Democratic policies. When he ran for office in 2018, Chesa Boudin, who served as the 29th District Attorney of San Francisco, announced, "We will not prosecute cases involving quality-of-life crimes. Crimes such as public camping, offering or soliciting sex, public urination, blocking a sidewalk, etc., should not and will not be prosecuted." Boudin described "open-air drug use" as a "victimless crime."

In other words, District Attorney Boudin—a man hired to enforce the law—was more than happy to allow the homeless to urinate, sell their bodies for sex, and block the sidewalk where your children play. In the eyes of progressives, that's what American greatness looks like.

But the data only tells one side of the story. It doesn't show us the real people who have to live, work, and raise their kids in this wasteland. These are people who are suffering.

"When Paneez Kosarian arrived at her condominium in downtown San Francisco around 1:40 a.m. on a Sunday morning in the late summer of 2019," writes Shellenberger, "she discovered a man blocking the entrance. His back was turned, and he was staring inside. The man, twenty-five-year-old Austin Vincent, said to Kosarian, 'I'm the only human left.' And, 'Everybody else is a robot.' He then said, 'What can I do to earn your trust? I'll kill anyone. I'll kill the robot to earn your trust.' By 'robot,' Vincent was referring to the woman at the front desk." The strange man grabs Kosarian. A struggle ensues. "I want to save your life!" he screams.

In his mugshot, Kosarian's attacker is smiling. The judge let him walk free. He didn't even have to wear an ankle monitor. "The court determined that Mr. Vincent was not a threat to public safety," explained his defense attorney. "Kosarian was shocked by the news. 'I'm scared. Terrified.' After all, Vincent knew where she lived. 'I don't understand what more it takes for the city and the judge to understand this man is a danger,' she said. She tweeted at California Governor Gavin Newsom, 'Please watch this video of me getting attacked at my front door less than 72-hrs ago. The man who attacked me was released this morning because the judge, Christine Van Aken believes that this man is not a danger to our community. PLEASE SAVE OUR CITY!!'"

The saddest part about Kosarian's night of terror is that it was a typical night in San Francisco. At this point, everyone who lives in San Francisco has their own horror stories. From carjackings to muggings and rapes, San Fran-Sicko has become the textbook example of what happens when Democratic politicians are given the keys to a city. If you want to see what happens when Democrats have their way, look no farther than the Bay Area. The Bay Area is the model for what the Democratic Party will do to the rest of the United States. With politicians like Zohran "police are 'a major threat to public safety'" Mamdani trying to seize the keys to other cities, there has perhaps never been a better time to study the irreparable damage done to San Francisco.

Of note, Shellenberger cut his teeth as a socialist. In the 1990s, he worked with eco-anarchists to save trees in California and the Pacific Northwest. Back then, he was on the streets of Seattle protesting economic globalization along with black bloc anarchists. A longtime resident of San Francisco, he had actually advocated for many of the policies that would later cripple his city. The genesis of his book was a question that many progressives began to ask themselves around the time Donald Trump first announced he was running for office: from homelessness to crime, why have all these problems gotten worse in the most progressive cities?

San Fran-Sicko, as Shellenberger calls it, is hardly an outlier. While people might not have liked the way President Trump described Baltimore—as a "disgusting, rat and rodent infested mess"—he wasn't off-track. And, vis-à-vis his liberal detractors, there was nothing racist about his comments. Kimberly Klacik, a black woman and a former congressional candidate who calls Baltimore County home, wasn't afraid to highlight what her city had devolved into under Democratic leadership. In a viral YouTube video, she explained, "Baltimore is one of the top five most dangerous cities in America. The murder rate in Baltimore is ten times the US average. The Baltimore poverty rate is over twenty percent. Homicide, drug, and alcohol deaths are skyrocketing in our city." While black lives matter to Democrats on election day, they matter very little on every other day of the year.

Trump has woken up many Americans to the reality of leftist policies that launch cities into a downward spiral.

It's not a political enigma why Baltimore is suffering. Even NPR had to acknowledge the truth. "Baltimore Residents Blame Record-High Murder Rate on Lower Police Presence," they recently wrote. Why is there lower police presence? "Some residents attribute the high murder rate to relaxed police patrols in the city following high-profile cases of police brutality. Officers have backed off in neighborhoods, like the one where Freddie Gray was arrested." Reverend Kinji Scott, a Baltimore pastor, expressed a sentiment shared by many people in his city, and by President Trump: "We wanted the police there. We wanted them engaged in the community. . . . We need the front line police officers . . ."

Chicago, San Francisco, Baltimore—what do these cities have in common? These are all cities that belong to the Democrats. Chicago hasn't had a Republican mayor since William Hale Thompson took office in 1927. San Francisco has been blue every year since Mayor George Christopher took office in 1956. Baltimore hasn't seen a Republican mayor since Theodore McKeldin was at the helm of Charm City in 1963. These are the cities where the Democrats have been able to pass virtually every piece of legislation they want to pass. The violent crime, the homelessness, and other related problems, like drug overdoses, haven't become worse *despite* Democratic policies—they have become worse *because* of them.

While we could proceed in this direction—going city by city, policy by policy, Democrat by Democrat—for another two thousand pages, the point is obvious: the Democratic Party, led by President Barack Obama, had failed to keep the American people safe. When Trump came down the escalator inside Trump Tower and announced his decision to run for president, the American people knew it was time for a radical change. When he announced his decision to run in 2024, they once again knew it was time for a radical change. The American people had given Joe Biden a chance that he didn't deserve, and by the end of 2024 it was clear that he and his administration had blown it—big time.

Whether we're talking about Portland, Oregon, where Antifa activists are quite literally burning the city to the ground, or the Big Apple, where Zohran Mamdani—the Democrat's Mayor of New York City—describes the police as "racist, anti-queer and a major threat to public safety," law and order has become the perennial target of the Democratic Party. No matter how disastrous their policies were for their constituencies, elected officials across the country always had support from the Obama and Biden administrations. Sanctuary city?

Sure. Decriminalize dangerous drugs? Go for it. Allow homeless people to camp outside your business and urinate on your windows? That sounds like progress.

"It's emotional for us," Raquel Santiago, a Mexican immigrant who came here legally, told *The Daily Signal* during an interview back in 2020, after leftist protests burned her family's ice cream shop to the ground. "When you see that your job, all you [have been] working for [for] years, not just you, [but also] your parents and the future, probably of your kids, burning down for something you have nothing to do [with] . . . This is just shocking." According to *The Signal*, about fifty businesses in Kenosha, Wisconsin, were hurt by the riots, which went on for two nights. "I don't even have words to describe what my family [is] going through."

When Trump promised to restore law and order in 2016, and again in 2024, he wasn't just appealing to right-wing partisans. He was connecting with Americans like Santiago. He was connecting with Americans on all sides of the political spectrum who have to deal with Antifa and other radical extremists, as well as the Democratic politicians who enable, protect, and—in many cases—encourage these left-wing terrorists. He especially connected with Americans who have to live, work, and raise their kids in cities like Chicago, San Francisco, and Baltimore. According to the data, most Americans don't believe the police are "racist, anti-queer and a major threat to public safety." They believe the police keep them safe.

The reason President Trump has been talking about sending National Guard troops to Baltimore is because Democratic politicians have failed to keep their own city clean and safe.

The reason Scott Presler, who leads Early Vote Action, and his volunteer movement have traveled to Baltimore is because children are playing in the Baltimore streets with used needles, human feces, and dead rats like this is a third-world country.

Donald Trump hasn't been sending National Guard troops to places like Memphis because he has nothing better to do. He's sending them because these Democratic politicians can't do their jobs.

It's embarrassing.

Instead of declaring a "constitutional crisis," these politicians should take a long hard look in the mirror and feel the shame for their failed leadership.

In 2021, the Pew Research Center conducted a survey of US adults. The percentage of Americans who said spending on policing in their area should be decreased was just 15 percent. A greater percentage of Americans said it should be "increased a lot." And what about the minorities who have to live in cities where their police departments have been defunded? What about the minorities who have to live with gang violence on a regular basis? Of those whom Pew surveyed, more black americans want to increase police funding than decrease it. More Hispanics want to increase police funding than decrease it.

Even among Democrats, the consensus is clear; according to the data accrued by Pew, more Democrats want more funding for the police, not less. It's telling that one year into the Biden administration, the American people were already expressing their disapproval with the way policing in the United States was being handled. Under Biden's leadership, America was once again gripped by the "defund the police" mass hysteria that defined President Obama's administration and that left our cities in shambles.

During the Biden years, Americans were seriously concerned about crime. In November 2023, Gallup reported that a "new high of 63% say US crime problem is extremely/very serious." And "majorities say US, local crime higher than a year ago." More tragically, "28% report their household has been victimized by crime." This was Joe Biden's America.

Later, in a spring 2024 poll, conducted on the verge of our most recent election, Harvard/Harris revealed that 75 percent of Americans have a favorable view of the police. Most Americans don't see the police as "racist, anti-queer and a major threat to public safety." They see them as what they are: the courageous protectors of our lives, our property, and our God-given freedoms. Without them, every city in America would look like Portland. With the exception of a relatively small handful of radical leftist activists and politicians, that's not what the American people want.

Interestingly, the Left seems to know that's not what people want, which is why they try to twist the truth when it serves their interests. During the "summer of love," they were the ones proclaiming their desire to "defund the police." After the police were defunded, and Americans were scared to leave their homes, they did an about-face. All of a sudden, they were presenting themselves as the party that supports law and order. Their turn, devoid of all evidence, is frankly astonishing.

The American Presidency Project, hosted at the University of California, Santa Barbara, an enclave of progressive misinformation, announced before the election that "President Biden has stood with law enforcement his entire career, and worked to ensure law enforcement serves all communities his entire career. And he has the results to show for it."

Notwithstanding the university's Orwellian effort to rewrite this particularly disastrous presidency as a win for law enforcement, the American people didn't buy into the deception. They weren't UC professors living in gated communities. They were the ones who had just witnessed their communities flooded with opioids and criminal illegal aliens for the past four years. They were the ones who had been suffering under Joe Biden's nonexistent response to crime. They were the ones who once again turned to President Trump for help.

Is it really any wonder that seventy-seven million Americans voted Donald Trump back into the Oval Office? Is it any wonder that he increased his share of the Hispanic vote? "Voter surveys from the Associated Press show that the president-elect won 43 percent of the overall Latino vote. That's an eight-point increase from 2020," reports PBS. Is it also any wonder that he increased his share of the black vote? "It is Trump, not Harris, who gained support among Black voters compared with the 2020 election," laments the far-left media outlet *Al Jazeera*.

After the eight-year disaster that was the Obama presidency, followed by four years of reprieve, and then four years of Biden asleep in the Oval Office—literally—the American people, especially minorities, were once again feeling unsafe, at risk, and left behind. After all, both Obama and Biden had put the safety of criminal illegal aliens over the safety of their own citizens—and the consequences were deadly.

As crime escalated and immigrants flooded cities across the US, Americans were, to borrow the title of sociologist Arlie Russell Hochschild's *New York Times* bestseller, feeling like *Strangers in Their Own Land.*

"The number of police officers killed in the line of duty has risen by almost 50% compared to this point last year," Trump reminded the American people in his first RNC address. "Nearly 180,000 illegal immigrants with criminal records, ordered deported from our country, are tonight roaming free to threaten peaceful citizens," Trump reminded his fellow Americans.

Under Biden's leadership, America was the land of lawlessness.

In fact, Trump could have delivered an almost verbatim reproduction of his 2016 RNC address in 2024 without missing a beat.

According to the House Committee on Oversight and Accountability and the House Committee on Homeland Security, "Under President Biden's watch, there have been over 8 million migrant encounters nationwide . . . Worse yet, over 1.7 million known got-aways—illegal immigrants who have evaded Border Control—are now living in the interior of the United States without documentation and without having undergone any vetting by immigration officials."

That's not putting Americans first.

That's not putting law and order first.

According to Chief Border Patrol Agents, who were interviewed for this report, this was something approximating the total absence of law and order. "[O]ur Sector Intelligence Unit estimates that the weekly revenue for illicit human smuggling in our sector along, the Del Rio Sector alone, is in excess of $30 million a week." "We have seen a ris[e] in the number of [Terrorist Screening Data Set] hits, which is individuals that have a record of potential terrorist ties. And in the last 2 years we've continued to see significantly more." Given the growing threat China poses to America, this last quote is particularly striking: "4,797 Chinese nationals were encountered at the southwest border. This represents a nearly 800% increase compared to November 2022."

That isn't a problem.

That's a national security crisis.

As the House Committee on Oversight and Accountability and the House Committee on Homeland Security conclude, "These staggering figures should send chills down the spine of every law enforcement officer in the nation. The Biden administration is solely responsible for the disastrous state of our southern border."

The 2016 and 2024 elections weren't just a rebuke of failed Democratic leadership in the Oval Office. They were a rebuke of the ascendent movement on the Left that wants to fundamentally reshape our country—not through policies that put Americans first, but through radical activism designed to erode law and order in the United States. The 2016 and 2024 elections weren't just battles for the Oval Office; they were battles to reclaim the vision put forth by America's Founding Fathers. They were battles to preserve the American way of life.

When Donald Trump promised the American people that he would restore law and order in the United States back in 2016, he was serious. And when he took office, it quickly became apparent that this wasn't an empty campaign gesture. He meant business. During his first term in office, according to the Trump White House website, "over 230 Federal judges were confirmed—each one committed to respecting the rule of law *as written*—and three new conservative justices sit on the Supreme Court. The Trump administration also achieved the most significant criminal justice reform in decades, resulting in the historic, bipartisan First Step Act."

The First Step Act was "the first landmark criminal justice reform legislation ever passed to reduce recidivism and help former inmates successfully rejoin society." The president "reversed decades-old ban on Second Chance Pell programs to provide postsecondary education to individuals who are incarcerated, expanding their skills and helping them to better succeed in the workforce upon re-entry," and he "awarded over $333 million in Department of Labor grants for reentry projects focused on career development services for justice-involved youth and adults who were formerly incarcerated."

Importantly, even as the president created a path back to society for offenders, he kept his promise about restoring law and order in the United States. It's that double focus, which combines strength and compassion, that made his first term in office so successful. Here are the stats from the National Archives' website page devoted to Law & Justice:

- In 2019, violent crime fell for the third consecutive year
- Since 2016, the violent crime rate has declined over 5 percent and the murder rate has fallen by over 7 percent
- Launched Operation Legend to combat a surge of violent crime in cities, resulting in more than 5,500 arrests
- Deployed the National Guard and federal law enforcement to Kenosha to stop the violence and restore public safety
- Provided $1 million to Kenosha law enforcement, nearly $4 million to support small businesses in Kenosha, and provided over $41 million to support law enforcement in the state of Wisconsin
- Deployed federal agents to save the courthouse in Portland from rioters
- Signed an executive order outlining ten-year prison sentences for destroying federal property and monuments
- Directed the Department of Justice (DOJ) to investigate and prosecute federal offenses related to ongoing violence
- DOJ provided nearly $400 million for new law enforcement hiring

- Endorsed by the 355,000 members of the Fraternal Order of Police
- Revitalized Project Safe Neighborhoods, which brings together federal, state, local, and tribal law enforcement officials to develop solutions to violent crime
- Improved first-responder communications by deploying the FirstNet National Public Safety Broadband Network, which serves more than 12,000 public safety agencies across the nation
- Established a new commission to evaluate best practices for recruiting, training, and supporting law enforcement officers
- Signed the Safe Policing for Safe Communities executive order to incentivize local police department reforms in line with law and order
- Made hundreds of millions of dollars' worth of surplus military equipment available to local law enforcement
- Signed an executive order to help prevent violence against law enforcement officers
- Secured permanent funding for the 9/11 Victim Compensation Fund for first responders
- The president was especially committed to stopping hate crimes, gun violence, and human trafficking. During his first term in office, he:
- Signed an executive order making clear that Title VI of the Civil Rights Act of 1964 applies to discrimination rooted in anti-Semitism
- Launched a centralized website to educate the public about hate crimes and encourage reporting
- Signed the Fix NICS Act to keep guns out of the hands of dangerous criminals
- Signed the STOP School Violence Act and created a Commission on School Safety to examine ways to make our schools safer
- Launched the Foster Youth to Independence initiative to prevent and end homelessness among young adults under the age of twenty-five who are in, or have recently left, the foster care system

- Signed the Trafficking Victims Protection Reauthorization Act, which tightened criteria for whether countries are meeting standards for eliminating trafficking
- Established a task force to help combat the tragedy of missing or murdered Native American women and girls
- Prioritized fighting for the voiceless and ending the scourge of human trafficking across the nation, through a whole of government back by legislation, executive action, and engagement with key industries
- Created the first-ever White House position focused solely on combating human trafficking

The president also fulfilled his campaign promise to protect unborn children from murder. He:

- Reinstated and expanded the Mexico City Policy, ensuring that taxpayer money is not used to fund abortion globally
- Issued a rule preventing Title X taxpayer funding from subsidizing the abortion industry
- Supported legislation to end late-term abortions
- Cut all funding to the United Nations population fund due to the fund's support for coercive abortion and forced sterilization
- Signed legislation overturning the previous administration's regulation that prohibited states from defunding abortion facilities as part of their family planning programs
- Fully enforced the requirement that taxpayer dollars do not support abortion coverage in Obamacare exchange plans
- Stopped the federal funding of fetal tissue research
- Worked to protect health care entities and individuals' conscience rights—ensuring that no medical professional is forced to participate in an abortion in violation of their beliefs
- Issued an executive order reinforcing the requirement that all hospitals in the United States provide medical treatment or an

emergency transfer for infants who are in need of emergency medical care, regardless of prematurity or disability

- Led a coalition of countries to sign the Geneva Consensus Declaration, declaring that there is no international right to abortion and committing to protecting women's health
- Became the first president in American history to attend the March for Life

The president also stood up for religious liberty, a foundational pillar of the American way of life, and one that has fallen by the wayside under Democratic leadership. The president:

- Protected the conscience rights of doctors, nurses, teachers, and groups like the Little Sisters of the Poor
- First president to convene a meeting at the United Nations to end religious persecution
- Established the White House Faith and Opportunity Initiative
- Stopped the Johnson Amendment from interfering with pastors' right to speak their minds
- Reversed the previous administration's policy that prevented the government from providing disaster relief to religious organizations
- Protected faith-based adoption and foster care providers, ensuring they can continue to serve their communities while following the teachings of their faith
- Reduced burdensome barriers to ensure Native Americans are free to keep spiritually and culturally significant eagle feathers found on their tribal lands
- Took action to ensure federal employees can take paid time off work to observe religious holy days
- Signed legislation to assist religious and ethnic groups targeted by ISIS for mass murder and genocide in Syria and Iraq
- Directed American assistance toward persecuted communities, including through faith-based programs

- Launched the International Religious Freedom Alliance—the first-ever alliance devoted to confronting religious persecution around the world
- Appointed a Special Envoy to monitor and combat anti-Semitism
- Imposed restrictions on certain Chinese officials, internal security units, and companies for their complicity in the persecution of Uighur Muslims in Xinjiang
- Issued an executive order to protect and promote religious freedom around the world

Finally, the president dealt with the elephant in the room: the opioid crisis. Under his leadership, the United States led the way in putting an end to the cartels and the deluge of drugs coming across our border and borders around the world. Some highlights from his first term office:

- In FY 2019, ICE HSI seized 12,466 pounds of opioids, including 3,688 pounds of fentanyl—an increase of 35 percent from FY 2018
- Seized tens of thousands [of] kilograms of heroin and thousands of kilograms of fentanyl since 2017
- The Department of Justice (DOJ) prosecuted more fentanyl traffickers than ever before, dismantled 3,000 drug trafficking organizations, and seized enough fentanyl to kill 105,000 Americans
- DOJ charged more than 65 defendants collectively responsible for distributing over 45 million opioid pills
- Brought kingpin designations against traffickers operating in China, India, Mexico, and more who have played a role in the epidemic in America
- Indicted major Chinese drug traffickers for distributing fentanyl in the United States for the first time ever, and convinced China to enact strict regulations to control the production and sale of fentanyl

When politicians, pundits, and the American people alike remember the president's first term in office as the most important term in the history of criminal justice reform, their memories are not an exaggeration. It was the most important term in the history of criminal justice reform.

When global leaders remember this as the period in which the United States led the way battling problems like religious persecution, illegal immigration, and global terrorism, they too are not misremembering these first four years that President Donald J. Trump was in office.

As the history books will no doubt acknowledge, this was *the* defining term for law and order, not just in the United States but around the world.

Under Trump 2.0, it's only going to get better.

Since taking office in 2025, President Trump has once again emerged as an unwavering leader in the war on crime—both at home and abroad.

"While little high-profile criminal justice reform legislation passed under President Biden," the Vera Institute of Justice, a progressive nonprofit, reflects: "AG Bondi wasted no time, issuing 14 memos on her first day rescinding Biden-era policies like the Garland Memo and ratcheting up 'tough-on-crime' policies, including directing prosecutors to pursue the highest charge justifiable by the evidence. Bondi also advanced Trump's executive order on 'Restoring the Death Penalty,' lifting the moratorium on federal executions and assisting states in pursuing capital cases against the 37 death row defendants whose sentences Biden commuted." As yet another sign of how divorced the Democrats are from the American people, the Vera report is not written as a celebration of the monumental job that AG Bondi and her team are doing, but as a critique. Indeed, they are upset she is ushering in a "tough on crime" era.

In their criticism of Trump, they write: "Chief among his enemies are so-called 'sanctuary' cities and states, which he has targeted with various lawsuits, attempts to withhold federal funding, and threats of prosecution. The administration has also sought to directly undermine big-city crime response. Department of Transportation Secretary Sean Duffy threatened federal funding to New York City and Washington, DC, if they did not crack down on transit crime and fare evasion."

"The trend of violent crime, homelessness, and other threats to public safety on one of our nation's most prominent metro systems is unacceptable. After years of soft-on-crime policies, our Department is stepping in to restore order," Duffy wrote. "Commuters are sick and tired of feeling like they have to jeopardize their safety to get to work, go to school, or to travel around the city. We will continue to fight to ensure their federal tax dollars are going towards a crime-free commute."

Isn't that what Americans deserve?

Don't they also deserve to fly without the stress that has become commonplace in American airports?

Newark Airport was an absolute disaster. Secretary Duffy turned it around. He is the first transportation secretary to take full responsibility for these issues. He is now leading the movement to revitalize air traffic control and all the staffing issues that are there. Secretary after secretary before him just passed the buck. This is a guy who's getting the job done. He's not neglecting our airports, just like he's not neglecting the crime on our subways. The buck stops with him.

This truly is a cabinet of consequence.

The Vera Institute also notes that "Trump also issued an executive order establishing a crime task force in Washington, DC, seeking to directly bolster law enforcement presence and immigration enforcement in the nation's capital." While Vera and the Democrats despise these actions, this is what the American people voted for. As virtually every poll suggests, Americans are sick and tired of the "soft on crime" approach of the Obama and Biden administrations. Nobody wants their city to look like San Francisco, the crime-ridden, drug-addled home of congresswoman Nancy Pelosi. For the second time, the American people voted for radical change.

Radical change is what Trump 2.0 is delivering.

On August 25, 2025, the president signed an executive order to help our brave service men and women crack down on crime in Washington, DC. As outlined on the White House's website:

- The order instructs the National Park Service to hire additional United States Park Police officers to support public safety in Washington, DC.
- It directs the US Attorney's Office for the District of Columbia to hire additional prosecutors to focus on violent and property crimes.
- It establishes an online portal for Americans with law enforcement experience or other relevant backgrounds to join federal law enforcement branches to support law enforcement operations in Washington, DC.
- It instructs law enforcement agencies that are members of the DC Safe and Beautiful Task Force to create and begin training, manning, hiring, and equipping specialized units that are dedicated to ensuring public safety and order in the nation's capital that can be deployed whenever the circumstances necessitate.
- The order directs the Secretary of Defense to create a specialized DC. National Guard unit trained to ensure public safety and order in the Nation's capital, when its activation becomes necessary, and ensure state National Guards are similarly trained and ready to assist in quelling civil disturbances nationwide. Further, the Secretary of Defense will ensure the availability of a National Guard quick reaction force for rapid nationwide deployment when circumstances warrant.
- The order directs the Department of Housing and Urban Development to investigate any noncompliance with crime prevention and safety requirements in HUD's agreements with the DC Housing Authority or landlords in vouchers to ensure

that housing providers are ensuring safe, decent, and sanitary conditions in housing and restricting tenants who engage in criminal activity like drug distribution, violent criminal activity, and domestic violence.

- It tasks the Secretary of Transportation with conducting inspections to address unsafe conditions in DC's federally funded transit services and take remedial action as needed.
- Finally, the order directs the Attorney General to request additional updates and modifications to the Metropolitan Police Department general orders from the mayor as necessary to address the crime emergency and ensure public safety.

This executive order is a long overdue win for the people of Washington, DC.

For decades, the people in our nation's capital have suffered.

Under Biden's failed leadership that suffering showed no signs of abetting.

As the White House site explains, "The local DC government has lost control of public safety in the city. In May, two embassy staffers were murdered. In June, a Congressional intern was fatally shot just a short distance from the White House. Just weeks ago, a Trump administration staffer was mercilessly beaten by a violent mob. Washington, DC, has a violent crime rate that is higher than some of the most dangerous places in the world. Washington, DC's 2024 murder rate (27.54 per 100K) is higher than Bogota (15.1), Mexico City (10.6), Islamabad (9.2), Lima (7.6), and major capitals like Paris (1.64), London (1.1), and Madrid (0.96). President Trump has a constitutional obligation to restore order so that citizens, tourists, and federal workers can live and work peacefully in the nation's capital. Our nation's capital should be the envy of the world, not a disgrace."

Having spent a large amount of time in DC, I could not agree more. Our capital should be our shining gem—a true city on a hill—not a dump.

"As a result of President Trump's decisive actions," explains the White House, "crime in D.C. has already started to fall, with robbery down 46%, carjacking down 83%, and violent crime down 22%." Furthermore, "dozens of homeless encampments have been cleared and graffiti is being cleaned up as the Trump administration works to restore glory and prestige to our nation's capital." Furthermore: "In just one week, 550 arrests have been made for crimes such as assault on a police officer, armed robbery, assault with a deadly weapon, involuntary manslaughter, child abuse, driving under the influence, and more. Authorities have also removed dozens of criminal illegal immigrants from the streets, including one MS-13 gang member and another charged with sex crimes against a child."

In late August, local news reported that "for the first time in a long time, DC has gone seven days without a homicide."

And DC is just the beginning.

No more excuses. Trump 2.0 is restoring law and order.

When Los Angeles was in turmoil in June 2025, as violent leftists tried to seize control of the city, the president sent in two thousand National Guard troops and seven hundred Marines.

In a social media post, the president accurately pointed out that the city would be "obliterated" without him. Spend more than five minutes in that city, and witness the protestors, the homeless encampments, and the violence, and you would no doubt agree. "The very incompetent 'Governor,' Gavin Newscum, and 'Mayor,' Karen Bass, should be saying, 'THANK YOU, PRESIDENT TRUMP, YOU ARE SO WONDERFUL. WE WOULD BE NOTHING WITHOUT YOU, SIR.'" You might not like how the president talks. And you might not think he's "nice." But he gets the job done—time and time again.

Above all, he listens.

When Americans like Paneez Kosarian have to tweet "PLEASE SAVE OUR CITY!!" at politicians like Gavin Newsom, it's an absolute embarrassment to the nation.

When leaders like Trump listen to citizens like Kosarian, Americans know they have an ally in the Oval Office. When Trump's team across the country listens, too, they know they have an ally in the House, in the Senate, in governors' offices, and in state legislatures where Republicans are working hard to keep their constituents safe.

In July 2024, Representative David Kustoff introduced H. Con. Res. 122, "Expressing the sense of Congress that Operation Legend was successful in reducing and combating violent crime in the largest cities of the United States and that a future presidential administration committed to enforcing and maintaining law and order should consider implementing a similar policy."

Fortunately for Representative Kustoff and the American people, Trump is back in the Oval Office.

And he's taking on district attorneys who are trying to thwart his administration's fight to stop senseless murders—like the murder of four-year old LeGend Taliferro, who was shot and killed inside his Kansas City apartment.

We should expect similar—and even better—policies and results during Trump's second term as commander in chief.

To hammer home the point: it's not just boots on the ground—like the Marines he sent to Los Angeles—that are making our cities, and ultimately our country, great again. It's also the legal battles that the Trump administration is waging to not only preserve law and order, but to preserve our Constitution.

"In recent months, the Justice Department has filed several lawsuits against sanctuary jurisdictions seeking to compel compliance with federal law, including one against New York City on July 24th. Recently, the Mayor of Louisville agreed to revoke their sanctuary policies following a letter from the Justice Department threatening legal action," explains the US Department of Justice.

These "sanctuary cities" aren't just unconstitutional, they're also some of the worst cities for violent crime, homelessness, and other preventable problems: San Francisco, Chicago, Portland, the list goes on.

What they have in common isn't just death and decay, the likes of which we would never see under a Republican president, but a total disdain for the foundational pillars of law and order.

If he were walking through these "sanctuary cities" today—stepping over passed out vagrants, used needles, and human excrement, as people who aren't even citizens hurl Molotov cocktails at a police station—George Washington would never be able to guess that he was in the United States. How could this possibly be the country he and the other Founding Fathers envisioned? How could this be a reflection of the US Constitution?

Honestly, the streets of Chicago, San Francisco, and Portland look like scenes from *Mad Max*.

In many ways, Trump personifies the strong leadership that made the United States what it is. He also personifies leadership that the United States once again needs. There's no doubt that the Founding Fathers would be standing shoulder to shoulder with our president.

George Lakoff, a cognitive linguist at the University of Chicago, has used the metaphor of the strict father figure to explain conservative morality. "In conservative, strict father morality," he writes, "evil is a palpable thing, a force in the world. To stand up to evil you have to be morally strong. If you're weak, you let evil triumph, so that weakness in itself is a form of evil, as is promoting weakness." As Lakoff concludes, "Not to show overwhelming strength is immoral, since it will induce evildoers to perform more evil deeds, because they'll think they can get away with it. To oppose a show of strength is therefore immoral."

By contrast, liberal morality revolves around the metaphor of the acquiescent mother. This is the mother who is hesitant to punish her children when they break the rules—talking back, acting out in the grocery store, and getting in trouble with their teachers and, eventually, the police. This is the mother who doesn't want her children to be upset with her. She doesn't want to be the one who has to enforce the rules; she wants to be their friend. It's pathological compassion. It doesn't just hurt her kids, it hurts the rest of us who have to encounter her kids. That is, it hurts society.

Within a few months of Trump leaving office back in 2021, protesters in Portland set a police union building on fire. That same week, protestors in Columbus broke into police headquarters. The doors were locked, and they breached them. In one video, a protestor hits a police officer with a club.

Do you think they would have had that gall if President Trump was in office?

Back in 2014, Donald Trump tweeted, "what separates the winners from the losers is how a person reacts to each new twist of fate."

How the president is cleaning up the mess left by President Biden, how he is tackling the crime wave in Washington, DC, Los Angeles, and other cities, how he is responding to the criminal illegal aliens at our southern border, it's what distinguishes him from the Democratic losers who have run this country into the ground.

It's what distinguishes him from men like Joe Biden.

And guess what?

The courts are making decisions to advance the Make America Great Again agenda as well.

Dobbs v. Jackson Women's Health Organization—goodbye federal government sanctioned murder.

The Ninth Circuit Court of Appeals rules in favor of the president's "Remain in Mexico" policy—goodbye unlawful immigration.

And the wins continue to come in.

"Supreme Court allows Trump administration to deport people to third countries for now," laments CBS News on June 21, 2025.

And, above all, there was the Supreme Court ruling that granted presidential immunity.

The judiciary is starting to correct course. They're affirming Trump policies they once blocked.

Of course, Trump will continue to have adversaries.

As CNN wrote in July 2025, "Two trends have emerged at the Supreme Court in recent weeks: President Donald Trump is on a winning streak and Justice Ketanji Brown Jackson, the court's junior-most justice, is having none of it."

The article says that Jackson's most recent dissent came "in the court's blockbuster decision last month that curbed the power of lower courts to issue temporary orders blocking the president's policy . . . Days earlier, dissenting from a decision that sided with fuel producers, Jackson wrote that [the] court's opinion left the impression that 'moneyed interests enjoy an easier road to relief in this Court than ordinary citizens.'"

No doubt Ketanji Jackson will continue to dissent, and continue to spread her own narrative about the Supreme Court's decisions to uphold what the American people voted for last November. The Democrats and the liberal media will continue to scream about a "constitutional crisis" (as if the Constitution says we should murder unborn babies and not have borders). The forces of the America Last movement are always going to be there, challenging us every step of the way.

As his presidency unfolds, it will be nothing short of exciting to see the many ways in which President Trump continues to win these battles against his adversaries and to keep our country not just safe—but prosperous.

"There can be no prosperity," proclaims President Trump, "without law and order."

Chapter 6

Education, Not Indoctrination

According to an *Inside Higher Ed*/Hanover Research poll, just 8 percent of university faculty backed Donald Trump over Kamala Harris in the 2024 election.

The partisan divide is even more drastic at our most elite universities.

When the *Yale Daily News* investigated Federal Elections Committee filings from 2023, they found that 3,041 "professors donated a total of roughly $127,000, of which 98.4 percent went to Democratic candidates and groups." Back in 2022, the *College Fix* found that "Democratic candidates and groups received 96 percent of total donations from Ivy League professors in the 2022 midterm elections." When you step foot in the Harvard Yard or the Princeton quad, it feels like you're stepping foot inside the Democratic National Convention.

In 2024, Duke University faculty were surveyed about their political identities. Over 23 percent identified as very liberal. About 40 percent identified as somewhat liberal. Just under 25 percent identified as centrists. Less than 10 percent identified as somewhat conservative. Under 4 percent identified as very conservative. Down the street at the University of North Carolina at Chapel Hill, a different report found that the state university has thirty-four times more registered Democrats than Republicans in the faculty ranks.

The partisan capture is most apparent inside the departments where students are taught how to think about politics, economics, and culture. According to a survey conducted by the Office for Survey Research Institute for Public Policy and Social Research at Michigan State University, these departments are wildly imbalanced.

In political science, just over 64 percent of research university professors identify as strong Democrats. Just under 15 percent identify as weak Democrats. About 8 percent identify as lean Democrat. By contrast, less than 1 percent lean Republican, less than 2 percent are weak Republicans, and less than 1 percent are strong Republicans.

In economics, about 50 percent of research university professors identify as strong Democrats; 19 percent identify as weak Democrats. 14 percent identify as lean Democrat. This is the most right-wing field, and still less than 3 percent lean Republican, less than 3 percent are weak Republicans, and less than 3 percent are strong Republicans. I'm hoping these studies begin to explain (or at least give me a good excuse) why I got a D in Econ 202 my sophomore year of college.

In anthropology, about 70 percent of research university professors identify as strong Democrats. Another 18 percent identify as weak Democrats and lean Democrat. Zero percent lean Republican. Zero percent are weak Republicans. And less than 1 percent are strong Republicans.

In sociology, where students are taught how society works (what's known as the empirical question) and how society should work (what's known as the normative question), the bias is even worse. More than 72 percent of research university professors identify as strong Democrats; 6 percent identify as weak Democrats, and 8 percent lean Democrat. Less than 1 percent identify as lean or weak Republican (0.86 percent combined). And less than 1 percent identify as strong Republicans (0.87 percent).

How do you think a course about crime, policing, and incarceration is going to be taught on an American college campus? How do you think a course about the communist economy of the Soviet Union is going to be taught? What do you think students are going to learn about the presidencies of strong Republican leaders like Theodore Roosevelt (at least the early years), Ronald Reagan, and George W. Bush? Do you think faculty who overwhelming identify as strong Democrats—many of whom see their teaching as a vehicle for their activism—are going to give these periods in American history their fair due? How do you think an institution made up almost entirely of left-wing academics is preparing the generation of American leaders?

Are students are going to be assigned conservative thinkers like Ann Coulter (whose lecture was censored at Cornell University, her own alma mater) and Charles Murray (whose lecture was violently censored at Middlebury College)? Of course not.

A typical syllabus for a college course in political science, economics, and various other fields like anthropology and sociology is going to include work by Karl Marx and Friedrich Engels, Richard D. Wolff and Robert Reich, Ibram X. Kendi and Robin DiAngelo, Judith Butler and Wendy Brown, and other thinkers who are even further left of mainstream Democrats.

If someone like Milton Friedman or Thomas Sowell makes an appearance, it is only to be chided.

At the University of Wisconsin–Madison, a university that depends on bipartisan support from taxpayers, students can take a course called "The Problem of Whiteness." According to one report, it was taught by a professor, whose salary also depends on bipartisan support from taxpayers, who "condones violence against law enforcement and compares white voters to the KKK."

At New York University, students can take a course in the fall 2025 semester called "Where/Who is Home? Trans/Queer Approaches to Domestic(ity)." In this course, the students—who pay $96,988 per year, according to NYU's website—can take in ideas that are so far left that even Alexandria Ocasio-Cortez might be confused. "Talking about home is more than talking about the architecture of dwelling," explains the professor, who promised to help students "develop trans and queer approaches to domesticity." On her faculty page, this professor identifies as an "LGBTI+ rights activist."

Race, gender, class—that's the holy trinity of a college education in America today.

Even in an English course, where you might expect students to be talking about truth and beauty and the differences between Mark Twain's realism and Don DeLillo's postmodernism, you find the same liberal garbage.

"Over the next four years, I grew increasingly disheartened by the volume of literary theory assigned throughout my English classes. I had arrived at Columbia intending to become a humanistic scholar, which is what was advertised to me during my application process. Yet, I found the vast majority of critical theory readings not only biased but also far off the mark: I was asked to understand Jane Austen's early 19th-century novel *Mansfield Park* under the 20th-century postcolonial lens of the notorious anti-Semite Edward Said, and I was fed Karl Marx in nine out of the sixteen literature courses that I took during my time as an undergraduate student," reflected a recent Columbia student.

But what should you expect when the faculty hiring process is so biased? In his systematic analysis of job advertisements in college English departments, Adam Szetela found nothing short of a far-left echo chamber. "Seventy-two out of seventy-four positions in North America seek applicants who specialize in race, ethnicity, sexuality, disability, indigeneity, and other identities," he writes in *That Book Is Dangerous! How Moral Panic, Social Media, and the Culture Wars Are Remaking Publishing*. English—like sociology, anthropology, and other fields that fund lifetime, tenured faculty positions for progressive activists—is a field where the pursuit of truth, and even beauty, takes a backseat to radical left-wing extremism.

What many Americans do not realize is that it's not just the professors who have turned our universities into left-wing indoctrination centers—it's also the administrators.

"I recently surveyed a nationally representative sample of roughly 900 'student-facing' administrators—those whose work concerns the quality and character of a student's experience on campus. I found that liberal staff members outnumber their conservative counterparts by the astonishing ratio of 12-to-one. Only 6 percent of campus administrators identified as conservative to some degree, while 71 percent classified themselves as liberal or very liberal. It's no wonder so much of the nonacademic programming on college campuses is politically one-sided," reports Sarah Lawrence political scientist Samuel Abrams.

After he reported his research, Abrams had his faculty door vandalized. Instead of defending him, Sarah Lawrence's president accused him of "attacking" members of the Sarah Lawrence "community."

Is it any wonder why so many Americans don't trust our universities?

According to a summer 2025 survey of registered American voters, "Trust in higher education is crumbling, and the system is in need of sweeping reform. Just 15% of voters say they have a great deal of trust in Ivy League colleges—less than almost every other major public institution, including the media. By a double-digit margin, and across a range of demographics, Americans believe that universities are on the wrong track, with overwhelming bipartisan and multiracial support for bold changes: banning disruptive protests, abolishing race-based admissions, reining in DEI, and restoring free speech and academic rigor. Despite deep political division, Americans agree that higher education has lost its way and that it is time to restore excellence."

Is anyone confused as to why 77,302,580 Americans voted Donald Trump back into office?

The indoctrination is no different in the K-12 public school systems, where nothing is studied outside the lenses of Marxism, feminism, and radical trans ideology.

Just look at the ubiquitous teaching of Boston University Professor Howard Zinn's anti-American screed, *A People's History of the United States.*

As the Goldwater Institute noted in a January 2025 report: "Authored by a self-described 'democratic socialist' who 'believe[s] in the wiping out of national boundaries,' Zinn's work has sold more than 2 million copies since its first publication in 1980. In conjunction with the affiliated online Zinn Education Project, its narrative informs the instruction provided to students in as many as 1 in 4 public school history classrooms across the country."

In his book, Professor Zinn explains that "there is no such thing as a pure fact," and that he wrote his *People's History of the United States* "to awaken a greater consciousness of class conflict, racial injustice, sexual inequality, and national arrogance."

Should that be the point of a history classroom?

Moreover, when America is presented as racist, sexist, and otherwise evil, how do you think young people are going to feel about their own country?

According to Gallup, "A record-low 58% of US adults say they are 'extremely' (41%) or 'very' (17%) proud to be an American, down nine percentage points from last year and five points below the prior low from 2020 . . . In January 2001, when Gallup first asked Americans how proud they were, 87% said they were extremely or very proud. After the 9/11 terrorist attacks, the figure increased to 90%, and it held at that level or higher between 2002 and 2004."

While Zinn and other socialists have been indoctrinating the American youth for decades, the indoctrination has become especially bad in recent years. Since the early 2010s—a period now known as the Great Awokening—both college and K-12 classrooms have become breeding grounds for leftist insanity.

What is the Declaration of Independence? Racist. What is the First Amendment? Evil. What is marriage? Sexist. Should men play women's sports? Of course. How do we make America safer? Defund the police. What is Israel? A terrorist organization. What about Hamas? They're angels. Who elected Donald Trump? Racists, sexists, homophobes, Islamophobes, transphobes, fascists, and otherwise evil people.

This is what students are taught from kindergarten to the time they step on stage to receive their college diplomas.

Christopher F. Rufo, a leading conservative strategist, has been documenting the rise of critical race theory in our schools for years. As he explains, all you have to do is read the foundational texts of this educational movement to see how insane it is. Here are the movement leaders' greatest hits:

"All white people are racist or complicit by virtue of benefiting from privileges that are not something they can voluntarily renounce." — Barbara Applebaum, *Being White, Being Good*

"White identity is inherently racist; white people do not exist outside the system of white supremacy." — Robin DiAngelo, *White Fragility*

"According to studies, babies at two to three years old, start internalizing racist ideas, start discerning and making decisions based on racist ideas . . . We're allowing our society to raise them to be racist." — Ibram X. Kendi, on KING5 News.

In his *New York Times* bestselling children's book, Kendi tells children to "confess when being racist" because "nothing disrupts racism more than when we confess the racist ideas that we sometimes express."

If you're wondering why teachers across the country have been telling children as young as three years old to confess their racism, you can thank Howard University Professor Ibram X. Kendi.

Fortunately, the war that President Trump began to wage against wokeness during his first administration carried on during the Biden years. The president set an example for politicians across the United States who continued the fight while he was out of office.

As the School of Law Critical Race Studies Program at UCLA laments, "Since September 2020, a total of 249 local, state, and federal government entities across the United States have introduced 870 anti-Critical Race Theory bills, resolutions, executive orders, opinion letters, statements, and other measures."

Under Trump 2.0, the war on wokeness will finally be won.

Within two months of taking office in 2025, President Trump published a report on the sorry state of American education. In the report, his administration notes:

- Math and reading scores for thirteen-year-olds are at the lowest level in decades.
- Six-in-ten fourth graders and nearly three-quarters of eighth graders are not proficient in math.
- Seven-in-ten fourth and eighth graders are not proficient in reading, while 40 percent of fourth grade students don't even meet basic reading levels.
- Standardized test scores have remained flat for decades.
- US students rank 28 out of 37 OECD member countries in math.

As I tweeted, "Parents should raise kids. Schools should teach math. Trump 2.0 will make that law."

I was right.

In his first month in office, President Trump signed an executive order promising to end "discriminatory equity ideology."

Of note, people on all sides of the political spectrum—including the Left—have been trying to end discriminatory equity ideology for years.

What makes President Trump's approach different is that he has used his presidential power to target their pocketbooks.

The title of Harvard law professor Alan Dershowitz's book says it all: *Trump to Harvard: Go Fund Yourself!*

Even just looking at the headlines, it's clear that President Trump is not here to play games. If you're not going to teach math, and science, and real American history, and you're going to instead teach nothing but antisemitism, and communism, and radical transgender ideology, then you can go fund yourself.

"Billions in grants frozen after Harvard pushes back against Trump's demands," reports PBS.

"Trump administration cancels $400 million in federal dollars for Columbia University," reports NPR.

"Trump is withholding $800 million from California schools," reports *CalMatters*.

He has also targeted Harvard's use of international visas. As reported in the *New York Times*, his "investigation targets the university's participation in the Exchange Visitor Program, which is designed to promote cultural and educational programs with visas for a variety of applicants, including students and professors as well as researchers, interns and au pairs."

As you can imagine, the *Times* hates this.

"Across government, a war is being waged in wordplay. It is fought in executive orders, official statements from the White House, press briefings and all manner of communiqués, internal and external. The very language that Mr. Trump and his administration are using to smash the federal bureaucracy is now also the official language of that bureaucracy, because it is being dictated by the man doing the smashing."

President Trump recognizes how important our nation's schools are to politics. As Andrew Breitbart famously said, "politics is downstream from culture." The latest campaign was proof of that. Now that he is back in office, Trump isn't just winning the educational war, he's planting the seeds to win the broader political war that will determine the future of our country.

Whereas Trump 1.0 left the culture war off the agenda, Trump 2.0 is waging a full-fledged attack on all fronts.

As a master of strategy, President Trump is reclaiming our universities with a multifaceted attack. As *US News & World Report* summarizes it, Trump's war on education has made use of nine different strategies:

- Influencing Policy Through Funding Threats and Lawsuits
- Dismantling the Education Department

- Revoking International Student Visas
- Student Loan Reform
- Canceling "Woke" Spending
- Cracking Down on DEI Policies and Programs
- Targeting Foreign Funds
- Accreditation Reform
- Barring Transgender Athletes from Women's Sports

Why has Trump been so effective implanting these nine strategies?

Simply put, he has the right people who understand the processes needed to implement the best policies.

And this time around, he also has a phenomenal team that wants to be led.

Secretary of Education Linda McMahon is leading that amazing team. As she told the American people after she was appointed: "President Trump nominated me to take the lead on one of his most momentous campaign promises to families. My vision is aligned with the President's: to send education back to the states and empower all parents to choose an excellent education for their children."

"After President Trump's inauguration last month," writes McMahon, "he steadily signed a slate of executive orders to keep his promises: combatting critical race theory, DEI, gender ideology, discrimination in admissions, promoting school choice for every child, and restoring patriotic education and civics. He has also been focused on eliminating waste, red tape, and harmful programs in the federal government. The Department of Education's role in this new era of accountability is to restore the rightful role of state oversight in education and to end the overreach from Washington."

As Secretary McMahon knows, "disruption leads to innovation and gets results."

From immigration reform to tariffs and policing, disruption is the theme of Trump 2.0.

This is not just going to be a disruption for the next three years.

It is going to be a disruption that has lasting effects well beyond Trump's second term in office.

Can you imagine if elementary school students were learning why the Declaration of Independence and the Constitution are so important instead of learning that "gender is a social construct" and "whiteness is bad"?

Can you imagine if high school students were learning about Martin Luther King Jr.'s colorblind vision for America instead of having to listen to their teachers glorify the racially divisive vision of Malcolm X and the Black Panther Party?

Can you imagine if college students were learning why capitalism is necessary to democracy instead of being forced to read *The Communist Manifesto* and *The Anarchist Cookbook*?

Do you think that ten, fifteen, and twenty years from now we might see a new generation of young conservatives ready to take up the fight for life, liberty, and pursuit of happiness?

The liberal media has been so hysterical about Trump's disruption of education because it may very well uproot the Left's most important institution for waging their fight: our schools.

It may very well end the decades of political indoctrination—funded by our tax dollars—that have given the Left a strategic advantage.

When Trump promised to "get rid of P.C.," he wasn't kidding.

What we're seeing with all these universities reforming themselves from the inside, it may very well mark the end of political correctness.

Perhaps better than anyone else, Chris Rufo understands why President Trump has targeted Harvard, Columbia, and these other elite universities. As Rufo explains, "You want to focus on elite universities because elite universities establish the cultural signals that then flow downward to the university sector as a whole. And what we know from Ivy League universities, including Harvard, Princeton, and Columbia, is that they are directly, flagrantly, and intentionally violating the Civil Rights Act of 1964. They're promoting from their central administrations racial discrimination, scapegoating, and even segregation."

"If you go back in history, President Eisenhower enforced the civil rights law at the time by sending federal troops into Little Rock High School. President Kennedy did the same thing, sending troops to desegregate University of Mississippi," explains Rufo. "So the president's threat under his Article II powers as president is not only legitimate, but I think it's really moderate, given the context of what's happening."

On September 9, 2025, the Foundation for Individual Rights and Expression (FIRE) published its 2026 report on college free speech. In their report, they note that 34 percent of students believe it is acceptable to stop a campus speech with violence.

The next day, Republican activist, author, and political commentator Charlie Kirk was assassinated while speaking at an event at Utah Valley University.

In his address to the nation, President Trump said:

"To my great fellow Americans, I am filled with grief and anger at the heinous assassination of Charlie Kirk on a college campus in Utah. Charlie inspired millions, and tonight all who knew him and loved him are united in shock and horror. Charlie was a patriot who devoted his life to the cause of open debate and the country that he loved so much, the United States of America.

"He fought for liberty, democracy, justice, and the American people. He's a martyr for truth and freedom, and there's never been anyone who was so respected by youth. Charlie was also a man of deep, deep faith, and we take comfort in the knowledge that he is now at peace with God in heaven. Our prayers are with his wife, Erika, the two young, beloved children, and his entire family who he loved more than anything in the world.

"We ask God to watch over them in this terrible hour of heartache and pain. This is a dark moment for America. Charlie Kirk traveled the nation, joyfully engaging with everyone interested in good faith debate. His mission was to bring young people into the political process—which he did better than anybody ever—share his love of country, and to spread the simple words of common sense on campuses nationwide. He championed his ideas with courage, logic, humor, and grace.

"It's long past time for all Americans and the media to confront the fact that violence and murder are the tragic consequence of demonizing those with whom you disagree day after day, year after year, in the most hateful and despicable way possible.

"For years, those on the radical Left have compared wonderful Americans like Charlie to Nazis and the world's worst mass murderers and criminals. This kind of rhetoric is directly responsible for the terrorism that we're seeing in our country today, and it must stop right now."

For too long, America's educational system has been the handmaiden of left-wing terrorism.

In Trump 2.0, that ends.

We're also seeing the end of the institutionalization of radical gender ideology. The president's executive order—Defending Women From Gender Ideology Extremism And Restoring Biological Truth To The Federal Government—isn't partisan. It's common sense. As the order notes, "'Gender ideology' replaces the biological category of sex with an ever-shifting concept of self-assessed gender identity, permitting the false claim that males can identify as and thus become women and vice versa, and requiring all institutions of society to regard this false claim as true."

The legal effect of this rollback on gender ideology for Title IX is crucial to protecting women in this country. "The prior administration argued that the Supreme Court's decision in *Bostock v. Clayton County* (2020), which addressed Title VII of the Civil Rights Act of 1964, requires gender identity-based access to single-sex spaces under, for example, Title IX of the Educational Amendments Act. This position is legally untenable and has harmed women."

Men should not be able to use women's bathrooms.

Men should not be able to play women's sports.

If a man wants to tell everyone he is a woman, he can be my guest.

I believe in the First Amendment as much as anyone.

But that doesn't mean our government and the American taxpayers have to fund his delusion.

For all their blather about protecting women and girls, the Left is intent on consistently putting them in harm's way.

In Trump 2.0, the antiscientific, pathologically nonsensical war on "cisgender women"—which is just a strange lefty term for "women"—comes to an end.

This is what real reform looks like in education.

And it's not just the educational system proper; it's also institutions like the John F. Kennedy Center for the Performing Arts. Richard Grenell, who is Special Presidential Envoy for Special Missions and President of the Kennedy Center, has been on Trump's side since day one. While the President of the Kennedy Center may not seem like the biggest job or the most important responsibility, it is an important cultural site. The first openly gay person to hold a cabinet-level position, Grenell wasn't appointed to fill an identity quota (like Pete Buttigieg). He was appointed because he is the most competent person for the job. And as we have all seen, he is shaking things up at the Kennedy Center.

This is another difference between Trump 1.0 and Trump 2.0.

During the first Trump administration, the Kennedy Center was largely written off. President Trump never attended an event there. He didn't participate in the traditional Kennedy Center Honors. This term, he fired the entire board. He named himself chairman of the board. He has attended events there—including a production of one of his favorite plays, the musical version of Victor Hugo's *Les Misérables*—because he now understands the cultural importance of the Kennedy Center. He even screened the premiere of the First Lady's movie *Melania* there in January 2026. So while it may not be the biggest policy issue, this time the president wants to lean into the cultural side of governance. In other words, he's now using all the tools in the presidential toolbox to Make America Great Again.

During the Biden years, Trump wasn't sitting around and reminiscing about all his monumental wins from his first administration.

He was planning how he would win even more during his second administration.

Trump 2.0 would have been monumental if it had occurred in sequential terms.

But because of that downtime—which gave Trump and his team time to plan—the second administration is surpassing even his own supporters' wildest expectations.

This isn't just the beginning of another administration.

This is the beginning of a new age of American greatness.

Chapter 7

The MAHA Policy Blueprint

On November 27, 1995, *New York* magazine published an issue featuring Robert F. Kennedy Jr. on the cover.

The title of the issue was "The Kennedy Who Matters."

Back then, Bobby Kennedy was the darling of the progressive left.

An environmental attorney—who, in *New York*'s words, had been the one to "save the city's water supply"—Kennedy had built his reputation as a man of the people.

As this liberal magazine proclaimed, Kennedy "believes in truth, and good and evil, and right and wrong." Kennedy, they went on, is the "de facto New York attorney general for the environment, enforcing laws that negligent or lazy prosecutors choose to ignore."

Back then, Kennedy had built his reputation not only speaking truth to power, as the old leftist saying goes, but reshaping the world to hold the powerful accountable. In many ways, Bobby Kennedy has long been the David standing up to the Goliaths of corporate America.

"The people of New York own the Hudson River," he told a journalist. "But General Electric owns every fish in that river because their PCBs are in every fish. They have taken away something of economic value. It's theft—General Electric is stealing those fish and that river from the people of New York."

In 2009, *Rolling Stone* declared Kennedy one of their "100 Agents of Change."

Time named him one of their "Heroes for the Planet."

A lot has changed since those days when everyone on the Left—from liberals to Marxists—was standing behind Bobby Kennedy, the environmental activist par excellence, the son of a Democratic senator, and the nephew of one of the most popular Democratic presidents in American history.

What happened?

Kennedy, as that 1995 quote suggests, has always cared about public health. But, in more recent years, he has shifted his focus from the environment to food and drugs.

To understand why he has become such a big target, by politicians on both the Left and the Right, but especially the Left, you really only have to understand one fact: Big Pharma and Big Food are among the most powerful lobbying groups in Washington, DC.

According to the DC-based nonprofit organization OpenSecrets, which tracks and publishes data on campaign finance and lobbying, these industries are truly the juggernauts of capitalism.

As of September 10, 2025, $226,783,485 has been spent on lobbying for pharmaceutical and health products. The pharmaceutical and health products industry has 562 clients. They have 1,672 lobbyists. Fifty-three percent of their lobbyists are former government employees. The revolving door is real. As OpenSecrets notes, the pharmaceutical and health products industry employees more than twice as many former government employees as lobbyists than the oil and gas industry. They employ more former government employees as lobbyists than the automative industry. Quite literally, the pharmaceutical and health products industry employs more former government employees as lobbyists than every other industry.

Big Pharma isn't just a juggernaut.

It's a juggernaut that is constantly increasing its size and its power.

In 2000, this industry spent $100.06 million on lobbing. By 2010, that number had climbed to $248.02 million. In 2020, it spent $319.09 million. In 2021, it spent $365.29 million. In 2022, it spent $380.46 million. In 2023, it spent $385.37 million. In 2024, it spent $391.04 million.

Who's paying for all of this?

The major drug companies.

Just past the halfway mark of 2025, the Pharmaceutical Research & Manufacturers of America (PhRMA) had already spent $20,635,000. For its part, Pfizer alone spent $7,850,000. Merck & Co spent $7,580,000. The list goes on, and on, and on.

At the end of 2025, this behemoth had spent $341,316,466.

In 2024, according to Statista, the pharmaceutical and health products lobby had spent more than the oil and gas lobby, the electric utilities lobby, the insurance lobby, the electronics manufacturing and equipment lobby, the business associations lobby, the air transport lobby, and the real estate lobby. They had, quite literally, outspent every single other lobby by more than $100 million dollars.

This juggernaut never sleeps.

It's insatiable, it's growing, and it's shaping public policies.

You might be wondering: What is the pharmaceutical and health products lobby spending hundreds of millions of dollars on?

They lobby politicians to protect their lucrative drug patents. They lobby politicians to prevent us from having access to cheaper Canadian drugs. They lobby on issues related to health care reform, drug pricing, and everything else that might affect their bottom line.

They're lining the coffers of every politician in DC. They fund presidential and congressional candidates, national party committees, and outside spending groups. They fund state candidates and committees. They don't care if you're blue or red. If you have the power to make them more money, you have their attention.

According to data from OpenSecrets for the 2023–2024 election cycle, the pharmaceutical and health products lobby contributed $16.55 million to Republican members of Congress. In that same cycle, they contributed even more money to Democratic members of Congress, $26.71 million.

Two hundred and eleven Democratic members of the House received an average contribution of $52,331. All together, those contributions totaled $11,041,869. Republicans, for their part, were in the same boat: 210 Republicans in the House received an average contribution of $46,744. Those contributions totaled $9,816,353. Together, they ran the bill to $20,858,222.

And what about the Senate?

It looks like a mirror image of the House. Forty-five Democrats received contributions from the pharmaceutical and health products industry. The average contribution was even higher. It was $84,527. Those contributions totaled $3,803,717. Fifty Republican Senators took home an average of $54,080 each. Together, that total hit $2,704,003.

If there is one thing Democrats and Republicans agree on, it's accepting money from the pharmaceutical and health products industry.

That said, there have been important changes in recent years. In 2012, 2014, 2016, and 2018, Republicans received more money. After Trump came to power, this industry shifted its focus to Democrats. In 2020, 2022, and 2024, they gave more money to Democrats. They understood that Trump represented a new direction for the GOP, and that direction was putting the American people—not their bottom line—first.

Can you guess who they gave the most money to in the most recent election?

The top recipient of their money in the 2023–2024 election cycle was our former vice president Kamala Harris. She was the top recipient by a landslide. How much money did they contribute to her? $8,652,114. In the 2019–2020 election cycle, their main man was presidential candidate Joe Biden. By a landslide, President Biden received the most money. Big Pharma put $9,002,834 in his pockets. As if this question even needs to be asked, who do you think was the top recipient of Big Pharma's money during the 2015–2016 election cycle? Hillary Clinton.

Again, Big Pharma has been—and continues to be—bipartisan. They like donkeys and elephants. They care about their profits. But since Donald Trump and the America First movement burst onto the scene like a bull in a china shop, the direction of that bipartisan spending has shifted in monumental ways. Big Pharma knows which politicians are going to put their interests first, and which politicians are going to put the American people first.

If you're still wondering why the swamp in Washington, DC, hates Robert F. Kennedy Jr., our new United States Secretary of Health and Human Services, please reread all those numbers.

When it comes to the pharmaceutical and health products industry, we're not talking about chump change. We're not even talking about enormous profits. We're talking about truly incomprehensible amounts of wealth.

To give you a sense of the landscape, in the first three months of 2024, President Biden's last year in the Oval Office, fifteen of the biggest drug companies reported $173 billion in revenue, according to the nonprofit organization Protect Our Care. They handed out over $28 billion to their shareholders. That's not $173 billion over a decade. That's not even $173 billion over the course of one year. That's $173 billion over the course of three months.

To be clear, I am a big fan of capitalism, I am all for companies making profits. But understanding how they make it is important.

As Protect Our Care explains, "they make billions while charging Americans prices up to four times higher than in other countries, forcing patients to cut pills and skip doses to make ends meet." As they note, "pharmaceutical manufacturers could lose $1 trillion in revenue over a decade and *still* be the most profitable industry."

There's a reason Big Pharma is referred to as a global cartel.

It's not just because they rake in the kind of wealth that makes El Chapo look broke.

Many of the drugs they produce are quite dangerous to people's health.

Just look at the Sackler family.

They have been called "the worst drug dealers in history."

They founded Purdue Pharma. They developed and marketed oxycontin. It's a drug that has killed hundreds of thousands of people and destroyed countless lives. According to an article by Arthur Gale in the journal *Missouri Medicine*, "it is estimated that in nearly one half of the cases drug addiction began with a doctor's prescription." As Gale notes, Purdue "used 'thought leaders' in medicine" to "promote the safety of opioids."

Of course, the only thing that is distinct about Purdue is the size of its profits and damage it has done to this country. There are an innumerable number of drugs that have unleashed havoc on the American people as well as our neighbors around the world. According to the European Federation of Pharmaceutical Industries and Associations, in 2024 "North America accounted for 54.8% of world pharmaceutical sales compared with 22.7% for Europe."

In 2024, David Ricks, CEO of Eli Lilly, was paid $29.2 million. Johnson and Johnson CEO Joaquin Duato took home $24.3 million. Pfizer CEO Albert Bourla cleaned $24.6 million. And Amgen CEO Robert Bradway made $24.4 million, while Gilead CEO Daniel O'Day made $23.7 million. The average CEO pay of the ten largest pharmaceutical companies, according to BioSpace, was $23 million.

According to survey data provided by KFF, formerly known as the Kaiser Family Foundation, in July 2025:

- The cost of prescription drugs prevents some people from filling prescriptions. About one in five adults (21%) say they have not filled a prescription because of the cost while a similar share (23%) say they have instead opted for over-the-counter alternatives. About one in seven adults say they have cut pills in half or skipped doses of medicine in the last year because of the cost. A third of all adults say they have taken at least one of these cost saving measures in the past year, including larger shares of women and those with lower incomes.

- Health care debt is a burden for a large share of Americans. In 2022, about four in ten adults (41%) reported having debt due to medical or dental bills including debts owed to credit cards, collections agencies, family and friends, banks, and other lenders to pay for their health care costs, with disproportionate shares of Black and Hispanic adults, women, parents, those with low incomes, and uninsured adults saying they have health care debt.

While it was nauseating to see the widespread celebration of Luigi Mangione, the vigilante who murdered UnitedHealthcare CEO Brian Thompson in cold blood, it's a sign of the times that "over 41 percent of respondents supported the Thompson assassination, or were at best ambivalent about it," according to *City Journal.*

The American people are angry.

To be clear, violence is never an acceptable means of settling the political score, but it's important to understand where we are as a society.

Something has gone very, very wrong in our country.

I imagine the billions of dollars that have been spent by the pharmaceutical and health products industry over the past three decades has something to do with it.

For all the money being spent on lobbying in the United States, you would expect Big Pharma's American profits to be large.

As American economist Brad Setser explains, "In a typical year, Pfizer reports losing money in the United States and making money abroad. And as a result, in a typical year, Pfizer pays a lot more in tax outside the United States than it pays inside the states. How do they do it? They license their intellectual property to an offshore subsidiary. Then they produce the high-value-added active ingredients in a factory in Ireland or Singapore. And finally they pretend like the profit is accrued to these offshore subsidiaries even though the sales are back to the United States." At the same time, "The top five American pharmaceutical companies all had more drug sales in the United States than they did in all the other countries put together."

As you can imagine, a US president who wants to put Americans first, and who wants to make sure American corporations are working for the American people, could not be a bigger threat to this industry.

That's why they threw boatloads of cash at Hillary Clinton, Joe Biden, and Kamala Harris.

When Robert F. Kennedy Jr. talks about draining the swamp, he's not just talking about the D.C. politicians who have been funded by Big Pharma. He's also talking about getting rid of the so-called "thought leaders." These are the experts embedded in institutions as different as the National Institutes of Health, the Ivy League universities, and the leading hospitals and research centers—like the pain center belonging to Russell Portenoy, MD, founder and chairman of the Department of Pain Medicine and Palliative Care at Beth Israel Medical Center in New York City, who received millions of dollars from Purdue and other pharmaceutical companies.

To be clear, the people in the swamp understand how to play the game.

You can't say: "RFK Jr. is going to hurt our bottom line—he must be crushed!" You can't say: "President Trump will reduce the amount of people addicted to our dangerous drugs—we need Kamala in office!" You can't say: "The Make America Great Again Movement has to be stopped because it's going to prevent us from robbing the American people blind!"

But you can say President Trump doesn't understand "the science."

You can say Secretary of Health and Human Services Robert F. Kennedy Jr. doesn't understand "the evidence."

There is a whole establishment—from politicians, to lobbyists, to CEOs, to doctors, to tenured professors, to think tanks, and media outlets—who see the Make America Healthy Again movement as a threat to their bottom line.

"We need to have somebody who is going to be grounded by science and evidence and not somebody who rejects it," proclaims John Maraganore, former chief executive of the Boston biotech firm Alnylam Pharmaceuticals.

"RFK Jr. is systematically undermining vaccine science and endangering health," contends the Center for American Progress, a liberal think tank that shapes public policy.

"RFK Jr.'s anti-science agenda will be catastrophic for the United States," declares Brooklyn College, City University of New York professor Moustafa Bayoumi.

"We can still avert disaster if we can understand the nature of the mounting anti-science threat and formulate a strategy to counter it," advises Baylor College professor Peter Hotez.

"The Junk Science of Robert F. Kennedy, Jr." reads a headline in *The New Yorker.*

"Given your dangerous views on vaccine safety and public health, including your baseless opposition to vaccines, and your inconsistent statements in important policy areas like reproductive rights access, I have serious concerns regarding your ability to oversee the Department," explained Senator Elizabeth Warren in her letter to RFK after his nomination to serve as the next Secretary of the Department of Health and Human Services.

As Kennedy noted in his exchange with Massachusetts Senator Elizabeth Warren at a recent Senate hearing on September 4, 2025, "I know you've taken $855,000 from pharmaceutical companies," which might be one reason Senator Warren has been relentlessly focused on stopping Secretary Kennedy.

As the novelist Upton Sinclair, who wrote *The Jungle*, his 1906 exposé of the meatpacking industry, put it: "it is difficult to get a man to understand something when his salary depends upon his not understanding it." Bingo.

To update Sinclair's acute observation, it is difficult to get Harvard Law School's "first woman of color" (as *Fordham Law Review* described her in a 1997 piece) to understand something when an $855,000 check depends on her not understanding it.

(We might also add that it's difficult to get a white woman to understand her own identity when a lucrative position at Harvard depends on her not understanding it. While Senator Warren accused Robert F. Kennedy Jr. of promoting "baseless conspiracies," it's hard to imagine a better description of her academic career as the Pocahontas of Harvard Law. According to the *Boston Globe*, Warren could be as much as 1/1,024th Native American, which is a more euphemistic way of saying her Native American ancestry is a baseless conspiracy created and promoted by her.)

Remember: It's the Democrats, not the Republicans, who have become the biggest recipients of contributions from the pharmaceutical and health products lobby.

That's why Democrats were so upset about Donald Trump's executive order prohibiting federal funding for COVID-19 vaccine mandates in schools. As the White House website explained, "President Trump is dedicated to ensuring that American students are not forced to choose between their education and their medical freedom."

That kind of executive order will make you no friends in the Big Pharma lobby.

And the influence of that lobby can be felt at every level of government.

When Secretary Kennedy fired six hundred employees at the Centers for Disease Control and Prevention, he was draining the swamp.

When he fired all seventeen members of the CDC Vaccine Advisory Committee, he was draining the swamp.

When he fired the director of the CDC, he was draining the swamp.

"The public must know that unbiased science guides the recommendations from our health agencies," he proclaimed.

And the liberal media cannot stand it.

"Kennedy, Rejecting Data, Fuels Distrust of His Own Agencies," read a *New York Times* headline.

"RFK Jr. wants all new vaccines tested against a placebo. Doctors say that isn't good science," reported PBS.

"Doctor reacts to RFK Jr.'s health report: 'Disjointed catalogue' with 'anti-science approaches,'" summarized MSNBC.

"'You're a charlatan': Cantwell slams RFK Jr. for rejecting vaccine science," noted the *Seattle Times*.

"How RFK Jr.'s misguided science on mRNA vaccines is shaping policy—a vaccine expert examines the false claims," wrote CNN.

To be fair, the liberal media establishment has good reason to be upset.

Remember the profits? It's not just Big Pharma's bottom line.

Big Pharma is a major source of the media's ad revenue. You can't miss all those drug ads when you are watching TV. Take a look at who sponsors the DC newsletters from *Axios* or *Politico*'s playbook. Chances are pretty good its Big Pharma itself or one its member companies. If you are a "reporter" and you see right in front of your face every day who is paying the bills, are you really going to take them on?

Investigative journalist Mark Hyman hit the nail on the head: "On November 15, 2024, CNN star [and former Hooters spokesman] Jake Tapper warned viewers 'I hope you like measles' when reporting [on] the Robert F. Kennedy, Jr. nomination to be HHS Secretary. Pharmaceutical company stock prices fell minutes after the Kennedy announcement. This is because Kennedy has been transparent about his goal to place the pharmaceutical industry under closer scrutiny. During his spiel, Tapper failed to disclose to viewers a giant-sized conflict-of-interest: Big Pharma is one of CNN's biggest advertisers. CNN and the other cable news outlets may be raking in one billion dollars or more from pharmaceutical advertising. Of course, CNN and other news programs are not about to bite the hand that feeds them."

Essentially, Big Pharma pays Jake Tapper's salary.

According to MediaRadar, "The pharmaceutical ad market contributed $10.8 billion in 2024, or 4% of total US ad spend, with 59% going to TV." Moreover, "when looking at just linear TV, prescription drugmakers spent an estimated $5.12 billion on national TV ads in 2024 and $2.97 billion in the first half of 2025."

That isn't chump change.

And this is why pundits and politicians see the Make America Healthy Again movement as the biggest threat that they have ever confronted.

In March 2025, the Campaign for Sustainable Rx Pricing released a new study of direct-to-consumer (DTC) advertising in the US, noting that "The 10 pharmaceutical companies analyzed spent a combined $13.8 billion on advertising and promotion (A&P) in 2023 alone in the US"

In 2023, three of the top five spenders on TV advertising were drug companies.

"Among some of the biggest recipients of the Big Pharma ad dollars," explains Hyman, "are cable news and broadcast (traditional) television news programs. Just how big is this spending? Just in the month of March 2023, the pharmaceutical industry spent nearly $15 million on *ABC World News Tonight with David Muir*, according to Ad Week. For an entire year this would be $180 million. For just one 30-minute newscast. That is quite the financial windfall."

This is important for a number of reasons.

As Hyman explains, "Other top 10 television drug advertising destinations were also news programs: *NBC Nightly News with Lester Holt*, *Good Morning America*, *CBS Evening News with Norah O'Donnell*, *Today* and *CBS Mornings*. Will David Muir, Lester Holt, Norah O'Donnell, and the other news anchors report to viewers a negative story about pharmaceutical companies such as Pfizer, Eli Lilly, Johnson & Johnson, or Novo Nordisk? Of course not. Big Pharma advertising is less about attracting new customers and more about buying silence from the news industry. In fact, it's not just silence, but compliance. This explains why news outlets go on the attack against anyone who questions pharmaceutical policies, such as vaccines."

In addition to the silence, as well as the attacks, brought to you by Big Pharma, there is also a financial windfall from all the advertisements they run.

The CSRxP found that "taxing or prohibiting DTC [direct to consumer] ads for the ten largest pharmaceutical companies in the US would result in increased federal tax revenue between $1.5 and $1.7 billion per year." Right now, "American taxpayers lose more than one billion each year in tax revenue as pharmaceutical companies write off these marketing expenses to further pad their bottom line."

The impact to the American people is more serious than that.

As many public health experts have concluded, DTC advertising undermines the doctor-patient relationship. A doctor might not believe a patient needs a particular prescription, or really any prescription at all. However, this patient may have been bombarded with advertisements for a drug they saw ads for over and over again. They may now believe that these drugs are what will solve the real problems they have or, in some cases, the fictitious problems that the drug industry has led them to believe they have. And instead of taking the advice of their doctor, they doctor shop until a doctor gives them what the ad convinced them they need.

In the current internet age, almost anyone can get linked up with a prescription-happy doctor in a matter of minutes. It doesn't take much effort to get what you want—even if it's not what you need.

What DTC advertising does is turn the American people into individual lobbyists for these products. There's a reason that the United States and New Zealand are the only countries that legally allow direct-to-consumer pharmaceutical advertising. The other countries have realized this is not a smart way to achieve a smart medical outcome, which is why these advertisements are banned across the world. But the pharmaceutical and health products lobby in the United States is strong, and they have long been able to get exactly what they want from politicians on both sides of the aisle.

Until now.

In September 2025, the FDA's new leader, Dr. Marty Makary, was clear in an editorial he wrote for the *Journal of the American Medical Association*. "Direct-to-consumer pharmaceutical advertising has evolved into a public health crisis demanding immediate action by the US Food and Drug Administration (FDA). For nearly 3 decades, pharmaceutical companies have exploited weak enforcement, flooding US consumers with promotional content that is often misleading."

On September 9, 2025, President Trump signed a memorandum targeting direct-to-consumer drug advertisements. In his memorandum, the president concludes: "These advertisements can mislead the public about the risks and benefits, encourage medications over lifestyle changes, inappropriately intervene in the physician-patient relationship, and advantage expensive drugs over cheaper generics."

Under the president's leadership, the FDA has been sending letters to drug manufacturers warning them that their advertisements must adhere to existing regulations. As President Trump notes, "the FDA has historically stipulated that a manufacturer, packer, or distributor must provide the public with materially complete information that fairly balances both the benefits and the risks of the drug," but recently drug companies have been including "less information, particularly in broadcast advertising."

Since Congress vested the Food and Drug Administration with the authority to regulate prescription drug advertising back in 1962, a lot has changed. Much of that change has occurred in the past decade. Social media influencers are paid to promote drug products without providing disclosures. Moreover, they're not liable to follow the same rules as the drug companies. They can promote drugs without acknowledging the side effects or the fact that they have been paid to promote these drugs.

The president has put everyone on notice.

If you're not here to Make America Healthy Again, if you're actively compromising the health of your fellow Americans, if you're putting profits over people, you're going to pay the price.

Ironically, the Left that has targeted DTC ads for decades.

But it's Trump who has actually put their backs against the wall.

As I have argued throughout this book, it's not just about good ideas—even the Left has them occasionally (or, to put it differently, even a fool can stumble on the truth).

It's also about having the people, the policies, and an understanding of the processes needed to make change happen.

Given the president's focus on DTC pharmaceutical ads, you would think the Democrats would be singing his praises. But that would go against the golden rule of their party—and really the only thing they have campaigned on for the past ten years: whatever Donald Trump is for, we are against.

Even his commitment to off-label drugs and his Right to Try Act have angered Democrats, some of whom once allegedly shared the president's commitment to expanding medical freedom.

But if Donald Trump is for it, the Democrats are now against it.

It's that kind of suicidal partisanship that has prevented any effective action in Washington—until now.

Donald Trump is not just giving us a new direction for public health, he is changing the processes by which things get done.

His commitment to promoting American-made prescription drugs, via an executive order, makes it clear that the Make America Healthy Again movement is part of the Make America Great Again Movement. As the White House notes, the order "directs the US Food and Drug Administration (FDA) to reduce the amount of time it takes to approve domestic pharmaceutical manufacturing plants by eliminating duplicative and unnecessary requirements, streamlining reviews, and working with domestic manufacturers to provide early support before facilities come online."

You can't disrupt the status quo this much without making enemies, and Donald Trump now has many.

It's not just Big Pharma that is waging an all-hands-on-deck crusade again President Trump, Secretary Kennedy, and the Make America Healthy Again movement.

It's also Big Food.

Like Big Pharma, they have all the resources to get exactly what they want.

And like Big Pharma, they don't care if you're on the Left, the Right, or in the center.

What they care about is their bottom line.

"They lobby about anything that's going to affect their business, no matter how remote," said Marion Nestle, a former professor of nutrition, food studies, and public health at New York University, who has researched lobbying in the soda industry. "I can't think of a single area of food or nutrition policy that isn't subjected to lobbying."

The food and beverage industry is more than willing to line any politician's coffers to protect their bottom line.

According to OpenSecrets, in 2024 they dropped a whopping $29,586,769 on lobbying.

Let's just be clear: this wasn't the celery, carrots, and tomatoes lobby.

This wasn't a lobby pushing politicians to subsidize apples, oranges, and pears.

This was the lobby on behalf of the big corporations that produce the most processed and unhealthiest products on the market.

Coca-Cola led the way, dropping $4,930,000. McDonald's added $2,950,000 to the effort. Candy maker Mars racked up a $2,000,000 bill. Keurig Dr Pepper threw in $870,000. The National Confectioners Association dropped $745,000. Hershey Co. added $684,000 to the total. Domino's Pizza came in at $320,000. And Red Bull GmbH was good for $260,000.

Great. ✓
Soda: ✓
Chicken nuggets, french fries, and McFlurries: ✓
Candy: ✓
More soda: ✓
More candy: ✓

Pizza: ✓

Is anyone wondering why 41.64 percent of the country is obese?

According to the Global Obesity Observatory, the United States is the tenth most obese country on a list of two hundred countries.

By contrast, Russia is #70.

Iran is #116.

And China is #149.

We won World War II. We won the Cold War. But we are losing the war on obesity.

If I was Vladimir Putin or Xi Jinping, I would be happy that Coca-Cola, McDonald's, and other companies are spending so much money to ensure their products are consumed by as many Americans as possible.

Do you think our enemies are cowering when they see images of Americans who are so out of shape they can't even make it down the candy aisle without an electric scooter?

Do these Americans look fit enough to defend the country?

As the new Department of Health and Human Services notes, "6 in 10 Americans have at least one chronic disease, 1 in 4 American children suffer from allergies, [and] 40% of Americans are diabetic or prediabetic."

Indeed, health problems are especially bad among young American children.

A study published in summer 2025, co-authored by researchers at the University of California, Los Angeles and Children's Hospital of Philadelphia, "found that US children and teens were nearly twice as likely to die as their peers in 18 other high-income countries between 2007 and 2022 . . . Chronic conditions also rose sharply: among 3- to 17-year-olds, the prevalence of chronic conditions increased from 39.9% to 45.7% in pediatric health systems, and from 25.8% to 31.0% in the general population. Diagnoses of anxiety, depression, and eating disorders more than tripled in some cases. Childhood obesity increased from 17.0% to 20.9%, and early onset of menstruation rose by over

60%. More children reported trouble sleeping, physical symptoms like fatigue and pain, and feelings of loneliness and sadness."

Is that what a healthy America looks like?

According to Dr. Neal Halfon of UCLA, "This study confirms what many pediatricians, educators, and parents have been sensing for years; that our children are facing a growing health crisis. The breadth and consistency of these declines across physical, mental, and developmental health indicators demand urgent national attention."

When Democrats take money from Big Pharma and Big Food, pushing agendas that put our children—and out nation's future—at risk, they need to be held accountable.

As I have said throughout this book, on my podcast, and in columns, there are forces eroding the United States from the inside.

But there are also forces rebuilding America from the inside.

The MAHA movement isn't the result of a new study.

It isn't the result of a new scientific finding on red dye, or processed foods, or seed oils like canola oil, or the scientifically dubious label of GRAS: generally recognized as safe.

Think of that term for a second: *generally recognized as safe*. I found this whole thing mind-blowing. It is a bunch of stuff we consume that industry has claimed that because it's been around a long time it's safe. "In 2010, the United States Government Accountability Office (GAO) published a report about potential deficiencies in the GRAS review process, giving four main areas of concern:

- the GRAS oversight process does not confirm the safety of all new ingredient assessments. This potential deficiency occurs because the FDA assesses GRAS petitions only if the manufacturer voluntarily notifies the FDA.
- the FDA has not provided guidance to companies for sufficiently documenting scientific evidence of safety in GRAS petitions.
- there is no final FDA regulation for criteria in the voluntary notification program, challenging credibility for GRAS status,

and there exists insufficient monitoring in the public market for the continued safety of GRAS substances.

- companies considering use of engineered nanomaterials in food can use the voluntary GRAS notification process, assuming full safety without the FDA having a complete assessment. In contrast to this absence of review, nanomaterials intended for use in foods must be fully reviewed for safety in Canada and the European Union before marketing."

Progress has been made since the 2010 report, in part because of leaders like Bobby Kennedy and so many of the millions of ordinary Americans who are fed up with the status quo—especially the MAHA moms who have been increasingly concerned about what their kids are being fed not just at home, but in our public schools.

As consumers, we were told by our own government what was healthy, and what was safe, and what we needed to consume—and we slowly learned none of that was true.

We learned just how little oversight there has been.

According to a New York University article published a few months before Donald Trump won his second election, "The current FDA process allows the food industry to regulate itself when it comes to thousands of added ingredients—by determining for itself which ingredients should be considered 'generally recognized as safe,' or GRAS—and deciding on their own whether or not to disclose the ingredients' use and the underlying safety data to the FDA. As a result, many new substances have been added to our food supply without any government oversight." According to Jennifer Pomeranz, associate professor of public health policy and management, "Both the FDA and the public are unaware of how many of these ingredients—which are most commonly found in ultra-processed foods—are in our food supply."

The American people are slowing learning more about what Big Pharma and Big Food have been doing—and they're not happy about it.

Donald Trump was elected by 77,302,580 people to put an end to the status quo.

If the problems are this bad, why has nothing been done to resolve them?

Why did it take outsiders like Donald Trump and Robert F. Kennedy Jr. to take them on?

It's the same reason there has been no traction when it comes to the pharmaceutical industry.

Our politicians are compromised.

That's not rhetoric.

That's a fact.

As OpenSecrets reveals, in 2024 the food and beverage industry deployed 327 lobbyists.

Do you think these lobbyists are being paid to make America healthy?

No, they are paid to make sure that these companies make money.

The close relationship between the food and beverage industry and Washington is exemplified by the fact that of those 327 lobbyists, 211 are what we call "revolvers." These are the people who have previously worked in the federal government. They are the people who make up the revolving door between politics and business.

Who was the biggest recipient of contributions from Big Food in 2024?

It was Democrat presidential candidate Kamala Harris.

The revolving door between the political swamp in DC, the news media, and the elite universities that are supposed to shine the light of truth on issues concerning public health is so well-established that it feels almost trite to acknowledge.

As Hyman explains, "Since 1981, 10 of the 11 Food and Drug Administration commissioners left the agency to take lucrative jobs with pharmaceutical companies. The exception was Dr. David Kessler who served under George H. W. Bush and Bill Clinton. After the FDA, Kessler became the dean of Yale School of Medicine."

For people who are willing to toe the line, there's no shortage of positions.

For people like Kennedy who aren't, the attacks could not be more vicious.

Indeed, there are few people who have been more outspoken against Big Pharma and Big Food than Robert F. Kennedy Jr.

Back in September 2024, on the eve of the election, Kennedy published a video of himself standing in a kitchen in front of a bottle of Tylenol, a bag of Doritos, a box of Cap'n Crunch, and other common household items.

In the video, which has now been seen millions of times by people across the world, Kennedy is clear:

"This is what most Americans innocently put into their bodies these days and most alarmingly into the bodies of their children. And it's no coincidence that Americans die earlier than Canadians, or Germans, or Italians, or Japanese, or Koreans, or Australians or most any other comparable country. And it wasn't always that way. Until the early 1990s, our life expectancy was the same or better than other developed countries. Then suddenly more and more Americans began suffering from chronic diseases from obesity, cancer, diabetes, kidney disease, Alzheimer's, heart disease, and all kinds of autoimmune diseases. Our maternal mortality rate soared to the highest of any developed country on Earth. Same with infant mortality. Like the frog and the slowly boiling water, we didn't really notice as we got sicker and sicker. We've grown now to accept chronic disease conditions as normal. But now in 2024 we're finally waking up to this cataclysm and we're asking ourselves how in the world did this happen."

Back then, Kennedy made a promise to the American people.

"The Democrats, who claim to be all about health care, have stood by watching other countries ban these poisons that make our kids sick," he explained. "Enough is enough. President Trump and I are going to stop the mass poisoning of American children."

Now, a year into this administration, President Trump and Secretary Kennedy have made good on that promise.

As reported on Whitehouse.gov, here are the highlights:

- The Trump administration has made incredible strides in its effort to Make America Healthy Again, with roughly 35% of the American food industry making a commitment to eliminate the use of artificial dyes, including Hershey, Consumer Brands and dozens of ice cream companies representing more than 90% of the ice cream volume sold in the US
- The Department of Health and Human Services revived its Task Force on Safer Childhood Vaccines.
- President Trump understands that America's health care system is largely focused on treating chronic illnesses rather than preventing them, leading to a growing health crisis with serious economic and national security consequences.
- Within weeks of taking office, President Trump established the Make America Healthy Again Commission, tasked with investigating and addressing the root causes of America's escalating health crisis, with an initial focus on childhood chronic diseases.
- President Trump has pledged to create the highest quality of life, build the safest and wealthiest and healthiest and most vital communities anywhere in the world.
- US Secretary of Agriculture Brooke Rollins signed a waiver to a restrict soda and energy drinks from food stamps in Nebraska. This ensures that American taxpayer funds are not used to subsidize unhealthy beverages.
- US Secretary of Health and Human Services Robert F. Kennedy Jr. announced a plan to phase out all petroleum-based dyes from the country's food supply by the end of 2026. This includes dyes like Red 40, Yellow 5, and Blue 1 that have been linked to negative health outcomes in children.

- The Department of Health and Human Services has removed COVID-19 vaccines from the list of shots recommended for healthy children and pregnant women. Unlike the previous administration, our federal government is committed to using gold-standard science when it comes to vaccine recommendations, especially for our youth.

As I tweeted, "Big Food is blinking. Nestlé, General Mills, Kellogg's—MAHA is working. Finally."

Because of the monumental victories that President Trump, Secretary Kennedy, and their super team have secured, the American's public's support for MAHA cuts across political lines.

In a May 2025 survey, the Department of Agricultural and Consumer Economics at the University of Illinois found that 35 percent of very liberal respondents had a very positive view of Make America Healthy Again. Those who identified as very conservative, for their part, were even more supportive: Fifty-three percent had a very positive view of MAHA.

This work isn't about politics.

It's about securing the health of our nation.

Whether we're talking about In-N-Out, which announced it will remove synthetic food dyes and artificial flavors from its menu items, or Steak & Shake, which has moved to 100 percent all-natural beef tallow and replaced its "buttery blend" with 100 percent Grade A Wisconsin butter, our country is transforming itself from the inside out.

The White House website posted a list of many of the steps companies have made since President Trump took office:

- Steak & Shake moved to 100% all-natural beef tallow and replaced its "buttery blend," which contained seed oils, with 100% Grade A Wisconsin butter.
- McCormick announced it will drop certain food dyes from its products.

- PepsiCo announced it will remove artificial ingredients from popular food items—including Lay's and Tostitos chips—by the end of the year.
- In-N-Out announced it will remove synthetic food dyes and artificial flavors from its menu items.
- Tyson Foods eliminated synthetic dyes in its food products.
- Mars removed titanium dioxide from its Skittles product.
- Sam's Club committed to removing 40 harmful ingredients — including artificial colors, additives, dyes, and high-fructose corn syrup — from its private-label products.
- Kraft-Heinz announced it will remove artificial dyes from its US products.
- General Mills announced it will remove artificial dyes from its US cereals and all foods served in K-12 schools.
- Nestlé announced it will remove all petroleum-based food dyes from its food and beverage products.
- Conagra Foods announced it will remove certain color additives from its frozen products, no longer offer products with artificial dyes in K-12 schools, and stop using artificial dyes in the manufacturing of its products.
- JM Smucker announced it will remove synthetic colors from its consumer food products.
- Hershey announced it will remove synthetic dyes from its snacks.
- Consumer Brands announced it will urge its members to remove artificial colors in food and beverage products served in schools.

Every new headline affirms the MAHA movement.

"Coca-Cola will launch version with US cane sugar after Trump push," reported NBC News.

"Hershey joins food makers in commitment to remove artificial dyes . . . Hershey's announcement comes after J.M. Smucker, Conagra Brands, General Mills, and Kraft Heinz have said they would remove synthetic colors by the end of 2027. Nestlé USA plans to fully remove artificial colors from its food and beverage portfolio by mid-2026," wrote the site *Food Dive.*

These aren't isolated events— something big is happening.

And it shows just how successful and far-reaching MAGA really is.

When Trump started the Make America Great Again movement, he didn't just mean our economy or our government—though he's fixing those too.

His administration is restoring American greatness in every possible way, from foreign policy to food supply.

Health policy isn't about profits. It's about people. MAHA is real.

Again, these changes aren't a result of new science. Companies are embracing these changes because they already know that dyes, artificial preservatives, and other additives aren't good for us or our children. They just needed to be pushed to make the changes.

Companies are following the leadership of this administration and fixing America's food supply.

That's not just good news in the short term.

It's something that will pay out dividends in American health for decades to come.

As the White House website reminds everyone, "President Donald J. Trump took office promising to confront the chronic health crisis plaguing Americans—and six months later, he is delivering on that promise by removing harmful chemicals from our food supply."

More recently, in September 2025, the Make America Healthy Again Commission released the Make Our Children Healthy Again Strategy. As they note, there are five key areas of the strategy:

- Restoring Science & Research: Expanding NIH and agency research into chronic disease prevention, nutrition and metabolic health, food quality, environmental exposures, autism, gut microbiome, precision agriculture, rural and tribal health, vaccine injury, and mental health.

- Historic Executive Actions: Reforming dietary guidelines; defining ultra-processed foods; improving food labeling; closing the GRAS loophole; raising infant formula standards; removing harmful chemicals from the food supply; increasing oversight and enforcement of direct-to-consumer prescription drug advertising laws; improving food served in schools, hospitals, and to veterans; and reforming Medicaid quality metrics to measure health outcomes.
- Process Reform & Deregulation: Streamlining organic certification; easing barriers to farm-to-school programs and direct-to-consumer sales; restoring whole milk in schools; supporting mobile grocery and processing units; modernizing FDA drug and device approval; and accelerating EPA approvals for innovative agricultural products.
- Public Awareness & Education: Launching school-based nutrition and fitness campaigns, Surgeon General initiatives on screen time, prioritizing pediatric mental health, and expanding access to reliable nutrition and health information for parents.
- Private Sector Collaboration: Promoting awareness of healthier meals at restaurants, soil health and land stewardship, and community-led initiatives, and scaling innovative solutions to address root causes of chronic disease.

As the first page of the MAHA report states: "To turn the tide and better protect our children, the United States must act decisively. During this administration, we will begin reversing the childhood chronic disease crisis by confronting its root causes—not just its symptoms. This means pursuing truth, embracing science, and enacting pro-growth policies and innovations to restore children's health. Today's children are tomorrow's workforce, caregivers, and leaders—we can no longer afford to ignore this crisis. After a century of costly and ineffective approaches, the federal government will lead a coordinated transformation of our food, health, and scientific systems. This strategic realignment will ensure that all Americans—today and in the future—live longer, healthier lives, supported by systems that prioritize prevention, wellbeing, and resilience."

Has there ever been an administration this committed to the health and well-being of our nation's children?

Has there ever been an administration that has been this effective at implementing seminal positive changes in such a short period of time?

Trump 2.0 is the first administration to not only have the monumental vision, but the people, the policies, and the processes in place needed to realize that vision.

Leaders like Robert F. Kennedy Jr. don't just talk the talk, they walk the walk.

There's a new regime in America.

It's a regime of safety, health, and strength.

As President Trump explained at a Make America Healthy Event on May 22, 2025, "Over the past few years, we've built an unstoppable coalition of moms and dads, doctors and young people and citizens of all backgrounds who have come together to protect our children. Very importantly, keep the dangerous chemicals out of our food supplies, get toxic substances out of our environment and deliver the American people the facts as to really where we're going. And we want to have what we deserve. And we want to be healthy. And we want to have a lot of good things happen. And I think we're going to have that. I think this is just the beginning."

MAHA specifically shows Trump's ability to put together a great team to accomplish goals.

He put Robert F. Kennedy Jr., a former card-carrying Democrat, at the head of HHS because he knew he could get the job done.

Add to that other key players like Dr. Marty Makary (US Commissioner of Food and Drugs), Dr. Mehmet Oz (Administrator for Medicare & Medicaid Services), Dr. Jay Bhattacharya (Director of the NIH), and Dr. Casey Means (who is awaiting confirmation as

Surgeon General), and you've got a team that's laser-focused on healing America from the inside out to make this the strongest country in the world.

That's one of the things Trump does best—finding great people with the right mission and agenda to get the job done.

Along with Marty, who has put direct-to-consumer advertising in his crosshairs, Dr. Oz is waging a war on the status quo as well by uncovering fraud in the Medicare system and finding ways to more effectively and efficiently deliver a better health care system for poorer and older Americans. Along with Secretary Kennedy, he made his views clear in a September 2025 piece for *USA Today*: "In the Working Families Tax Cut Act, Congress created the Rural Health Transformation (RHT) Program to address the underlying problems that cause rural health care to fail. President Trump and congressional lawmakers have entrusted us with stewardship of $50 billion to transform rural health care delivery across all 50 states." As they explain, "Rather than repeating the mistakes of the past, President Donald Trump's administration will deliver unprecedented investments to rebuild rural health care infrastructure and address the root causes of the health care crisis facing rural America."

Casey Means fits right in with this super team. She has, in her words, committed her life to helping people learn "how to eat and live for truly optimal health of the mind, body, spirit, and planet." Her number one *New York Times* bestselling book *Good Energy: The Surprising Connection Between Metabolism and Limitless Health* isn't just a helpful resource for individuals; it is a central text in the growing Make America Healthy Again movement. Along with her brother, Calley Means (who is known as "the man who linked MAGA and MAHA"), and *House Inhabit* author Jessica Reed Kraus (who is known as the "the MAHA maven"), she is here to disrupt business as usual in DC.

Dr. Jay Bhattacharya is likewise a disruptor. When the lockdowns took over America, this Stanford University professor was an outspoken critic of the liberal dogma that had engulfed his university and many parts of the country. The mainstream public health establishment dismissed him. Now he's in charge. "The first and most important thing," he told *Politico*, "is that dissenting voices need to be heard and allowed."

That's what real scientific inquiry is all about.

That is what Trump 2.0 is all about.

We're overturning orthodoxies that were not allowed to be questioned. We're cutting through the spin. And we're working every day to put this country back on the right course.

This isn't just the beginning of a new administration.

The is the beginning of a new direction for the greatest country on earth.

Chapter 8

DOGE, Finally

On May 5, 1984, President Ronald Reagan delivered a radio address to the nation.

What was the focus of his address?

Waste, fraud, abuse, and mismanagement in the federal government.

"When I spoke to you a week ago we were in China working to strengthen cooperation between our two countries, increase opportunities for jobs and a better life for our people, and improve the prospects for a more peaceful world. As I told the citizens of Alaska when we arrived back in the States, I feel we made significant progress. Today I'd like to speak about our efforts toward another goal, one that might not get the headlines of a trip to China, but that nonetheless has an important impact on our lives. I'm talking about reducing waste, fraud, abuse, and mismanagement in government—problems that for too long were permitted to grow and spread like an unchecked cancer, plundering your pocketbooks and hindering government's ability to provide essential public services in an efficient and timely manner."

While much has changed since President Reagan left office in 1989, a lot has remained the same.

The news media loves headlines about our government's relationships with other countries: Russia, Ukraine, Israel, Iran, and even China, the list goes on.

Yet, what doesn't make the headlines is what's happening in our own backyard. But what's happening in our own backyard has a significant impact on our lives.

For too long, as President Reagan himself noted, the United States government has been mired in waste, fraud, abuse, and mismanagement.

According to the Cato Institute's Fiscal Policy National Survey in 2025, "Perceptions of government waste may have reached an all-time high. Americans estimate that 59 cents of every dollar the federal government spends is wasted. This is higher than Gallup has recorded since it began asking the question in 1979."

In the eyes of the American people, what is the source of all this waste?

"51 percent believe the federal government employs too many workers, and they estimate that 34 percent of federal jobs are unnecessary."

To be sure, that number would be a lot higher if it wasn't for Republicans like Ronald Reagan.

In 1982, the president established a private-sector commission to uncover wasteful spending and improve government efficiency. President Reagan's Private Sector Survey on Cost Control was formed to deal with a problem that previous administrations had not dealt with.

Executive Order 12369 sought to bring in leaders in the private sector to improve the management of government resources and to reduce costs.

The private sector leaders were appointed by executive order to serve without compensation. At the helm was industrialist Joseph Peter Grace, the CEO of W. R. Grace & Company, who convinced President Reagan to undertake this endeavor at the federal level.

The Grace Commission, as it came to be known, was funded by $76 million in private-sector contributions. It included more than 150

CEOs and senior corporate leaders, spread out across thirty-six task forces, who were committed to reducing the excess fat that had crippled the American government by the time President Reagan entered office.

Of note, there were no federal employees in the commission.

While there are many government employees committed to making the United States government as efficient as possible, there are just as many who aren't. Both Reagan and Grace understood that many of these employees were actually committed to maintaining, and even expanding, the government bloat.

As I previously noted, the novelist Upton Sinclair put it best: "It is difficult to get a man to understand something when his salary depends upon his not understanding it."

With this super team applying modern business practices to improve the efficiency and effectiveness of federal agencies, waste was cut.

"For 18 months, the commission hunted for wastefulness and inefficiencies before issuing its formal findings on January 16, 1984. In a report that filled 47 volumes and 23,000 pages, the commission made 2,478 cost-cutting and revenue-enhancing recommendations that it estimated would result in $424 billion in savings over three years," writes historian Christopher Klein.

"The federal government is suffering from a critical case of inefficient and ineffective management, evidenced particularly by the hemorrhaging of billions of tax dollars and mounting deficits," the Grace Commission's report stated.

You might be wondering: What did this waste look like?

According to Klein, "While scandalous examples of profligate spending by the Department of Defense, such as $436 for a claw hammer and $511 for a 60-cent light bulb, grabbed headlines, the commission pinpointed more mundane, but fruitful, targets. It flagged the Federal Power Marketing Administration for selling subsidized power in the Northwest at one-third of market rates and recommended that cash seized by the Justice Department be placed in interest-earning bank accounts. It found the Treasury Department could save $1.3 billion over three years by paying bills when they were due instead of when they were received and estimated that individuals and corporations failed to pay $81.5 billion in taxes in 1981. The Grace Commission also reported that civil service retirees received three times the benefits of the best private-sector plans, with military employees receiving six times the benefits. In addition, federal employees retired at considerably younger ages and received pensions fully indexed for inflation, a rarity in the private sector. The commission estimated federal pension reform could result in more than $60 billion in three-year savings."

To be sure, President Reagan wasn't the first president to point his crosshairs at government waste and inefficiency. The Heritage Foundation, which has written extensively about this issue, points back to another Republican president, Dwight D. Eisenhower. As they explain, "Eisenhower targeted growing problems with waste and inefficiency with a three-pronged strategy. First, drawing from his military background, he sought to implement a military-like efficiency in the Executive Office itself. Second, he successfully achieved both spending cuts and reductions in agency personnel. Of course, this led agencies to complain (sound familiar?) that they were being forced to do more with less. Third, in a move foreshadowing the Department of Government Efficiency (DOGE), Eisenhower announced that he had created a three-man committee named the President's Advisory Committee on Government Organization. Eisenhower's DOGE was composed of Eisenhower's brother Milton, Nelson Rockefeller, and Arthur Flemming. Rockefeller, as we all know, was a very rich, successful businessman (sound familiar?), while Flemming was then serving as the Civil Service Commissioner. Milton Eisenhower recounted in his book, *The President Is Calling*, that Eisenhower saw many federal programs as 'wasteful and inefficient.'"

While President Eisenhower set the stage for Ronald Reagan, his results fell short. As the Heritage Foundation notes, "History proved that ultimately, cutting waste and inefficiency wasn't enough. The 1960s brought a wave of new regulations as existing agencies flexed *their de facto* lawmaking powers. And subsequent Republican administrations did little to rein them in, or to stop the plethora of new agencies, commissions, and boards from being created, as the federal administrative state has become a bloated monstrosity." That bloated monstrosity, like a horror movie monster, has kept itself alive for decades—feeding on taxpayer money like a vampire feeds on blood.

As you might expect, critics went after President Reagan and his Grace Commission just like they went after President Eisenhower and his Advisory Committee on Government Organization. The Left targeted Reagan with a viciousness that Upton Sinclair might have forecasted. After all, the Reagan administration was unearthing a mountain of waste, and it was proposing watershed cuts to the American government. If there is one thing that unites government employees, it's the commitment to not only retaining but expanding their scope—and, consequently, the money they are allocated. And it doesn't matter to them if that money is used effectively, in a way that maximizes return for the American people.

"If you put the federal government in charge of the Sahara Desert," the economist Milton Friedman is purported to have said, "in five years there'd be a shortage of sand."

Even in the face of criticism, and a countermovement to protect government waste, the Reagan administration still came out on top.

According to Citizens Against Government Waste, which was founded back in the 1980s, "Reagan saved more than $100 billion by implementing Grace Commission proposals through executive orders."

Under the banner of the Department of Government Efficiency, Trump 2.0 has already surpassed that $100 billion.

It is, in more ways than one, the restoration of efficiency to the US government that men like Reagan, Grace, and their supporters across the country could only dream about.

Indeed, this has long been a focus of the Republican Party.

In the 1990s, Newt Gingrich, Speaker of the United States House of Representatives from 1995 to 1999, was always talking about restoring sanity to the federal budget. He was always talking about how out of touch his colleagues in Washington, DC, had become. I still remember him, in the lead-up to the 1994 Contract With America, campaigning around the country with an ice bucket. The ice bucket was a physical symbol of bureaucratic waste, the ineffectiveness, inefficiency, and outdatedness of what going on in the Capitol.

Newt explained that every day, every member of Congress had someone deliver ice to their office. Four hundred–plus offices, twice a day, every day. Now here we were in the middle of the 1990s when every member of Congress already had a refrigerator with a freezer attached to it in their office. They didn't need ice! It was so profoundly stupid. But it created several political patronage jobs for some member of Congress. The grand cost to American taxpayers was about $200,000. $200,000 was being spent to deliver ice that no one needed.

While a couple hundred thousand was not going to make a dent in eliminating the deficit or debt, Newt's point was the ice delivery was a clear symbol of what was going on in Washington. If these people don't care about, you know, $200,000, what makes you think they care about $2 million? What makes you think they care about $20 million? The ice delivery was a lasting symbol of the stupidity in our Capitol, the stupidity of how our elected representatives spend our money. The 1994 Republican Congress may have ended ice delivery in the Capitol, but there are thousands of programs today that are way more expensive. Waste is as much a part of the American government as baseballs and bats are a part of Major League Baseball.

Donald Trump formed DOGE for the same reasons that Dwight D. Eisenhower formed the Advisory Committee on Government Organization and Ronald Reagan formed the Grace Commission.

As he explained on November 12, 2024, DOGE "will pave the way for my administration to dismantle Government Bureaucracy, slash excess regulations, cut wasteful expenditures, and restructure Federal

Agencies—Essential to the 'Save America' Movement . . . Republican politicians have dreamed about the objectives of 'DOGE' for a very long time. To drive this kind of drastic change, the Department of Government Efficiency will provide advice and guidance from outside of Government, and will partner with the White House and Office of Management & Budget to drive large scale structural reform, and create an entrepreneurial approach to Government never seen before."

In the president's words, DOGE is "potentially, 'The Manhattan Project' of our time."

The American government should work for the American people. It shouldn't be a bloated bureaucracy wasting taxpayer dollars. It shouldn't be another wasteful financial burden on the American people's shoulders.

When President Trump announced the new department, he reminded the American people what they voted for. They voted to drain the swamp.

"Making changes to the Federal Bureaucracy with an eye on efficiency and, at the same time, making life better for all Americans," that's what DOGE is all about. As the President forecasted, "we will drive out the massive waste and fraud which exists throughout our annual $6.5 Trillion Dollars of Government Spending. They will work together to liberate our Economy, and make the US Government accountable to 'WE THE PEOPLE.' Their work will conclude no later than July 4, 2026—A smaller Government, with more efficiency and less bureaucracy, will be the perfect gift to America on the 250th Anniversary of The Declaration of Independence. I am confident they will succeed!"

As of September 2025, DOGE has not just fulfilled the president's promise to the American people, it has surpassed it.

According to DOGE.gov, the savings for the American people are historically unprecedented. As of January 19, 2026:

$215 billion in estimated savings.

$1,335.40 saved per taxpayer.

Where did all these savings come from?

Whitehouse.gov, with its new commitment to radical transparency under our new president, provides the receipts.

You can browse the 13,440 entries listed under contracts.

You can browse the 15,887 entries listed under grants.

You can browse the 264 entries listed under leases.

It's all there for the American people to see.

Here's a sample:

Gavi, the Vaccine Alliance, received a $2,630,000,000 grant from USAID to strive toward its partisan vision to "leave no one behind with immunization." Cutting this overseas program saved the American taxpayers $1,750,000,000.

As Secretary of State Marco Rubio put it, "After a 6 week review we are officially cancelling 83% of the programs at USAID. The 5,200 contracts that are now cancelled spent tens of billions of dollars in ways that did not serve, (and in some cases even harmed), the core national interests of the United States."

For its part, Walgreens lost their $3,372,581,217 contract to provide access to no-cost COVID-19 testing and no-cost vaccines, while CVS lost their $3,448,342,863 contract to increase community access to testing, treatment, and response. When Secretary of Health Robert F. Kennedy Jr. talks about the close relationship between the drug business and the American government, he's not exaggerating.

But it's not just USAID and the Department of Health and Human Services who felt the blow from DOGE.

The Social Security Administration felt the heat, too. DOGE "marked approximately 3.2 million Social Security number-holders for people aged 120 and older as 'deceased' as part of ongoing efforts to root out fraud." The table posted by the department showed 3,261,057 number-holders being removed from the "living" count. As Elon noted, "Maybe *Twilight* is real and there are a lot of vampires collecting Social Security." In reality, as he also noted, the Social Security program "might be the biggest fraud in history."

The Department of the Interior lost a $3,329,900,357 contract to provide facilities and full wraparound childcare and case management services for undocumented immigrants.

For its part, the Department of Defense lost the remainder of a $12,500,000,000 contract, which saved the American people $4,000,000,000.

The biggest area of waste, said Secretary of War Pete Hegseth, was clear. "Part of what we've uncovered is that the Defense Department has become very much overreliant on management consultants and contractors," he said. "We found that we likely have more contractors than we have civilian employees.

"Together with DOGE, the DOD found another $5 billion in savings, bringing our total savings to over $10 billion. All this money will be reinvested in readiness, capability, training and the troops."

As Secretary Hegseth noted, "We need to replace wasteful spending in favor of a culture focused on . . . actual financial responsibility and stewardship so that our limited funds are spent better on . . . things like health care and mission-related programs for our warfighters and their families."

This is a historically unprecedented effort to reshape the American government.

As the Heritage Foundation observed, "DOGE's goals are far from a historical anomaly. But DOGE is novel in a different respect. For perhaps the first time in the administrative state's history, America is looking to dismantle an until-now unquestioned and unchecked bureaucracy."

In previous administrations, department leaders like Hegseth would be fighting these cuts tooth and nail. They would be up in arms if even one nickel rolled out of their budget. That's what leaders of these departments and agencies have historically done—they have protected their bottom line, even at the expense of the American people.

But this administration is different.

Every leader who President Trump has appointed to office is on board with the Trump 2.0 agenda.

They're here to put Americans—not the bureaucracy—first.

DOGE even rounded up the strangest and most baffling misuses of government funding.

A $620,000 grant was devoted to "adapting an LGB+ inclusive teen pregnancy prevention program for transgender boys."

An $814,000 grant was allocated to a "daily diary examination of the influence of intersectional stigma on blood pressure."

A $697,000 grant provided to "black and Latinx parents leading reform and advancing racial justice in elementary mathematics."

A $664,000 grant went to "sustainable racial equity: creating a new generation of engineering education DEI leaders."

An $801,000 grant funded research attempting "to shed light on the extent and the manner in which structural racism and discrimination shapes older gay men's health."

A $500,000 grant was going to be spent on "the racialized basis of trait judgments from faces."

A $250,000 grant was allotted to "paid leave programs based on racial equity."

A $6.9 million grant was designated by the Department of Education to be spent on "teaching social and emotional learning and foundations of mental health development from an antiracist approach."

Another $10 million grant was given by the Department of Education to be spent on "decolonizing the curriculum."

You can't make this stuff up.

To say that the Left was pillaging the United States government to fund its stupidity really doesn't quite get at the stakes of these DOGE cuts.

Many of these grant allocations were not just nonsense—they were actively harmful to America.

When you're funding racially divisive K-12 and college education, transgender programs that undermine the mental and physical health of children, and outright socialism, you're eroding America from the inside.

If I was Vladimir Putin and Xi Jinping, these are the programs I would love to see the United States government funding.

After all, this is money that is not going to science, technology, mathematics, or engineering.

This is money that isn't going to repair our roads, bridges, and public parks.

It's money that is not helping Doug Collins, our Secretary of Veterans Affairs, who wants to get care to veterans in a more productive and effective way.

This isn't money that is going to fund medical expenses for our brave men and women serving in our military, who every day are ensuring that our freedoms are protected from countries like Russia and China.

This is money being spent to teach Americans why they should hate America, why we should be divided along tribalistic lines of race and gender, and why capitalism should be overthrown.

If you wanted to see the collapse of the United States, these are the programs you would fund.

Fortunately, the era of insane lefty lunacy—sponsored by our own government—is over.

The era of Trump 2.0 is here.

The waste that DOGE has uncovered, the fraudulent activities that it has illuminated, and the cuts that is had made—$215 billion in estimated savings and $1,335.40 saved per taxpayer—mean one thing: President Trump was right.

This is the Manhattan Project of our generation.

As I have said a million times, Trump's strength isn't chaos—it's clarity. He gets to the "why" faster than anyone I've worked with.

Why are we funding billion-dollar vaccine programs when the science regarding their efficacy and unintended effects is still being debated?

Why are we funding million-dollar educational programs designed to divide us according to race?

When President Trump took office, he and his America First team had been asking these "why" questions for the four years that President Biden was in power.

That's why they were prepared to dismantle this infrastructure as soon as the president retook the Oval Office.

DOGE truly is the Manhattan Project of our generation.

But you wouldn't know that from the left-wing media.

At every step of the second Trump administration, the left-wing media has slammed DOGE.

"Some Dems are excited about Musk and Ramaswamy's DOGE. Their optimism feels naive," forecasted MSNBC.

"Elon Musk's DOGE is dumb. it could also do serious damage," *Jacobin* more ominously predicted.

"How Musk and DOGE could end up costing more than they save," added CNN.

"100 days into Trump's second term, DOGE has not delivered on its promised savings, efficiency or transparency in meaningful ways," announced NPR.

"Like most tech-bro schemes, DOGE is a rip-off," surmised *Mother Jones*.

"Elon Musk's special project has fueled mass layoffs, widespread confusion and may not have even saved a dime," reflected the *HuffPost*.

"DOGE overstated the savings of its largest cuts by 97%, analysis finds," reported the *CBS Evening News*.

"DOGE is far short of its goal, and still overstating its progress," writes the *New York Times*.

"DOGE vowed to make government more 'efficient'—but it's doing the opposite," adds the *Washington Post*.

"What seems farther away than ever in the chaos . . . is Musk's promise to make the government more efficient and better serve the public," writes the *Guardian*.

"DOGE is the most wasteful federal agency," declares *CounterPunch*.

"DOGE Was Bad," concludes the *Atlantic*.

This is the media ecosystem from the center left to the far left.

And it could not be more wrong.

The American people can just look at the data.

Unlike the backdoor dealings that defined the Biden administration—the dealings that not only concealed the administration's financial activities, but Biden's disintegrating psychological competence—all of DOGE's findings are readily available and downloadable on their website.

They're not offering meaningless rhetoric.

They're providing the receipts.

Perhaps *Jacobin*, NPR, the *New York Times*, the *Washington Post*, the *Guardian*, and the *Atlantic* journalists should read them.

After all, it takes an extraordinary amount of ignorance to conclude that DOGE was bad.

In fact, the only people who seem to have reached that conclusion are the left-wing journalists and professors who have seen their funding cut.

The only other people are the wasteful and, in some cases, nefarious bureaucrats who are the reason DOGE was established in the first place.

As Elon Musk forecasted, "This will send shockwaves through the system, and anyone involved in Government waste, which is a lot of people!"

He was right.

And the people who benefit from government waste aren't happy.

Like the liberal media, they are more interested in trying to assassinate the characters of President Trump, Elon, and other leaders in this movement, than accounting for the decades of waste, fraud, and disservice to the American taxpayers that have been unearthed.

"Elon Musk and Donald Trump care about one thing: lining their own pockets. Not government efficiency, and certainly not making things better for everyday Americans," American Federation of Government Employees National President Everett Kelley claimed.

Like the left-wing media, Kelly couldn't be more misleading and wrong.

But that doesn't mean the shockwaves aren't real.

The shockwaves can be felt from the Department of War, to the Department of Health and Human Services, to the Department of Interior Services, all the way to the Public Broadcasting Service and National Public Radio.

Congress cut $1.1 billion in funding for PBS and NPR.

No wonder they're upset.

But here's the deal: This is what the American people voted for.

They knew our government was bloated, inefficient, and, in many cases, laundering their money to left-wing causes they don't support.

To believe that PBS and NPR are some sort of bipartisan source of truth for Americans on all sides of the spectrum, you really have to be blind to reality.

Even their own employees have accused them of abandoning the pursuit of truth in their own pursuit of a progressive agenda.

Uri Berliner, a senior editor who has been at NPR for twenty-five years, said as much in a *Free Press* article. "NPR has always had a liberal bent," admits Berliner, but it's got especially worse in recent years. By 2024, he writes, "We weren't just losing conservatives; we were also losing moderates and traditional liberals."

Do I have to ask the obvious question?

Why should conservatives, moderates, and traditional liberals have to fund NPR?

Why do we have to fund an institution that clearly doesn't reflect our values, interests, and hopes for the future of our country?

Beyond that, why should the government be in the media business at all? While all these outlets are left-wing, I am more opposed to them on a philosophical basis. The government should not be in this at all, regardless of the ideological bent. We have plenty of media sources. State-backed media should not be one of them.

Here's another way to think about this: Do you think progressive taxpayers want to fund the Manhattan Institute? Do you think they want to fund the American Enterprise Institute? What about the

Heritage Foundation? More to the point, do you think they want to see their tax dollars go to journalists at *Breitbart*, *National Review*, and Fox News? Of course they don't. They understandably don't want to pay for partisan institutions that don't share their values, interests, and hopes for the future of our country.

So why should a conservative farmer in southern Idaho have to fund PBS? Why should a single mother in Miami, who has never voted for a Democrat, have to fund NPR? Why should these hardworking Americans, many of whom are living paycheck to paycheck, have to pay the salaries of people who call them backward, ignorant, racist, sexist, fascist, and evil? Why do they have to fund institutions working tirelessly to ensure their political candidates don't get elected to office? Why should they fund institutions working tirelessly to thwart their candidates who do get elected to office? Beyond the partisan argument, why is the government in the media business, especially in this day and age?

I mean, seriously, just look at NPR's reporting about Trump.

These are the headlines:

"Trump's racist comments find support in Montana."

"How Trump is relying on a racist conspiracy theory to question election results."

"Trump escalates racist rhetoric and plays on white grievance at recent rallies."

"It's gotten a lot harder to act like whiteness doesn't shape our politics."

"Understanding multiracial whiteness and Trump supporters."

In the last one, NPR educates Americans about "multiracial whiteness." This is a phenomenon by which "people of other races and ethnicities want to benefit from white privilege by supporting it." If you're confused, you're not alone. Fortunately, the folks at NPR explain it. "All of these scholars share a view that I share, that whiteness is not the same thing as white people and that whiteness is actually better understood as a political project that has emerged historically, and that is dynamic and that is always changing. And so whiteness as an ideology is rooted in America's history of white supremacy." In plain English, it's a cheap way to attack people of color who vote for Trump. They too must be white supremacists (even though they're not white)!

You can't make this stuff up.

But if you do know how to make it up, you can get a job as a "journalist" at NPR.

You can also get a job as a "scholar" at Harvard, Yale, and Princeton.

As the NPR reports suggest, all of this stuff is connected.

The left-wing professors get lifetime jobs at our universities—private universities that get enormous tax breaks because of their nonprofit status or public universities that get outright funded by the government, like the prestigious University of California, Berkeley. They then apply for government grants from the NIH, the Department of Education, and so on. These grants then fund their research, like all this research on "multiracial whiteness." Their research then gets picked up by left-wing organizations like NPR, which are also funded by taxpayers.

In an article in the *Wall Street Journal*, former Portland State University professor Peter Boghossian refers to this process by which "nonsensical jargon like 'intersectionality,' and 'cisgender,' is imbued with an air of false authority" as "idea laundering." As Trump and DOGE know, this idea laundering occurs on the taxpayer's dime. It's the taxpayers on all sides of the political spectrum who provide the money needed to keep this idea laundering empire afloat.

But not anymore.

Just because the Left keeps calling their journalism "open-minded," "objective," and "the light in the age of darkness" doesn't make it true.

In fact, much of the so-called journalism that comes out of PBS and NPR looks like verbatim speeches from the Democratic National Committee.

As Berliner himself notes, much of what NPR has produced in recent years just looks like anti-Trump disinformation. "The rise of advocacy took off with Donald Trump. As in many newsrooms, his election in 2016 was greeted at NPR with a mixture of disbelief, anger, and despair. (Just to note, I eagerly voted against Trump twice but felt we were obliged to cover him fairly.) [Our coverage] veered toward efforts to damage or topple Trump's presidency. Persistent rumors that the Trump campaign colluded with Russia over the election became the catnip that drove reporting.

"It is one thing to swing and miss on a major story. Unfortunately, it happens. You follow the wrong leads, you get misled by sources you trusted, you're emotionally invested in a narrative, and bits of circumstantial evidence never add up. It's bad to blow a big story. What's worse is to pretend it never happened, to move on with no mea culpas, no self-reflection. Especially when you expect high standards of transparency from public figures and institutions, but don't practice those standards yourself. That's what shatters trust and engenders cynicism about the media."

As if Berliner even has to say this, "Russiagate was not NPR's only miscue."

So, again.

Do we have to ask the obvious question?

At a moment when Americans across the political spectrum unanimously agree the government is spending too much of their money, why do conservatives, moderates, and traditional liberals have to fund "journalism" that so transparently doesn't even attempt to reflect their values, interests, and hopes for the country?

Why do Americans have to fund "journalism" that is not interested in telling the truth?

As NPR's own editor explains, "There's an unspoken consensus about the stories we should pursue and how they should be framed. It's frictionless—one story after another about instances of supposed racism, transphobia, signs of the climate apocalypse, Israel doing something bad, and the dire threat of Republican policies. It's almost like an assembly line."

He's right.

Language matters and the Left and the media get this.

Ever heard of the left-wing group "Third Way"? It hasn't been in the news much, not until recently. But they caught my attention when they sent out a memo that said the quiet part out loud: The Left's language is losing them voters.

Let's be honest. The Democrats and mainstream media have been weaponizing language for decades. It's how they kept their narrative front and center—and how they silenced or cancelled people who dared to push back. But with the rise of alternative media and platforms for free discourse like X, that strategy is backfiring big time.

Americans are seeing through the charade.

They're not just seeing through it. The language is now turning them away from the Democratic Party.

There's been a legacy of lying language. And now the Left is panicking.

For decades, Democrats and the media have weaponized language. Every story is tilted their way. Standing up for unborn lives? That's dubbed anti-choice, even anti-woman. Supporting the Second Amendment? Well, you must be against sensible efforts to stop killing. Even now, in seemingly clear-cut cases, the Left still finds a way to spin the story to fit their agenda.

Exhibit A: In their book, Kilmar Abrego Garcia is a "Maryland man." In reality, he is an illegal alien with alleged gang affiliations, and with numerous accusations of beating his wife. But they make him out to be a saint, targeted by a vicious administration. This kind of blatant dishonesty in language would be bad enough, but there's more. Not only is the Left twisting language, it's using it to police your speech too. Buzzwords like "privilege" and "microagression" are used to silence opposition, while words like "birthing person" or "pregnant people" push an agenda that demands you accept unreality as truth.

It's madness.

And the Left is finally waking up to the fact that they've gone too far.

While there are plenty on the Left who are still completely bought into this perversion of language, some of these progressives are backtracking the insanity. Some, including Third Way, are realizing how much their language is alienating their own supporters. You can read their memo in full. It's a pretty strong indictment of the Democrats' status quo: "For a party that spends billions of dollars trying to find the perfect language to connect to voters, Democrats and their allies use an awful lot of words and phrases no ordinary person would ever dream of saying . . . to please the few, we have alienated the many."

It's finally hit them. Nobody talks like they do. And what's more, nobody likes being lied to. And that's exactly what the Left has been doing for decades. Maybe party leaders will heed the memo, maybe they won't. But one thing's for sure: if they keep going down the path they're on, they won't have to worry about party language because there won't be much of a party left.

The bottom line is this: The language battle has been brewing for years.

This is what Newt Gingrich dealt with during the Contract with America, and it's what today's Right continues to be faced with. The good news? The deception is ringing hollow. The radicalism of the Left, coupled with increased transparency and dialogue in new media and platforms like X, is giving the American people the full picture. And like you can read in the piece by Third Way, Democrats are scrambling. If they were smart, they'd change course and work to rebuild credibility with their audience. But it seems that for most on the Left, the strategy is to double down on their spins and deception.

I, for one, am not complaining.

The deeper they dig themselves into this hole, the better 2026—and 2028—look for Republicans.

Dig away.

You don't even have to read the articles.

Just look at the headlines:

"'Not Racist' Is Not Enough: Putting in the Work to Be Anti-Racist."

"The History of Trans Misogyny Is the History of Segregation."

"Climate Change Is Boosting the Risk of Sleep Apnea."

"Netanyahu Defends Israel's Plan to Seize Gaza City, Despite Global Condemnation."

That's not journalism.

That's propaganda for the Left.

And when it comes to NPR and PBS, the hardworking American people shouldn't have to fund it.

At a moment when most Americans believe our government spending needs to be reined in, I can't imagine any Americans—outside of a Yale University professor or a radical Antifa activist breaking windows on the streets of Seattle—who actually believe their tax money should line the coffers of PBS and NPR.

According to that same Cato survey, "more than three-fourths (76 percent) of Americans believe the federal government 'spends too much money.'" A lot of this spending is on the salaries of people who shouldn't ever be employed by the government. And the American people know this. "62 percent support cutting the number of federal employees to reduce spending."

This isn't a sample of Republicans.

This is a sample of the American people.

When I say that Trump's decision to trim the government fat isn't partisan, I'm not exaggerating.

When I say that DOGE isn't partisan, I'm not being hyperbolic.

According to Cato, 80 percent of Independents, and even 59 percent of Democrats, say "the government spends too much money."

As they note, "89 percent favor auditing all government spending to root out waste, fraud, and abuse; Americans would cut 40 percent across the board."

The audits, the cuts, and the rest of the agenda implemented by President Trump and the Department of Government Efficiency—this is what the American people want.

This is what they voted for.

In the words of DOGE's X account, "the people voted for major reform."

Major reform is what Trump 2.0 promised.

Major reform is what Trump 2.0 has delivered.

And it's only going to get better.

DOGE represents the first truly successful attempt to really look under the hood of the American government, to expose the excessive waste, the inefficiencies, the ineffectiveness, and the outdatedness that has become endemic to the US government, our departments and our agencies, and many of the people who work for them—and even lead them.

The stuff that DOGE uncovered has been pretty amazing.

We will be writing about it in history books for decades to come.

That said, the process by which they did it definitely earned them some criticism, and in some cases, rightly so. The speed at which they did things, the haphazard nature—it warranted some legitimate critiques. DOGE was by no means perfect. But to be perfectly frank, that's the cost of change at this level.

Remember, through all this we are $38 trillion dollars in debt and are running almost $2 trillion a year in deficit spending on a yearly budget of roughly $6.75 trillion. The real outrage should be that this did not happen before 2025, and that it's not more aggressive.

DOGE wasn't the product of some milquetoast bill or haphazard reform we would all forget about in less than a week.

It was the beginning of a new epoch in American governance.

Trump 2.0.

What all this really gets down to is long overdue respect that our government needs to have for the American taxpayer.

If I'm punching my time clock ever day of the week—harvesting crops, delivering oil, restocking the grocery store shelves, and keeping this country afloat, day in and day out—I shouldn't have to worry about keeping my own household afloat to fund a professor at Princeton who wants $500,000 to research "multiracial white supremacy."

That's not partisan politics.

That's common sense.

And it's the reason the majority of Democrats agree that their government is spending too much of their hard-earned money.

At the end of the day, we need roads and bridges that allow for interstate commerce to flow freely.

We need a strong military that can defend us from threats abroad.

We need a strong police force that can defend us from threats at home.

We need doctors, and scientists, and engineers, and other people to keep the gears of our country moving toward greater wealth and prosperity.

And we need the educational infrastructure to produce the next generation of innovators, trailblazers, and leaders.

We don't need to fund K-12 curricula materials that teach students about "the epistemologies of the Latin/x diaspora," "the harmful toxicity of masculinity," why "math is racist," and "the need for socialism."

If you want to read about that stuff on your own time, be my guest.

But you're not going to force that on our children.

We need to protect parental rights.

And you most certainly are not going to fund it with that farmer's paycheck.

It's telling that it took an outsider like Elon Musk, appointed by an outsider like Donald Trump, to rein all this stuff in.

As I've argued elsewhere, the president's use of SGEs—special government employees like Elon, who can work in government for up to 130 days a year but don't have to give up their civilian careers—has been a seismic advantage over previous administrations. Because of SGEs, the president can bring in America's leading figures to share their expertise and their insights to improve our government.

The use of SGE's is not new, but the degree to which Trump 2.0 has utilized them shows a big difference between now and Trump's first term. It bears repeating: four years out of office allowed Team Trump to really think through and strategize how different, how much more effective a second term could be with the right people, process, and policies. All of this did not happen by accident.

For too long the establishment tone of the DC power players hasn't cut it.

Donald Trump may not do it the "D.C. way"—but he gets things *done.*

He is delivering the populist results that the American populace wants.

Finally, the country is catching up to him.

The fact that we need people like Elon, because our government leaders are so inept and compromised by outside influences, many of whom do not put Americans first, is a real challenge—and while it's a challenge that DOGE has confronted head-on, it's not a challenge that will disappear as quickly as a million-dollar grant to "decolonize the curriculum."

And that's part of the problem.

There are a million sacred cows in Washington, DC.

They have been grazing there for decades.

As stupid as many of these grant-funded projects were, they all had a constituency.

Those constituencies are still active in our nation's capital.

They still have their lobbyists, they still have the ears of our politicians, and they still have influence.

They still control our universities and many of our journalistic outlets.

That is why DOGE can't be the end of the road.

As the Heritage Foundation noted, "DOGE is a first step, and a necessary one, in dismantling the administrative state. But more must be done. That will take endurance, unrelenting effort by the president and his cabinet secretaries, and ultimately cooperation from Congress to achieve the objectives that the president can't accomplish alone through his constitutional authority as the head of the executive branch. But until then, we can only wish DOGE success in pursuing its rather unoriginal goals—to make our government an effective instrument that doesn't waste taxpayer money on ridiculous, duplicative, and unnecessary programs (like transgender comic books in Peru) and doesn't abuse its power to tyrannize our citizens."

That is why we have to remain vigilant against every new threat.

We have to maintain a DOGE approach not just to our federal government, but to our state governments, our public school systems, and other corners of American life.

We have to nip problems in the bud before they have time to grow into invasive species that hurt the American people—invasive species that reproduce and that become increasingly difficult to eradicate over time.

We shouldn't have to recover what remains of a $1 billion grant to fund waste. We should never again be funding waste in the first place.

In the conclusion to his radio address to the nation back on May 5, 1984, President Ronald Reagan announced: "The progress we've made is a good start, but it's little more than a ripple in the river of waste, fraud, and abuse that's been rising for years. That's why it's clear the way to reduce the deficit is by strong economic growth and by reducing wasteful bloated government, not by raising taxes on you, the people." As he put it, "our administration is determined to reverse the years of neglect and get this monster under control so we can have a government of, by, and for the people again, not the other way around."

By the end of Trump's first year back in office, an *Axios* analysis of Bureau of Labor Statistics revealed that there are "271,000 fewer federal employees than there were at the start of 2025—about a 9% drop. The sharp decline is a result of President Trump's efforts—initially spearheaded by Elon Musk's DOGE—to drastically reduce the size of the federal government."

A government of, by, and for the people again, not the other way around—that is what will make America great again.

That is Trump 2.0.

Chapter 9

Taking Back the Media

We learned a lot on November 5, 2024. But two things stand out. First, the support for President Trump and his policies resonated in places and with people many didn't think possible.

Second, if you are getting your information from left-wing media sources (the *Washington Post, Politico, Axios,* CNN, the *New York Times,* CBS, NBC, etc.), they proved once and for all how useless and biased they are.

When you look at the election results, it's clear that support for President Trump grew across the whole country. From New Jersey to California, states got redder and redder. In fact, when you actually shade the country by county and city, it's clear we don't have red states and blue states, we have a red country and blue cities. The Democratic Party has become the party of the cities. It is truly now just a geographical party.

The liberal media loves to give the impression that the Republican Party is just the party of white men—"evil" billionaires and "evil" hillbillies, rednecks, and pieces of white trash from the Midwest. The liberals love to give the impression that these white men, the ones who voted for Trump, are morally deficient, ignorant, or some combination of the two.

This has been the Democratic playbook for decades.

From 2004's *What's the Matter with Kansas? How Conservatives Won the Heart of America* by Thomas Frank to 2024's *Stolen Pride: Loss, Shame, and the Rise of the Right* by Arlie Russell Hochschild, there has been a concerted—and, frankly, well-funded—effort to depict Republicans as the party for Ku Klux Klansmen from midwestern and southern shantytowns, and nefarious capitalists on par with the Once-ler, the infamous antagonist in Dr. Seuss's *The Lorax*, his heavy-handed parable about corporate greed.

I'm not exaggerating.

Just read the headlines.

On November 15, 2016, *Slate* ran an article titled "There's No Such Thing as a Good Trump Voter." In it, Jamelle Bouie wrote, "Donald Trump ran a campaign of racist demagoguery against Muslim Americans, Hispanic immigrants, and black protesters. He indulged the worst instincts of the American psyche and winked to the stream of white nationalists and anti-Semites who backed his bid for the White House. Millions of Americans voted for this campaign, thus elevating white nationalism and white reaction to the Oval Office." More succinctly put, Bouie claimed: "People voted for a racist who promised racist outcomes. They don't deserve your empathy."

In short, 63 million Americans are the dirt beneath your feet.

If this kind of "journalism" is new terrain for you, you have to understand that Bouie's broadside isn't a deviation from the norm; on the Left, this is the norm. Jamelle Bouie isn't some fringe writer who managed to slip this insane piece through the otherwise watchful gatekeepers of rigorous and fact-based journalism at *Slate*. Quite the opposite. Bouie was *Slate*'s chief political correspondent. As a reward for producing these kinds of unhinged tirades, he moved up to the highest echelon of liberal journalism: he is now a columnist at the *New York Times*.

Since arriving at the *Times*, he's continued to write the same article—over, and over, and over again. He's produced such original pieces as "The Unreal Spectacle of Trump's Authoritarianism," "We Are Not 'Property' of Donald Trump," "Why Trump Always Wants a Crisis," "Trump Wants to Be a Strongman, but He's Actually a Weak Man," and "Maybe Trump and Miller Don't Understand Americans as Well as They Think They Do." Instead of trashing the president, maybe Bouie should be thanking the president for giving him a job. After all, Bouie seems entirely incapable of writing anything besides yet another article about Donald Trump.

But that's how you get a job at the paper of record.

Just look at what gets churned out by the other newspapers, magazines, and websites. It all looks like a concerted effort to produce the same misleading narrative about Trump's support from the American people. After 2016, *The Conversation* announced "the real reason Trump won: white fright." *Vox*, for its part, concluded that "Donald Trump's victory is part of a global white backlash" and, more emphatically, "Trump's win is a reminder of the incredible, unbeatable power of racism." *The Los Angeles Times* asked: "Trump supporters say they're not racist. So why did they vote for someone who spouted racism?" *Newsweek* published an article about "how Donald Trump's nationalism won over white Americans" right after the result came in. Not to be outdone, the *Washington Post* announced that "yes, half of Trump supporters are racist." As they conclude, in the sheer absence of empirical data to support their argument, "Hillary Clinton may have been unwise to say half of Donald Trump's supporters are racists and other 'deplorables.' But she wasn't wrong."

If these are your sources for what's going on in the world, you can be forgiven for thinking that not a single racial or ethnic minority voted for Trump in the 2016 election.

The Left loves this quote from Karl Marx's book *The German Ideology*: "The class which has the means of material production at its disposal, has control at the same time over the means of mental production, so that thereby, generally speaking, the ideas of those who lack the means of mental production are subject to it."

Has anyone told them that the quote is a fitting description of *their* control of the media?

I'm not a Marxist. But, as I have said before, even a broken clock is right twice a day.

Almost a decade later, the same false narrative is being spun about the 2024 election.

It couldn't be more wrong.

To begin, look at the data for Hispanics—the people who, according to the liberal media, would be most harmed by a second Trump presidency. Both nationally and in the key states, the numbers are clear: Trump crushed it.

According to a Pew Research Center survey conducted November 12 through November 17, 2024, 48 percent of Hispanics said they voted for President Trump in our most recent election. In 2020, it was 36 percent. In 2016, it was 28 percent. In other words, Trump has been *increasing* his support among Hispanics every time he runs.

In other words, Hispanics are *leaving* the Democratic Party.

But you wouldn't know it from the liberal media.

Going into the 2024 election, you would think that Trump had no chance among Hispanics. His wall, his promise to deport millions of criminal illegal aliens, and his commitment to otherwise make America's borders mean something again was described as an "attack on Hispanics." It was described as an "assault on the Latinx community." It was described as fascism.

And yet, the very people who we were repeatedly told would be hurt the most by Trump—the Hispanics—voted him into office. Moreover, their enthusiasm for his agenda has been utterly rhapsodic. He has seen so much support from the Hispanic community not *despite* his policies, but *because* of them.

When Trump said "nobody loves our Latino community more than I do" at a 2024 rally in Pennsylvania on the eve of the election, he wasn't kidding.

Guess what?

The Hispanics of Pennsylvania knew he wasn't kidding.

Between 2024 and 2028, they moved from the left to the right.

Even though the liberal media establishment said it couldn't be done, the president took Pennsylvania from the Democratic Party—and, as the trend suggests, the Republican Party isn't going to give it back in 2028.

On that note, just look at the six states with the largest percentage of Hispanics: Texas, Arizona, Nevada, Florida, New Mexico, and California.

President Trump won Texas.

President Trump won Arizona

President Trump won Nevada.

President Trump won Florida.

While the president did not win New Mexico, it's not unreasonable to believe that state could flip Republican in 2028, just as Pennsylvania flipped in 2024.

The trend, as virtually every data set shows, is one in which Hispanic Americans—across the country—are moving right.

But what about California?

What about that stronghold of the Democratic Party?

It's the state with 54 electoral college votes.

It's the state that voted Kamala Harris into power as a senator. She is the one who, on October 16, 2024, a month before the 2024 election, ominously warned Hispanics: "His Project 2025 Agenda would give him virtually unchecked power to implement policies that would disproportionately harm Black and Latino communities."

CalMatters, a resource for California politics, policy, and political news, analyzed the state voting data. According to their analysis, "Most—if not all—of California's 12 Latino-majority counties gave a larger share of their vote to Trump compared to 2020, and counties with a higher share of Latino population swung further toward Trump. Trump also expanded his vote share in most other counties in California."

And the Democrats' fear-mongering about "disproportionate harm to Black and Latino communities," as Vice President Harris learned, isn't panning out.

After the election, the Americas Society/Council of the Americas highlighted the most important findings. "19 of the 26 counties along the US border voted for Trump. This includes half the border counties in Arizona, all but one in New Mexico, and 12 of 14 in Texas . . . 7 of the 10 most Hispanic counties voted for Trump. These counties are all in Texas, with 88 to 98 percent of their electorate being Hispanic. In 2020, all voted for Biden. Miami-Dade County swung 19 percentage points to Trump from 2020 to 2024. Trump won 55 percent of votes in this county, which is 68 percent Hispanic."

The data doesn't lie.

But the liberal media does.

Already, after three straight elections in which Trump increased his share of the Hispanic vote, the liberal media is suggesting that he's actually losing it.

"Republicans are losing Latino voters," proclaims *Newsweek* in an August 2025 column.

"High prices and health care costs may turn Latino voters away from Republicans in 2026," forecasts NPR.

"Hispanics helped Trump retake the White House. Now their support is waning," declares Reuters.

"Republicans are making a very simple, unforced mistake with Latino voters. Does Trump know he's blowing up the GOP's future?" asked *Vox*.

"Trump's failing Latino voters," proclaims MSNBC.

Remember when the liberal media confidently predicted that Hillary Clinton was going to win the 2016 election?

Remember all those polls that unanimously concluded that Trump wasn't going to win the election?

We saw a similar narrative in 2024.

On October 14, 2024, *CBS News* reported that Harris was ahead of Trump nationally with 51 percent of the vote while Trump had 48 percent of the vote. They also reported that Harris was leading Trump in the battleground states 50 percent to 49 percent. *ABC News*, for its part, had Harris taking 50 percent of the vote while Trump was taking 49 percent of the vote. Yahoo News had Harris ahead of Trump 50 percent to 45 percent. The *New York Times* once again forecasted that Trump would be defeated by a 49 percent to 46 percent margin.

For the record, Trump won the popular vote, won all seven swing states, and increased his margin in every state.

And now we're supposed to believe that liberal journalists are the political experts on how Americans feel about the second Trump administration?

We're supposed to believe that they're the experts on how Trump is doing with the Hispanic community—a community that has only increased their support for the president from 2016 to 2024?

Give me a break.

In the liberal media, there's a belief that if you write a lie enough times it becomes true.

The Democratic politicians aren't any different.

Their claims are so similar to *Vox*, MSNBC, the *New York Times*, and other outlets that you might think that the journalists in the liberal media were writing their interviews, campaign speeches, and podcast diatribes for them.

Arizona Senator Ruben Gallego, a Democrat, recently told *CBS News* that Hispanic supporters are having "buyer's remorse." Apparently, they're saying "this is not what we voted for."

Hispanics themselves know this is a lie.

To believe that Trump is losing support among Hispanics because of his "racism," or just as nonsensically, his economic policies, you'd have to be living on another planet—let's call it the MSNBC newsroom.

The same is true with other voters of color.

For decades, the liberal media has been misrepresenting the views of African Americans.

For decades, they have been pandering to African Americans.

The liberal media, which is primarily made up of affluent white people from elite colleges and universities, think that all African Americans want to hear about is racism.

This was essentially the *New York Times'* 1619 Project in a nutshell.

"In August of 1619, a ship appeared on this horizon, near Point Comfort, a coastal port in the English colony of Virginia. It carried more than 20 enslaved Africans, who were sold to the colonists. No aspect of the country that would be formed here has been untouched by the years of slavery that followed."

When they write that no aspect of our country has been untouched by slavery, they really believe it.

From the perspective of the liberal media, every single bad thing in every single corner of the country is a result of slavery.

Racism is the original sin that America can't escape—a sin that will haunt us forever.

Why are there so many homeless African Americans in San Francisco? Racism. Why do some African Americans get fired from their jobs and evicted from their homes? Racism. Why do African Americans commit murder at much higher rates than white Americans? Racism. Why are African Americans overrepresented in prison? Racism. Why are there relatively few African American scientists? Racism. Why do African American children perform worse in math? Well, it's because math is racist.

During President Biden's administration, the Smithsonian's National Museum of African American History and Culture created a helpful handout to educate their fellow Americans about racism. In the handout—titled "Aspects and Assumptions of Whiteness & White Culture in the United States"—they proclaim that a host of normal values, and, I would argue, laudatory values, are racist. According to them, "rugged individualism" and "self-reliance" are racist. A "nuclear family" is racist. The "scientific method" is racist. "Objective, rational linear thinking" is racist. A "quantitative emphasis" is racist. The "written tradition," that too is racist. So is the idea that one should "be polite" and "respect authority." Even "wealth" is racist. Under Biden's leadership, the Smithsonian declared that the foundation of the American dream—"hard work is the key to success"—is actually racist.

These are the kinds of bizarre, and frankly racist, ideas that the liberal media—in cahoots with the Biden administration, the nonprofit industrial complex, and our public schools—has worked hard to institutionalize. This is the world that our children are educated in when their teachers require them to read and memorize material from the *New York Times*' 1619 Project, one of the most influential anti-American projects that the liberal media establishment has ever produced. This is a world in which college students are required to take courses in "antiracist sociology," "radical feminist epistemologies," and "decolonial resistance"—required courses where students have to watch *Democracy Now!* while memorizing the so-called journalism published by extremist socialist magazines like *Dissent*, *CounterPunch*, and *Jacobin.* The relationship between our publicly funded education institutions and the liberal media establishment is so close that we should really call it a marriage. I know because I've read through the syllabi. I know because this is what parents across the country are complaining about at school board meetings and town halls. I know because I've spent my life trying to counter the world of disinformation institutionalized by the radical left.

This a world in which up is down, left is right, and right is wrong. Hard work? That's evil. Personal responsibility? Forget about it. Math? You must be a white supremacist.

Whether it's a handout about "whiteness" produced by the Smithsonian, or an article about "white fragility" in the *New York Times*, or an assignment in a journalism course at Columbia University's Graduate School of Journalism that asks students to "decolonize whiteness," whatever that means, the Left has created an *Alice in Wonderland* landscape where their attempts to pander to minorities have backfired big time.

Most African Americans know that hard work matters. They know that wealth matters. They know that learning calculus, trigonometry, and statistics are not racist. It's what will help them solve problems, get a job, and otherwise make the world a better place. They know that the Democrats who pander to them in increasingly bizarre ways are full of it.

Their disdain for the Democrats is showing more and more in the voting booths.

"Trump won with a voter coalition that was more racially and ethnically diverse than in 2020 or 2016," concluded a Pew Research Center analysis of the 2024 electorate. "Among Hispanic voters, Trump battled to near parity in 2024 (51% Harris, 48% Trump) after losing to Joe Biden 61%–36% in 2020. Trump won 15% of Black voters—up from 8% four years earlier. Trump also did better among Asian voters. While a majority of Asian voters (57%) backed Harris, 40% supported Trump. This was a narrower margin than Biden's in 2020 (70% to 30%)."

While the Democrats *love* identity—as PBS gloated, "Kamala Harris' racial and cultural background took stage throughout the Democratic convention"—most Americans could not care less whether Kamala Harris is half Indian, half black, or half albino. They want actual policies that will improve their lives and make them safer.

These are the kinds of policies that were not supported under Joe Biden's administration. They are also the kinds of policies—tougher immigration laws to protect native-born workers, the end of indoctrination in our public schools, lower taxes, and the like—that Trump and his team are working day in and day out to enact.

Even among Harris's own demographic—Indian Americans—the Democratic Party is losing ground. Going into the 2024 election, about a third of Indian Americans were planning to vote against Harris. According to data from the Carnegie Endowment for International Peace, "their attachment has declined."

Even when Democrats run the daughter of an Indian immigrant, they still can't connect to Indian Americans.

Appealing to someone solely on the basis of identity is not a winning strategy.

In particular, young minorities—who understand that they will have no future under a Democratic president—were clear last November.

They want substance—not someone who shares their "historically marginalized identity."

They want substance—not someone who, as Kamala Harris put it on *The View*, wouldn't have done a single thing different than Joe Biden.

They want substance—not memes.

The Cook Political Report summarized it best: "Even as many in the TikTok generation embraced Harris' 'coconut tree' meme, she failed to capture the imagination or support from young voters that Biden enjoyed in 2020. Among all young voters, Harris underperformed Biden by six points, but the gap was much larger among younger Latino (-12) and AAPI (-9) voters. Among Black and white younger voters, the drop-off in support from 2020 was less severe (-4)."

If you were trying to understand America through the lens provided by the liberal media, you would have no idea that Hispanics, African Americans, Asian Americans, and Indian Americans have been moving right for years. Instead, you would be confronted with a near bottomless well of new stories that portray Trump as a racist who hates Hispanics, African Americans, Asian Americans, Indian Americans, and every other minority group.

Even after the 2024 election dealt a fatal blow to that narrative, the liberal media has been relentless in its zombie-like commitment to manufacturing new stories out of thin air about Trump's love of "racism," "xenophobia," and "whiteness."

On August 30, 2025, Rashad Robinson said in the pages of *The Guardian*: "We live in a very diverse country, a country with many different types of people that come from many different backgrounds, and the president exhibits his values by who he puts in office. This is not simply that Donald Trump has put only one Black person in his cabinet. It's that Donald Trump has gone out of his way to find some of the most unqualified and ill-equipped people to put in those jobs as a way to actually avoid having to put Black people in his cabinet."

Really?

Is anyone buying this?

Does the *Guardian* really believe this kind of pandering is going to bring African Americans back to the Democratic Party?

It didn't work in 2016.

It didn't work in 2020.

It didn't work in 2024.

And it's not going to work in 2028.

They're trying to manufacture the reality they want.

But, as the data shows, they're failing—big time.

"Trump's tariffs risk destroying his winning coalition," forecasted *Vox*.

"Trump gained some minority voters, but the GOP is hardly a multiracial coalition," declared the Brookings Institution.

As the Brookings Institution knows: If you have to admit the truth, then you better spin it.

Sure, Trump has rapidly won the hearts and minds of racial and ethnic minorities across the country—but now he's losing their support!

Because he's a racist!

And a xenophobe!

And a fascist!

And he didn't put enough people with the right amount of melanin in his cabinet!

I've said it before, and I'll no doubt say it again: The liberal media isn't interested in representing the truth. It's interested in creating their version of the truth.

Often attributed to Joseph Goebbels, the quote about the big lie—"if you tell a lie big enough and keep repeating it, people will eventually come to believe it"—is the unwritten rule of the liberal media establishment.

From Benghazi to the Russia Hoax—which Trump, Tulsi Gabbard, and their team are now unearthing for the American people—the liberal media has done the truth no favors. To the contrary, it has created enormous obstacles to the truth.

Interestingly enough, in the rare instance that the liberal media does acknowledge the truth—yes, racial and ethnic minorities are fleeing the Democratic Party in droves, and that trend shows no sign of abating—they spin it in a way that further isolates them from racial and ethnic minorities.

According to the liberal media, Hispanics, African Americans, Asian Americans, and other minorities aren't leaving the Democrats because they want better policies.

They are leaving the Democrats because they don't understand their own interests.

This is what Marxists call "false consciousness."

It's the idea that all these groups—the minorities who the DNC romanticize—are, in fact, not intelligent enough to recognize the Democrats as their saviors.

This is what the liberal media's deluge of articles about "messaging" is all about.

It presumes that the Democratic Party is the only party for—fill in the blank—African Americans, Asian Americans, and so on; the Democrats just have to do a better job of explaining this to these people.

It's paternalistic, it's condescending, and it's frankly offensive.

It basically treats minorities not as the Democrats' equals, but as their children.

You see the viciousness of the liberal media when their "messaging" doesn't work.

Just look at how they treat racial and ethnic minorities who fail to toe the line.

Thomas Sowell is a race traitor. Glenn Loury is a sellout. So is John McWhorter. And so on.

Just look at what happened to Coleman Hughes when he went on *The View*.

The liberal media has a whole dictionary it uses against minorities who step out of line.

"You have unconscious racism against your own people."

"You have internalized white supremacy."

The liberal media romanticize minorities—until they run away from the Democratic plantation.

Then they're evil, stupid, or both.

If you're Coleman Hughes, the Democrats see you as no better than how they see the poor and working-class white people working in the mines of West Virginia and on the farms of New Hampshire.

In short, you're not a good minority—or even a good person—unless you vote for the Democrats.

But if you are a minority who is willing to the toe the line, there's no shortage of opportunities to appear on TV, in the pages of the *Washington Post*, or anywhere else the Democrats are trying to pander.

Just look at the career trajectories of people like Roxane Gay, Ta-Nehisi Coates, and Ibram X. Kendi—the author of *How to Be An Antiracist*—to get a sense of the landscape.

Trump, on the other hand, is appealing to racial and ethnic minorities not because he's confessing his "white privilege," or babbling ad nauseam about "white supremacy," but because he treats racial and ethnic minorities as his equals.

He treats everyone in this country—regardless of whether they are African American, Asian American, Hispanic American, or Indian American—as an American first.

This is one of the many reasons his campaign has been so popular.

It's also why so many Americans are shutting off MSNOW (formerly MSNBC), and CNN, and ending their subscriptions to the *New York Times* and the *Washington Post.*

They're sick of media that divides us based on race, gender, and other categories.

They're sick of stoking the tribalism that has torn apart so many great nations—the tribalism that increasingly poses an internal threat to the United States.

There is a reason that the Fox News Channel, which is home to thirteen of the fifteen most watched cable news shows, is so popular. There is a reason it has been the number one network in basic cable for the last eight years and the most-watched television news channel for more than twenty-three consecutive years. There's a reason that the data from Pew Research Center shows that even "Black Democrats are less dependent than white Democrats on *New York Times*, NPR; more likely to turn to Fox News."

Fox covers issues and stories that go unnoticed by the left-wing legacy outlets.

Moreover, it's not catering to elites.

One the greatest ironies about the left-wing media is that it consistently represents itself as "the voice of the people."

It's "speaking truth to power."

It's "holding the elites responsible."

Yet, the data suggests it is the voice of elites.

In her book *Bad News: How Woke Media Is Undermining Democracy*, Baya Ungar-Sargon has a whole chapter titled "The Abandonment of the Working Class." In it, she looks at the numbers. According to the income profile of news audiences from 2012, 38 percent of those who consumed the *New York Times* made $75,000 or more per year. By contrast, just 23 percent of Fox News consumers made that same amount. MSNBC, CNN, and even the *Colbert Report* all reported higher top incomes for their audiences than Fox.

And what about education, that other proxy for class?

According to the data set that Ungar-Sargon explores in her book, 56 percent of the *New York Times*' audience is a college grad or more. Just 24 percent of Fox News consumers have the same level of education.

More recently, according to 2020 data, a whopping 68 percent of NPR consumers and a whopping 72 percent of *New York Times* consumers are in the "college+" stratum. Just 27 percent for Fox News.

In the past decade, the Republican Party has definitively become the party of working-class Americans.

And the conservative media has become their media of choice.

As Ungar-Sargon admits, "The truth is, Fox News is not making anyone conservative. It is conservative because it caters to the working class—a working class long abandoned by the liberal press."

And "The truth is, much of the outrage against Fox News for its alleged racism is not for actual racism, but for things that have increasingly been lumped under the ever expanding category of what counts as racism. Proof of its 'white supremacy' ranges from things like criticizing any person of color—even if they are a member of US government, and even when the criticism is itself coming from a person of color; to questioning liberal policies and explanations for things; to criticizing the lax immigration laws that have governed this country for so many years."

Likewise, Joe Rogan has the number one podcast in the world because he is not here to divide us. And he is certainly not here to produce biased, partisan narratives that serve the interests of the elites. He's here to tell the truth. That's why the Democrats cannot stand him, and it's why they cannot stand the growing number of podcasts like his.

But that doesn't mean they're going to go down without a fight.

It's telling that so much of the liberal media establishment is devoted to trying to discredit independent media.

Just at look at what they write about Rogan. He's a "prophet of dangerous disinformation" because he asked legitimate questions about the COVID-19 vaccines. He's a "toxic male influence" because he believes men should work out, delay gratification, and pull themselves up by their bootstraps to achieve their goals. He's a transphobe because he's a father of three daughters who doesn't want men competing against women in sports—especially in mixed martial arts, where the consequences can be, quite literally, deadly. He is also, you guessed it, a racist. Because anyone who even mildly questions the motivations, the reporting, and the conclusions of the liberal media is unquestionably a racist.

Here's the funniest part: The Democrats probably could have had Rogan on their side in the 2024 election if they didn't attack him.

But it wasn't just Rogan; they ignored their own base.

After Joe Biden admitted he wasn't capable of being the Democratic nominee, the DNC chose to forgo a primary process that would have involved their own voters and instead went the path of coordination with Kamala Harris. Where were the leaders of the Democratic Party demanding a primary? Where were the liberal journalists outraged at this breach in the basic rules of democratic elections?

In cahoots with the Democratic National Committee, the liberal media decided that Kamala Harris, a candidate who no one voted to run against the former president, should be the only person to run against the former president. On the eve of the election, the *New York Times* proclaimed that Kamala Harris was "the only patriotic choice for president."

"As a dedicated public servant who has demonstrated care, competence and an unwavering commitment to the Constitution, Ms. Harris stands alone in this race. . . . Many Americans remain deeply concerned about their prospects and their children's in an unstable and unforgiving world. For them, Ms. Harris is clearly the better choice."

By the end of this full-throated endorsement, one was left wondering whether Harris was the candidate who no one voted to run against Donald Trump, or if she was some kind of omnibenevolent saint who would rescue America from the hell that Trump had created.

By contrast, Trump is portrayed as a vicious dictator—absolutely committed to destroying everything beautiful, and righteous, and true in the world. Saint Harris is depicted by the *NYT* as someone who walks on water, ready to take on the problems she ignored for the previous four years.

Is that what the American people should expect from the paper of record?

If you think I'm exaggerating, I encourage you to read that piece from the *New York Times* editorial board. You won't find nicer words spoken about Vladamir Putin on the television network Russia Today, which is state-run media.

Even after the liberal media utterly distorted reality in the lead up to the 2024 election, it still did an about-face when their efforts failed. According to their post-election narrative, Trump didn't win despite attacks from the media. He won *because* of the media. Specifically, he won because media personalities like Joe Rogan had tricked the American public into voting for a fascist.

The liberal media is most vicious toward the media that doesn't play by its rules.

In an interview with standup comedian Tim Dillon, another podcaster and close friend of Joe Rogan, CNN journalist Elle Reeve, the author of *Black Pill: How I Witnessed the Darkest Corners of the Internet Come to Life, Poison Society, and Capture American Politics*, seemed utterly incapable of accepting the idea that millions of Americans voted for Donald Trump because they liked his policies and his vision for America.

Instead, she tried to scapegoat Dillon and the network of popular podcasts of which he is a part.

"Do you feel like you're part of a new establishment?" Reeves asked Dillon in their viral interview.

"I don't think I'm part of a new establishment," he explained to her, "I know it's a popular thing right now, especially in certain media circles, to say that, after running an incredibly unpopular candidate, who was introduced very late in the race because an elderly man who could not be the president, who everyone told was functioning for the president for four years, decided to [drop out] . . . She was somewhat unpopular, and she was not a star in Democratic politics before this *at all* . . . So to hang this defeat all on a few podcasts, and to say that they were the problem, I just don't buy the narrative."

But that is the narrative that the liberal media has been spinning in the wake of their 2024 defeat.

Kamala Harris didn't lose because Americans didn't believe in her or her vision for the future of the United States.

She lost because stand-up comedians like Joe Rogan, Tim Dillon, and Theo Von had put lipstick on a pig.

They had deceived the American public into voting for Donald Trump.

Since they now, apparently, have more power than the liberal media establishment and the DNC—that's why Trump is back in office.

It's crazy, I know.

But this is the narrative.

You can't make this stuff up.

All of a sudden—in the wake of the 2024 loss—the liberal media establishment, the DNC, and Kamala Harris are portraying themselves and each other as victims of the "new establishment," one that, according to journalist Elle Reeves, is more powerful than all these Democratic elites combined.

Fortunately, there are people like Tim Dillon who aren't going to let that narrative be promoted as truth.

"If you weigh, again, a few comedians with podcasts verse all of the people that supported Kamala Harris—you know, Democrat donors, billionaires, big people—if the idea that me and a few comedians have more power than multibillionaires, huge media institutions, a whole political party apparatus, I just don't think most people are going to buy that."

He's right.

Just read the top comments on this video—"Elle Reeve to Tim Dillon: Do you think you are part of a new establishment?"—which was produced and published by CNN.

"This is the first time I've ever clicked on a CNN video."

"The fact this woman is 44 years old is astounding. She has the wisdom of a 19 year old."

"Tim Dillon looks like he's teaching his niece how the world works."

"You can tell around the CNN office, the staff talks about Joe Rogan like he's Voldemort."

But what else should you expect from CNN?

As Dillon later revealed, "They said to me at CNN, 'we're editing the interview.' I said, 'put that hour out.' I sat there for an hour. . . . It's wrong to have someone come in and talk for an hour, and then use five minutes."

The liberal media is as committed to truth—and providing the whole story to the American people—as the propagandists are in George Orwell's *1984*.

Much like the Ministry of Truth, these outlets have no discernible interest in discovering, much less telling the truth.

In this era, it's relatively unsurprising that Americans would rather get their news from people like Tim Dillon.

Unlike the liberal media establishment, he doesn't have a preconceived political agenda.

He's not there to repeat the same liberal talking points over, and over, and over again.

He's not there to condense a one-hour conversation into a five-minute soundbite that can be used to advance a preconceived political agenda.

His only agenda is getting to the bottom of things and figuring out which politicians are going to do what is best for America.

That's also what Joe Rogan's agenda is.

After the 2024 election, the liberal media harangued him for having Donald Trump on his podcast. ABC News lamented that "Trump was reelected with help from podcasters like Joe Rogan." *Slate* added that "Joe Rogan just showed us who he's really been all along" in their article chiding "every young male MAGA dipshit."

Most viciously, they attacked Rogan for having Donald Trump on his podcast instead of Kamala Harris.

What they overlooked—deliberately or not—is that Rogan wanted to have Harris on his podcast.

"She had an opportunity to come here when she was in Texas. I literally gave them an open invitation. I said 'anytime.' I said if she's done at 10:00, we'll come back here at 10:00. I go, 'I'll do it at 9:00 in the morning. I'll do it at 10:00 p.m., I'll do it at midnight.'" Rogan said "Great, I would love to talk to her."

Yet, her team wanted Rogan to change the format of *The Joe Rogan Experience* to paint her in a better light.

When he refused to do that, the liberal media then painted him as a villain who didn't want to platform her.

As he explains in his podcast with Dan Richards: "There was a thing that came out recently. There was a book that was some book about the Kamala Harris campaign, where they talked about her getting on this show. And they said a bunch of things that weren't true."

What did they say?

"Supposedly they talked to like 150 different people about her and, you know, what happened with her coming on the show. . . . They didn't talk to us. Which is kind of crazy. They didn't even ask. But they said things that just weren't true. One of the things they said that weren't true was that we lied about the day that Trump was coming on. No, we just didn't tell you that Trump was coming on. He was already booked a long time ago.

"This is how it worked. Trump was *really* easy to book. Like super easy. We offered one day. He said yes. That was it. There was no 'What are we going to talk about?' "How long is it going to be?' 'Is it going to be edited?' There was nothing."

By contrast, the Harris team "never committed to doing the show." So, "all this talk, there was another thing they said, that the reason they did the Beyoncé thing, the Beyoncé event in Houston, was so that they could be in Texas to do my show. They never agreed to do the show. None of that's true. They never agreed.

"They also said that they sent someone down here to the studio to do a walkthrough of the set. That's not true. The Trump administration did. . . . They're the only ones that had a date to do the show. These people didn't have [a date]. They never agreed to do the show."

To give you a sense of how difficult it is to work with the Harris campaign, and the extent to which they'll go to try to shape the narrative, consider Rogan's frustration with her team.

"Even after Trump went on, they offered for me to come to DC and do a show with Kamala. But even then, it was the same deal. It was only like forty-five minutes to an hour. And, you know, it was not on my set. And I said that, 'Look, he did it here. We should probably do it here.' Like, if it's possible to do it here. Obviously when he did it, it had an enormous result. I'm willing to do the same thing for her."

But her team wanted to work with Rogan to create an artificial episode of *The Joe Rogan Experience*, and Rogan was not on board with that. "It's got to be the actual, real show. It shouldn't be some fake version of it where I'm sitting in a conference room. Also, they wanted a stenographer in the room. They wanted staff in the room . . . They wanted it very controlled . . . It's got to be in the studio. And it's got to be real. It's got to be a real conversation."

By contrast, "Trump was just in here by himself. Just me, him, and Jamie [Rogan's A/V specialist]. That's it. For three hours."

Can you imagine Kamala Harris talking to Joe Rogan for three hours?

I can't.

Without a teleprompter and carriers by her side, I can't imagine her making it through the first ten minutes.

The Democrats—like their media—struggle without authenticity.

Whether you love President Trump or you hate President Trump, there's no ambiguity about who President Trump is. He says what he believes—even if it upsets people—and he is willing to defend it with absolute conviction. He is always his authentic self.

That's why he can sit down and have a normal conversation with Joe Rogan for three hours.

The American people want authenticity.

They don't want Gavin Newsom pretending to be his version of Donald Trump because he thinks it will get him votes.

This issue of authenticity—it's why the Harris team was so concerned.

It's why they were trying to limit the interview to forty-five minutes, to keep her team in the room, to do it outside of Joe Rogan's studio, and to take every other measure possible to create a fake podcast episode.

You can fake your way through a presidential debate. You can fake your way through a forty-five-minute interview with CNN anchor Anderson Cooper. You can't fake your way through a three-hour—one-on-one, mano-y-mano—unscripted conversation.

The Harris team knew that. Way too many word salads were on the menu in that scenario.

They knew that Harris going on Rogan would be as disastrous for her campaign as Joe Biden's decision to debate Donald Trump. Whereas the debate showed the world that Biden was unfit to be president, the same thing would have occurred had Harris gone on *The Joe Rogan Experience.*

Harris would rather do the *Call Her Daddy* podcast on a fake set.

Interestingly, most people felt that the podcast was totally contrived (because it was).

By contrast, Trump is the opposite of contrived.

On May 9, 2025, I had Alex Bruesewitz on *The Sean Spicer Show.* Alex was the architect behind the Trump campaign's digital podcast, independent media strategy. "He's very in touch with the pop culture," Alex explained. "He pays attention to who's popular, who's not. He leans into certain issues. He's got great political instincts. He picked on Taylor Swift, right? Everybody said, 'Oh, Trump can't touch Taylor Swift. She's an icon. She's icon.'"

And what happened? "Donald Trump posted in all caps, 'I HATE TAYLOR SWIFT!' Right? The Democrats thought, 'Oh my God, every young girl in America is going to come out and vote against Donald Trump.' Trump's instincts on that were right. The very next day, ABC came out with a poll that said, 'Taylor Swift's endorsement, does it help or hurt Kamala Harris?' Seven percent said helps. Eight percent say hurts. And the rest said, 'We don't care about Taylor Swift.'"

His instincts on *The Joe Rogan Experience, This Past Weekend* with Theo Von, and the NELK podcast were also right.

Kamala Harris's instincts have been dead wrong.

But since Trump's appearance on *The Joe Rogan Experience* has been linked to his November victory, her team is now doing an about-face, pretending that it was Rogan who stopped that podcast from happening.

They keep trying to give the impression that Harris is some kind of everywoman, a real representative of the people, who would have loved to connect with Rogan and his young male listeners.

I find that hard to believe. In fact, I'm guessing that this would have been the most awkward three hours of Joe Rogan's life. Harris, in addition to her bad politics, personifies the humorless, snobbish, and out of touch liberal elite. She is the very antithesis of Rogan.

Given the generous invitation Rogan extended to her and her team, even offering to rearrange his schedule for them, it's sad to see them trying to scapegoat him for their election loss.

As Rogan notes, "They keep pretending that I lied, or I did this, or I did that. . . . We have all the receipts by the way. I have a whole list of conversations that took place. They never said she was going to do it. So there's a whole idea that we ****** her over, and that we ****** her over for Trump. Incorrect. Just not true."

Rogan wanted Kamala on his podcast. He also wanted to release both podcasts on the same day. That was his goal. He even offered to host

Kamala that same day that Trump was in the studio—after he left—so that the American people could listen to both podcasts back-to-back. It was an enormous gesture on Rogan's part, one in which he really wanted the American people to see who these candidates are, and to decide for themselves who was the best person for the job of US president.

The Harris team rejected that gesture, and then they just spun a narrative—with the help of the liberal media—that said Harris wanted to do the podcast, but Rogan, who has since been presented as a Trump lackey, wouldn't have her on.

If these are the lies they'll manufacture about a podcast episode, do you think these people are telling you the truth about the economy, the border, the war in Ukraine, Israel's war with Palestine, and other challenges we as a country are confronting?

Whereas booking Harris was an absolute nightmare, Trump was as easy as pie. He came on for three hours. They talked, they laughed, and the American people left the episode with a better understanding of who Trump is, what he is about, and why he is fighting so hard to make America great again.

As of January 21, 2026, Trump's episode with Rogan has 61 million views on YouTube.

And that is despite the fact that Rogan has said "there's an issue with searching for this episode on YouTube."

Just 28.9 million people watched Harris's speech at the Democratic National Convention.

The Democratic Party—once again—blew an opportunity to connect with ordinary Americans who they might have been able to sway. They once again blew an opportunity with young men, a demographic who is fleeing their party like the plague. And they once again blew an opportunity to embed themselves in this new media ecosystem.

Ironically enough, the table was set for them not to blow it. As Rogan himself acknowledges, "I was a Bernie supporter . . . I always considered myself a left-wing person. I never thought I would ever vote right-wing."

But a lot has changed over the past ten years.

Now instead of trying to win back Rogan, the Democrats are trying to create a Manchurian Joe Rogan.

As reported, "Six months after the Democratic Party's crushing 2024 defeat, the party's megadonors are being inundated with overtures to spend tens of millions of dollars to develop an army of left-leaning online influencers."

They are, as the saying goes, trying to create the "liberal Joe Rogan."

And they're throwing bags of money at people to make it happen.

One of the organizations is Project Bullhorn. It will "pool contributions to back creator projects. The money is running through Jason Berkenfeld, who has advised the political giving of Eric Schmidt, the billionaire former Google chief executive, and others. Mr. Berkenfeld pitched the project to major Democratic contributors at a briefing this month featuring Senator Cory Booker of New Jersey. Mr. Berkenfeld is seeking to raise $35 million in the first year for Project Bullhorn and aligned work, according to two people who have spoken to him. He is largely trying to amplify existing influencer networks: An early recipient of the money he raises will be a fund backing left-leaning creators on YouTube. Another will be a 'matchmaking service' to book these creators on YouTube shows and podcasts."

The Democrats think they can buy public opinion.

"One of the top aides on former Vice President Kamala Harris's 2024 campaign, Rob Flaherty, and a digital media executive, Mike Vainisi, have been in conversations with donors in recent weeks ahead of what is expected to be a multimillion-dollar fund-raising round for a new for-profit company called Channel Zero. The group is meant to provide back-office services to content creators who already have large followings. Mr. Flaherty is also advising Project Echo, a new four-year $52 million influencer program from People for the American Way, a progressive nonprofit group.

"The group is spending about $10 million of its own money and pitching donors for the rest, according to its president, Svante Myrick.

A program called Double Tap Democracy, meanwhile, is working with 2,000 mostly apolitical creators who generally have smaller followings. The project was started by Rachel Irwin, who led a $30 million influencer program last cycle for Future Forward, the biggest Democratic super PAC."

Instead of spending tens of millions of dollars in order to create the liberal Joe Rogan, why don't Democrats try being honest with themselves? They had the liberal Joe Rogan. His name was Joe Rogan.

And he left the Left for the same reason that so many other Americans have left the Left.

The Left's problem is not a lack of influencers or platforms; it's them. As the saying goes, I have met the enemy and he is us. Or to put this in terms most Democrats would understand, their beloved surrogate Taylor Swift said, "It's me, hi, I'm the problem, it's me." Until Democrats understand that their policies and their leaders are the problem, they will continue to lose.

Refusing to accept reality doesn't serve their interests or the interests of the country.

You don't need to spend tens of millions of dollars to realize the truth.

This kind of astroturfing approach—which, like most DNC initiatives, smacks of inauthenticity—is only going to further alienate the Democratic Party from normal Americans, especially the young American men who can smell the DNC's ruse from a mile away.

It's oxymoronic to think you can buy a Joe Rogan.

Rogan is so popular because he isn't a shill.

Love him or hate him: he's not for sale.

The same is true for Trump.

From Rogan to Tulsi and RFK, Trump is connecting with people who have long been on the other side of the political aisle.

Given the widespread dissatisfaction with the Democratic Party and the liberal media, that shouldn't be a surprise.

Again, the new media—with *The Joe Rogan Experience* at the center—isn't a partisan enterprise. It's not MSNBC. And it's not Fox News either. It's a decentralized ecosystem of people who are trying to make objective sense of the world. It is people, like the ordinary Americans who tune in to listen to them every week, who are just trying to get to the bottom of things.

As Rogan said, "My whole goal with her and with him [President Trump] is just talk, just sit, have a conversation like a human being—you find out things about people, you get a sense of them at least, a real sense."

You also get a sense, a real sense, of the stakes of these elections.

What should the future of the United States look like?

How do we get there?

Who are the best politicians for the job?

Back in the day, asking these questions was the function of the legacy media.

It's a sad sign of the times that truth telling is now considered the terrain of an evil "new establishment."

When I hear liberals like Elle Reeve use the word "establishment" when they're slamming podcasters like Dillon and Rogan, it's hard not to think about what happened on the Left in the lead up to the 2024 election.

Basically, the DNC—with aid in the form of positive and uncritical coverage from the liberal media establishment—decided that its own constituents shouldn't have the right to vote for their own presidential candidate.

Where was the deluge of CNN coverage critically examining that decision?

The powers that be chose DNC stooge Kamala Harris. And they told their own constituents to shut up and accept it.

There would be no primaries. There would be no other presidential candidate.

If it wasn't already clear before the 2024 election—and, if you were paying attention, it should have been—the DNC decides. The voters in the Democratic Party don't.

The liberal media, for its part, simply exists to grease the wheels.

This is most apparent in what the DNC, and its lackeys at outlets like the *New York Times* and the *Washington Post*, did to Bernie Sanders.

Have we ever seen a more concerted effort by one of America's two major political parties to destroy the reputation of an enormously popular politician in their own party?

Even Trump, who is by no means a fan of the socialist, has observed the way the Democrats will destroy anyone in their ranks who steps out of line.

Back on February 14, 2020, he tweeted: "It is happening again to Crazy Bernie, just like last time, only far more obvious. They are taking the Democrat Nomination away from him, and there's very little he can do. A Rigged System!"

It really is a sign of the times that a Republican president has to be the one to shine a light on the internal corruption of the Democratic Party.

Shouldn't that be the job of progressive journalists?

Isn't the *Washington Post*'s slogan "Democracy dies in darkness"?

What happened to all their talk about "speaking truth to power"?

"It is no great secret that the Republican party is winning more and more support from working people," Senator Sanders has said. "In too many ways the Democratic party has turned its back on the working class."

That's why the liberal media hates him.

It's also why they hate President Trump.

Despite their differences, both Trump and Sanders have called the Democrats out for their abandonment of the working class.

More to the point, they have called out the liberal media—time and time again.

That is why you will never see the *New York Times* endorsing Bernie Sanders or Donald Trump like they have endorsed Kamala Harris, Joe Biden, Hillary Clinton, and Barack Obama.

That's why you're not going to see the *Washington Post*, *Vice*, or *Salon* singing their praises.

The liberal media is just as much a part of the swamp as these politicians.

It's their job to preserve the swamp.

For them, there is nothing more threatening than a popular candidate—a political outsider—who wants to come into DC to drain it.

There were similar forces at work on the Right, as evidenced by the Never Trump movement of Republicans.

But the difference between the Left and the Right is that the Right has a diverse media system.

Sure, there were Never Trump pundits and journalists.

But there were also pundits and journalists who fiercely defended the president.

Like a real environmental ecosystem, where you have different species, the Right has its libertarians, religious conservatives, free-market capitalists, and the like. Unlike the Left, it has actual diversity of thought.

Above all, the Republican National Committee didn't try to destroy Donald Trump like the Democratic National Committee destroyed Bernie Sanders.

As I told PBS on December 8, 2016, our job at the RNC "was to let the voters choose a nominee, and then fully support that nominee, and give them the resources necessary to win. . . . And so our job was to be neutral through the primary, and then be as supportive as we could be once we had that nominee. And that's what we did. And once Trump was clearly going to secure that nomination, we did everything we could to make sure that his team was surrounded with the infrastructure and resources needed to win."

Interestingly enough, perhaps the biggest difference between the liberal media's explanation for Trump's win in 2016 and his win in 2024 is the degree to which "sexism" has become central to their explanation.

Having failed to popularize the narrative that Trump is the enemy of minorities—as evinced by the growing number of racial and ethnic minorities who turned out for him at the polls in 2024—the liberal media has shifted gears to gender.

Now, we are repeatedly told, Trump hates women.

And he is colluding with "the Manosphere"—the network of popular podcasts like *The Joe Rogan Experience, This Past Weekend,* and *The Tim Dillon Show*—to roll back their rights.

This time, their narrative goes, it's not just racism—it's also sexism that brought us Trump 2.0.

In the leadup to the 2024 election, the president was a guest on a number of podcasts that are popular among young men. From *The Joe Rogan Experience* to *This Past Weekend* with Theo Von, and even the NELK podcast, he was embraced by young men, many of whom saw hope in his strength, his intelligence, and his demonstrated ability to lead. They saw a better future for America with him at helm of this ship.

While the liberal media should have been trying to understand Trump's appeal among young men—after all, their shift right is one of the most fascinating aspects of the 2024 election—they were instead too busy branding Trump and his followers as sexists. The liberal media spun the president's success among young men as evidence that he was not only the candidate for Klansmen, he was also the candidate for the Harvey Weinsteins of the world.

If you were a man who voted against Harris, you were a sexist. You were someone who couldn't accept a woman president. You were someone who wanted to Make America Misogynistic Again.

And if you were a woman who voted for Trump, you had "internalized sexism."

You were the "handmaiden of misogyny."

You were a "puppet of the patriarchy."

This was the narrative after 2024.

As Kate Manne, a Cornell University professor who has perpetuated her insane narratives both inside her Ivy League classroom as well as the pages of the *New York Times* and the *Washington Post*, wrote on November 10, 2024, "Trump's election is a triumph of rape culture. People are trying to normalize his election victory, blaming it on failures of Kamala Harris's campaign or problems in the Democratic Party. Don't let them."

A "triumph of rape culture"? Is that not one of the most offensive things you have ever heard? Zero pushback.

Again, you don't even have to waste your time reading their articles.

Just look at the headlines.

The AP News reported that an "emboldened 'manosphere' accelerates threats and demeaning language toward women after US election."

"The result of the US election unleashed a ferocious feminist backlash," announced *The Guardian*.

President Biden, for his part, "wasn't surprised" that "sexist" attacks cost Kamala Harris the election.

Kamala even titled her book *107 Days* to make it clear it was a time issue. Never mind that she blew one and a half billion dollars and still came up short (and oh, by the way, went into debt, which the DNC is still paying off). Beyond the timing issue, her book introduces a list of grievances, blaming everyone but herself for her loss.

I mean, seriously, standup comedian Tim Dillon offered a better analysis of the outcome of the 2024 election than all these experts combined.

The American people, including millions of women, voted for Trump not because they hate women.

But because Kamala Harris offered them nothing by way of policies that would improve their lives.

And let's face it: many women don't support abortion.

Notwithstanding what the media says, millions of women don't see abortion as empowerment.

They see it as murder.

According to data from Pew in 2024, 33 percent of women say it should be illegal in all or most cases.

Women are just as diverse as African Americans and other historically marginalized groups in their views on the most pressing issues of our time.

And guess what? They too are fleeing the Democratic plantation in droves.

Pew reported that "46% of women voted for Trump in 2024, compared with 44% of women four years earlier."

That is, the president *increased* his support among women.

Just as you could be forgiven for thinking that not a single racial or ethnic minority voted for Trump, if the liberal media was your only source for the election results you could be forgiven for thinking that not a single woman voted for the president.

The reality is much, much different.

Even in 2020, his results among women were remarkable.

As the sociologist Musa al-Gharbi summarized it, "Trump won white women by a margin of 9 percentage points. This year, he won by 11 percentage points. In 2016, Democrats won Hispanic and Latina women by 44 percentage points; in 2020 they won by 39. Last cycle, Democrats won black women by 90 percentage points. This year, by 81 points. That is, in a year when a black woman was on a major party ticket for the first time in US history, the margin between Democrats and Republicans among black women shifted 9 percentage points in the other direction—towards Trump."

As Pew notes, the trend continued in 2024: "Black men and women alike were more likely to vote for Trump in 2024 than in 2020."

In the words of the Women for Trump Coalition, "President Trump's policies will continue his legacy of empowering women and establishing a United States with greater equality and opportunity for all." As they note, "Under President Trump, unemployment for women hit its lowest rate in nearly 70 years," and "President Trump established a task force to help combat the tragedy of missing or murdered Native American women and girls," and "President Trump signed the INSPIRE Act which encouraged NASA to have more women and girls participate in STEM and seek careers in aerospace," and "President Trump led a coalition of countries to sign the Geneva Consensus Declaration, declaring that there is no international right to abortion and committing to protecting women's health."

In their words, "President Trump did more for Women than any administration in history!"

Good luck finding that conclusion in the *New York Times.*

If you want to know what black women think about Trump, just ask them. Herneitha Rochelle Hardaway Richardson (who passed away in January 2023) and her sister Ineitha Lynnette Hardaway, better known as Diamond and Silk, were once Democrats. They have more than once explained why they and so many black women have left the Democratic Party to support President Trump. "He's going to protect us all!" they proclaimed at a rally in Phoenix, Arizona.

But you never win in the world of the liberal media.

As *Business Insider* contends, "For Trump and his supporters, they were a way to sidestep accusations of racism." "It's a discourse about Blackness where actual Black participants are almost secondary characters," one of their "experts," a professor of sociology, noted. In other words, you're not an "actual" black American unless you vote for Democrats.

If you want to know what progressives believe black americans should think about Trump, take a listen to how NPR frames the issue. One listen and you will hear no shortage of commentary about how black americans, especially black women, and other racial and ethnic minorities are voting against their own interests—and how they should be voting better. Thank goodness Congress finally ended taxpayer financing of NPR and PBS.

You'll find no shortage of "intersectional" commentary about why progressives need to educate black women, so they understand how they are being harmed by the "racism" and "sexism" of the Trump administration.

Even though women showed up for Trump in historically unprecedented numbers, institutions like NPR continue to give the impression that this is some kind of fluke—one might say a glitch in the Matrix—that will pass.

As President Trump warned us back in 2021: "Our media is not free. It's not fair. It suppresses thought. It suppresses speech, and it's become the enemy of the people. It's become the enemy of the people. It's the biggest problem we have in this country. No third world countries would even attempt to do what we caught them doing."

And it's not just the legacy media institutions.

It's also big tech.

"And just like the radical left tries to blacklist you on social media. Every time I put out a tweet, that's, even if it's totally correct, totally correct, I get a flag. I get a flag. And they also don't let you get out. You know, on Twitter, it's very hard to come onto my account. It's very hard to get out a message. They don't let the message get out nearly like they should. But I've had many people say, 'I can't get on your Twitter.' I don't care about Twitter. Twitter's bad news. They're all bad news. But you know what, if you want to, if you want to get out a message and if you want to go through big tech, social media, they are really, if you're a conservative, if you're a Republican, if you have a big voice, I guess they call it shadow banned, right? Shadow banned. They shadow ban you, and it should be illegal."

He's right.

And the Hearing on the Weaponizing of the Federal Government proved that.

Michael Shellenberger, in his testimony before Congress, summarized what this landscape looked like:

"Many insist that all we identified in the Twitter Files, the Facebook Files, and the CTIL Files were legal activities by social media platforms to take down content that violated their terms of service. Facebook, X (formerly Twitter), and other Big Tech companies are privately owned and free to censor content. And government officials are free to point out wrong information, they argue. But the First Amendment prohibits the government from abridging freedom of speech, the Supreme Court has ruled that the government 'may not induce, encourage or promote private persons to accomplish what it is constitutionally forbidden to accomplish,' and there is now a large body of evidence proving that the government did precisely that. . . . What's more, the whistleblower who delivered the CTIL Files to us says that its leader, a 'former' British intelligence analyst, was 'in the room' at the Obama White House in 2017 when she received the instructions to create a counter-disinformation project to stop a 'repeat of 2016.'"

Matt Taibbi, one of the last great American journalists, was similarly caustic in his testimony. "There's been a dramatic shift in attitudes about speech," he noted, "and many politicians now clearly believe the bulk of Americans can't be trusted to digest information. This mindset imagines that if we see one clip from RT we'll stop being patriots, that once exposed to hate speech we'll become bigots ourselves, that if we read even one Donald Trump tweet we'll become insurrectionists. Having come to this conclusion, the kind of people who do 'antidisinformation' work have taken upon themselves the paternalistic responsibility to sort out what is and is not safe."

Often what is "not safe" are mainstream conservative views.

Often what is "not safe" for consumption are stories that reveal the truth about the Democratic Party's corruption.

As Taibbi notes, the people who are allowed to censor the rest of us are not ordinary Americans. "Whether America continues the informal *sub rosa* censorship system seen in the Twitter Files or formally adopts something like Europe's draconian new Digital Services Act, it's already clear who *won't* be involved. There'll be no dockworkers doing content flagging, no poor people from inner city neighborhoods, no single moms pulling multiple waitressing jobs, no immigrant store owners or Uber drivers, etc. These programs will always feature a tiny, rarefied sliver of affluent professional-class America censoring a huge and ever-expanding pool of everyone else."

The stakes are high.

"Take away the highfalutin talk about 'countering hate' and 'reducing harm' and 'antidisinformation' is just a bluntly elitist gatekeeping exercise. If you prefer to think in progressive terms, it's class war. The math is simple. If one small demographic over here has broad control over the speech landscape, and a great big one over there does not, it follows that one group will end up with more political power than the other. Which one is the winner?"

The winner is not the American people.

It's the Democratic Party.

Of course, it's not just Twitter and Facebook.

It's the whole ecosystem of social media, which is almost entirely based in the hyper-progressive enclave of San Francisco.

Birds of a feather flock together.

And the hyper-progressive tech wizards who run our social media platforms, from the CEOs down to the programmers and even the interns fresh out of Stanford, are not here to promote the widest possible range of views.

They're here to control the narrative.

As of September 2025, Joe Rogan still pins his podcast episode with Donald Trump at the top of his X page because, as he notes, "there's an issue with searching for this episode on YouTube."

YouTube outright removed the NELK Boys podcast with Donald Trump from their platform because of "misinformation." In their world, misinformation is anything that strays from the left-wing narrative.

These aren't fringe websites. These are the biggest websites on planet earth. They are the modern public square. YouTube alone has more than 2.5 billion monthly active users. These are platforms where people get their information, where they debate, and where they develop and refine their views.

When you remove a podcast episode with Donald Trump, or you make it difficult for people to find the episode, you're limiting the scope of free speech. In the case of Trump, you're limiting a presidential candidate, and former president, whom millions of people want to hear.

This is the sort of censorship we might expect in a third world country, or a dystopian novel like *1984*, not the greatest country on earth.

It's a shame that Donald Trump, the 45th and 47th US President, has been banned on Twitter, Facebook, Instagram, Twitch, and Snapchat.

Imagine if they did this to United Kingdom prime minister Keir Starmer, or German President Frank-Walter Steinmeier, or French President Emmanuel Macron. Institutions like the *New York Times* and the *Washington Post* would be up in arms.

Imagine if they did this to Barack Obama.

The liberal media would have declared a state of emergency. They would have accused these platforms of throwing free speech—and democracy itself—under the bus. They would have accused them of trying to distort public opinion and shape the election.

Yet, they unanimously lauded these platforms as heroes for censoring Donald Trump.

They didn't just censor the president.

They censored Americans who support him.

Reddit banned the subreddit r/DonaldTrump. Shopify banned stores affiliated with Trump. TikTok removed content and redirected hashtags like #patriotparty to their community guidelines. Discord banned the server The Donald. Apple suspended Parler from its App Store, thereby preventing the president's supporters from communicating with each other—at the very moment when other social media platforms had stifled their voices.

And, again, they were lauded as heroes by the liberal media.

This will go down as one of the most shameful periods in American history, one that really pushed our Democracy to the brink of collapse.

Fortunately, there are Republican lawmakers who have tried to rein in big tech, tech leaders like Mark Zuckerberg who are acting like the great robber barons of their generation.

In his letter to Facebook CEO Zuckerberg, on the eve of the 2020 election, Senator Josh Hawley wrote, "Today, the *New York Post* released a story revealing that Hunter Biden facilitated a meeting with a Ukrainian energy executive and his father, who was then serving as Vice President. In it, the *Post* offers evidence that directly contradicts the claims of the Democratic nominee for president, who had previously stated that he has 'never spoken to my son about his overseas business dealings.' Yet it has come to my attention that this news report—one clearly relevant to the public interest—has been censored on Facebook."

To be fair, the Biden administration is behind much of this.

While Zuckerberg doesn't deserve a get out of jail free card, it's important to note that he himself was pressured by the former US president to comply with the Democrats' agenda.

As he later admitted, the Biden administration would "call up the guys on our team and yell at them and cursing and threatening repercussions if we don't take down things that are true." He also described his own company's "fact-checking" process as "something out of *1984*."

After President Trump returned to office, leftist tech leaders like Zuckerberg have shifted gears, knowing that liberty and freedom are once again going to be defended by the Oval Office. For what it's worth, I believe strongly that Zuckerberg is making a purely business move and will revert back to his leftist ways when Trump leaves office. In January, just a few months after the 2024 election, Facebook ended its DEI programs. As they noted: "The legal and policy landscape surrounding diversity, equity and inclusion efforts in the United States is changing. The Supreme Court of the United States has recently made decisions signaling a shift in how courts will approach DEI. It reaffirms longstanding principles that discrimination should not be tolerated or promoted on the basis of inherent characteristics."

Good.

And that's just the beginning.

The problem of conservative, and even moderate, voices being censored by big tech has been so pervasive that Hawley had to write a book about it.

As he explains his reasoning for writing *The Tyranny of Big Tech,* he notes: "At a time when these platforms are determining elections, banning inconvenient political views, lining politicians' pockets with hundreds of millions of dollars, and addicting our kids to screens, I want to draw attention to the robber barons of the modern era. This is the fight to recover America's populist democracy. That is why I am writing this book."

His book should be required reading in every American classroom.

Indeed, it's a miracle that it was even published.

As Adam Szetela recently exposed in his 2025 book, *That Book Is Dangerous! How Moral Panic, Social Media, and the Culture Wars Are Remaking Publishing,* progressives have utterly taken over the Big Five publishers: Penguin Random House, Hachette, HarperCollins, Macmillan, and Simon & Schuster. A president at one of the Big Five publishers admitted that his publisher is hiring people "at the very, very, very farthest edges of the cultural police." These radical progressives ensure that conservative books will not be acquired.

Just look at what happened to Mike Pence and Jordan Peterson.

Inside Penguin Random House, employees tried to prevent the publication of Jordan Peterson's self-help book *Beyond Order: 12 More Rules for Life.* While the content of the book is as controversial as a bake sale, Peterson's opinions of trans people are controversial. Accordingly, these progressives felt he shouldn't be allowed to publish a book. As part of their attempt to pressure Penguin Random House to censor Peterson, they held a town hall. During the town hall, some of these adult liberals cried. On social media, the narrative circulated that Peterson was evil, and any righteous person should do what they could to stop his book from being published.

It's the same tactic that was used at Simon & Schuster to try to stop the publication of Mike Pence's memoir, *So Help Me God.* In an open letter, these employees accused their own publisher of standing "on the wrong side of justice." "By choosing to publish Mike Pence," they went on, "Simon & Schuster is generating wealth for a central figure of a presidency that unequivocally advocated for racism, sexism, homophobia, transphobia, anti-Blackness, xenophobia, misogyny, ableism, islamophobia, antisemitism, and violence." "This is not a difference of opinions; this is legitimising bigotry," as reported in *The Guardian*.

Fortunately, both books were published.

But these are the rare exceptions that prove the rule.

The rule is that the progressives who control the mainstream publishers are not interested in publishing conservative voices—unless those voices have huge platforms that will guarantee unprecedented levels of sales. As one vice president at a Big Five publisher explained to Szetela, "I would say anyone who is incentivized to make money is in support of conservative imprints because they have tended to be very lucrative. That's the reason they continue to exist. But, if you put it to an internal vote, it wouldn't even be close. It would be 8–1 in favor of disbanding the conservative imprint or banning, you know, Fox personalities and Republican politicians."

And what about Hollywood?

American conservative political commentator Ben Shapiro was born in the shadow of the Hollywood sign. Both his parents work in Hollywood. As he writes: "Imagine a group of activists so powerful that they could beam their propaganda directly into your brain. Now also imagine that they're so sophisticated, they actually get you to pay them to do it. Unfortunately, you don't have to imagine it. It's real. It's Hollywood."

Shapiro knows the landscape better than most.

As he reflects, "As big as the Internet has become, Hollywood—and here, I'm talking specifically about television—is still king. Not only does it reach hundreds of millions of people with its messaging, it embeds that messaging in seemingly innocuous stories—stories that distract us from the hardships of daily life; stories that make us feel good, compassionate, and decent."

And what kinds of stories get churned out ad nauseam by Hollywood?

"They spin out hour after hour of slickly-produced left-wing propaganda and give themselves awards for doing it. They applaud each other's 'courage,' even though all their friends think exactly as they do. I spoke with nearly a hundred members of the Hollywood community when I wrote my book, *Primetime Propaganda*, and many of them openly admitted they inserted 'social justice' messages into their shows."

"How they do it," continues Shapiro, "is both clever and effective. Hollywood writers, producers, directors, actors create characters we keep wanting to spend time with, then have those characters act in ways most of us would judge wrong. Then, in effect, they ask us a question: Isn't it really okay that Rachel from *Friends* decided to have a baby without first marrying Ross? After all, you like Ross and you like Rachel! How can what they do be bad?"

In the wake of the so-called of Summer of Love, the summer of 2020 in which the radical Left, led by Antifa, burned businesses to the ground, Hollywood has been especially committed to "antiracism." That was the period Netflix pledged $5 million to support black creators. That was the period in which every movie theater in America was showing films that in some way, shape, or form were designed to make white people feel guilty.

But it's hasn't always been like this.

As Shapiro notes, Hollywood used to be a source for American values and patriotism. It used to believe that yes, America is imperfect, but it's still the land of the free and the home of the brave—it's still a country everyone should be proud to live in.

"For decades, Hollywood promoted traditional American values. That changed, as did so much else in the late 1960s and '70s, when Hollywood stopped celebrating American values and started transforming them. For example, in the early 1970s, abortion was a hotly-contested issue. A year before the *Roe v. Wade* Supreme Court case, the top-rated TV sitcom, *Maude*, featured a storyline in which the title character of the show has an abortion. *The LA Times* described it as 'a watershed moment' in TV history. Why? Well, because it removed the stigma of abortion. Millions of Americans, sitting in their living rooms, saw a beloved character do something they did not approve of—and felt sympathy."

As Shapiro notes, "It isn't just social issues. Chevy Chase likes to boast that he helped Jimmy Carter defeat Gerald Ford in 1976. He may be right. Week after week on *Saturday Night Live*, Chase portrayed Ford, probably the most athletic president in American history, as a bumbling, uncoordinated idiot. In the early 2000s, Comedy Central had a show, *That's My Bush!*, that openly mocked the 43rd president. And, of course, Hollywood despises Donald Trump. From crime dramas to the late-night comedy shows, he's relentlessly ridiculed."

When Hillary lost the election, comedian Rob Schneider, a former *SNL* cast member, felt that the show had finally hammered the last nail into its own coffin.

"I hate to crap on my own show. But when I saw, when Hillary Clinton lost, which is understandable—she's not exactly the most likable person in the room—and then when Kate McKinnon went out there on *Saturday Night Live* from the cold opening, and she started dressed as Hillary Clinton, and she starts playing 'Hallelujah,' and I said, I literally prayed, 'Please have a joke at the end. Don't do this. Please don't go down there.' And there was no joke at the end. And I went, it's over. This is not going to come back. It's gone."

It's not just *SNL*.

As Schneider, no stranger to late night, observes: "You can take the comedy routines—'the comedy routines'—you can take the comedic indoctrination process happening with each of the late night hosts, and you can exchange them with each other, that's how you know that's not interesting anymore."

There's a reason *The Late Show with Stephen Colbert* is getting kicked off the air.

And it's not because Trump is "censoring" him.

It's because, as two insiders revealed to the *New York Post*, "the show was on the trajectory of losing more than the $40 million to $50 million it lost last year."

It's not an interesting show.

It's predictable. It's hackneyed. It's nauseatingly partisan—to the point where one has to wonder if Colbert receives talking points from the speechwriters at the Democratic National Committee.

On July 21, 2025, he had CNN's Anderson Cooper on his show.

At this point, you can't tell the difference between Cooper and Colbert.

And as Colbert is now realizing, offending half the nation's audience with jokes so redundant that they look AI generated—that's not a sustainable business model.

The show is simply not doing what it's supposed to be doing: generating money by making people laugh.

Do any of these guys get math? Clearly they don't get funny.

In essence: it's journalism, it's social media, it's the biggest publishers on planet Earth, it's Hollywood—it's the many-headed hydra of the Democratic establishment that has devoured our media ecosystem.

And the heads of this blue hydra are united by their commitment to silencing the truth, to distorting the truth, and to otherwise keeping ordinary Americans asleep as their democracy—and their country—falls apart.

Just look at the media targeting of law firms that defended Donald Trump. Who in their right mind would call that journalism? Who could possibly see that as the kind of media central to a thriving democracy? That kind of media is the antithesis of democracy—and America itself.

They tried to make defending Donald Trump illegal.

They lost.

Donald Trump, leading the best team in the history of American politics, is wielding a broadsword and cutting off the heads of this hydra one by one.

PBS with its 330 stations: cut their federal funding.

NPR with its 246 stations: cut their funding.

The National Endowment for the Arts with its fellowship for creative writers who write stories that do little more than promote radical left-wing ideologies: cut their funding.

The American people have spoken.

They're not going to fund indoctrination.

That's not what taxes are for.

To be clear, Trump is not trying to "destroy the media."

He's trying to make it great again.

Even the radically left-wing NEA is still getting funding; but the funding is going be put toward projects that align with the president's priorities, like celebrating the 250th anniversary of American independence.

The US government shouldn't be funding art projects that promote hatred toward America.

We already get enough of those projects from the Big Five Publishers, Hollywood, and the *New York Times.*

From the legacy media to social media, and everything in between, there is a reason the liberal media is now frequently described as the Matrix, that artificial reality at the center of the 1999 film that keeps millions of people enslaved in an unreality of delusion.

In the end, for a candidate the left-wing media has repeatedly called Hitler, Donald J. Trump sure did pretty well among groups that would stand to lose the most if he was actually the reincarnation of the Führer.

And for a guy who Mark Cuban said doesn't surround himself with strong women, Trump has sure picked an awful lot of impressive women for high-level positions.

Evidently, the liberal media aren't familiar with White House Chief of Staff Susie Wiles, who has been absolutely vital to coordinating the staff effort and response. Wiles, who directed Trump's campaign to victory in Florida in 2016, is—in Trump's words—"tough, smart, innovative, and is universally admired and respected." She is, in the president's words, "the most powerful woman anywhere in the world." Is Mark Cuban paying attention? Maybe he should go back to running his failed powdered milk business.

If he wants to chime in on national politics, and Trump's relationship with powerful women, maybe Cuban should talk to Secretary of Education Linda McMahon, or White House press secretary Karoline Leavitt, an incredibly strong woman who is now the youngest press secretary the White House has ever had. Unlike Biden, who appointed Kamala Harris as his vice president for no other discernible reason than her gender and race, these women were appointed because they are the most competent individuals for their respective jobs. They were appointed not to check off a census box, but to Make America Great Again.

When Mark Cuban hurls criticism at the president hoping something sticks—"you never see him around strong, intelligent women, ever, it's very simple, they're intimidating to him"—it says less about the president's sexism, which doesn't exist, and more about Mark Cuban's sexism. After all, you would have to be a sexist to look at women like Wiles, McMahon, and Leavitt, and then take Cuban's criticism seriously. And I could keep going, adding Agriculture Secretary Brooke Rollins and Attorney General Pam Bondi to a long list of tough, smart, effective women serving in Trump 2.0.

Ben Carson, himself an African American who has been a vocal defender of women's rights, and who served in Trump's first administration, put it eloquently in an interview: "President Trump does not like to surround himself with 'yes' people." The president wants winners, regardless of their race or their gender, who understand the processes needed to pass the policies America needs.

In plain English, President Trump doesn't care whether you have XY chromosomes or XX chromosomes.

He does"t care about the amount of melanin in your skin.

He cares about what's inside your head and your heart; he cares about your commitment to this country and your ability to enact an America First agenda at a level this country has never seen.

That's why McMahon is in office.

That's why Wiles is in office.

That's why Leavitt is in office.

It's why organizations like Moms for Liberty, a multiracial grassroots organization committed to protecting America's sons and daughters, love President Trump.

It's why moms across the country were knocking on doors, calling prospective voters, and trying to get people out to the polls for him in November 2024.

As he often says, he wants winners—the best of the very best—on his team.

Let's zoom out: The bigger point is that, despite all this noise, the American people saw through the media's lies that Trump wasn't going to be supported by racial and ethnic minorities and women going into the election.

And they're now seeing through the current wave of disinformation that is telling the world that Trump is losing support among racial and ethnic minorities and women.

They're seeing through Stephen Colbert, who is now out of a job.

They're seeing through the writers at *Saturday Night Live*, a show that recently aired its lowest-rated episode among adults eighteen to forty-nine in the show's fifty-year history.

They're seeing through platforms like Facebook and Instagram, which have long been the arbiters of censorship.

Regardless of their race or gender, millions of Americans voted for the only candidate who they knew would get better results for the country—and the only candidate who had the desire to drain the media's swamp.

Under Trump's leadership—and the multiracial coalition of men and women who came out to support him—this is the first time the GOP has won the popular vote since Americans elected George W. Bush to office in 2001.

And that happened despite censorship from social media, a deluge of Hollywood narratives normalizing the insanity of the Left, a publishing industry that would rather burn conservative books than publish them, and a journalistic ecosystem that is as polluted as the Hudson River.

Generously, we might say there are two types of political pundits: those who acknowledge that the GOP has been gaining ground for years and those who haven't looked at the data.

More cynically, we might say there is a third type of political pundit: those who have looked at the data but refuse to accept it.

Those folks get jobs at MSNBC, the *New York Times*, and PBS.

They're especially likely to get those jobs when they spout racist views.

Doreen St. Félix, who recently called Sydney Sweeney an "Aryan princess," built her career spouting racist, sexist, and antisemitic views.

That's how she won a National Magazine Award for Columns and Commentary,

That's how she got her job as a staff writer at the *New Yorker*.

On white men, St. Félix has written: "You all are the worst. Go nurse your f–king Oedipal complexes and leave the earth to the browns and the women."

She also declared that she "would be heartbroken if I had kids with a white guy."

"Whiteness," she explains, "must be abolished."

She's also written that "White people['s] . . . lack of hygiene literally started the bubonic plague, lice, syphilis."

And more concisely, she has stated: "I hate white men."

Most bizarrely, St. Félix has claimed that "we lived in perfect harmony w/ the earth pre whiteness," and that the cause of environmental destruction is "white capitalism."

That's how you get a job at the *New Yorker*.

That's how you win a National Magazine Award for Columns and Commentary.

These aren't just baseless falsehoods that have as much truth in them as a Stephen King novel.

They're pure hate.

But as we have known for years, especially since the 2016 election, the so-called journalists have been spewing their hatred for white men, capitalism, and the like long before Trump ever walked onto the scene.

It's not an aberration from what they do.

It is what they are paid to do.

But Trump is no stranger to criticism.

Strong men aren't.

And our president, he doesn't back down.

He can dismiss these attacks by pointing to his record of results from his first term, and the growing support he is garnering from Americans of all races, genders, sexualities, religions, and the like.

Trump is the great uniter.

And Trump 2.0 is only going to deliver more results.

In the face of the liberal media's attacks, these results are going to be better than ever.

In the end, the liberal media establishment is on its last legs.

They pretended Trump supporters didn't exist. They had panels and guests that painted a picture of Democrats who despised him and Republicans who all repudiated him. Instead, what the results showed last November was that the president's support has grown massively. He went around the legacy outlets and used long-form podcasts and independent media in a way no one has. He rendered the legacy media useless (remember him blowing off *60 Minutes* because they lied about the Hunter Biden laptop?).

The liberal media and their buddies in the DNC focus on Trump's tactics and tone, but Trump focuses on what matters.

Trump reshaped politics. Now he reshapes government.

He is all about results—not rituals.

They mocked the tone. But they can't deny the results.

That's Trump 2.0.

On that note, is it any wonder that the president also shook up the White House briefing room? What assistant press secretary Taylor

Rogers calls "the archaic White House press corps" is no longer allowed to have a monopoly on press coverage. Press Secretary Karoline Leavitt announced this historic change during the press briefing on January 29, 2025.

"Starting today, this seat in the front of the room, which is usually occupied by the press secretary staff, will be called the 'new media' seat. So, in light of these announcements, our first questions for today's briefing will go to these new media members whose outlets, despite being some of the most viewed news websites in the country, have not been given seats in this room."

Karoline was clear: "It's essential to our team that we share President Trump's message everywhere and adapt this White House to the new media landscape in 2025. . . . This White House believes strongly in the First Amendment, so it's why our team will work diligently to restore the press passes of the 440 journalists whose passes were wrongly revoked by the previous administration."

When the White House stripped the White House Correspondents' Association of its ability to manage the White House press pool, they didn't do it to create an echo chamber. They did it to break the echo chamber. In the same way the president is against grotesque monopolies in other corners of American life, he is against the liberal media's monopoly over press coverage.

The White House press pool is the designated group of select reporters on any given day that represent the larger group that covers the White House. As you can imagine, only so many people can ride on Air Force One or fit into the Oval Office so the Correspondents' Association chose which reporters were allowed in on a daily basis. So, if you control who gets access you control the narrative. Only the likes of ABC, NBC, the *Washington Post*, *New York Times*, and *Politico* were eligible to be part of the pool. Independent media need not apply. That stranglehold has ended. The White House press office now sets the pool schedule and has opened up who can join, allowing for independent voices and conservative media to be part of it.

The WHCA can have their poorly attended annual White House Correspondents' dinner, which has become little more than another Democratic Party gala. But real journalists—a diverse group of journalists—are going to have historic access to the White House press room.

As for dinners, there's a host of other events that real journalists can attend.

Substack, a newsletter platform that I use for seanspicer.com, held a true black-tie affair to compete with the White House Correspondents Dinner—and it was packed. The interesting thing about this alternative dinner was that it spanned the spectrum. You had writers and creators from the far left and far right there—everyone together in the same room, enjoying each other's company, and having a great event celebrating the ability to exercise our First Amendment rights.

Alternatively, the White House Correspondents' Dinner continues to be a place where you invite left-wing comedians to hate on Donald Trump and conservatives.

The good news in all of this is that the coming reforms will be hard to turn back. This White House has embraced independent media in a way that will be hard for any future administration to undermine. They deserve a lot of credit for how they have embraced and welcomed this new media.

The White House Correspondents' Association and the White House Correspondents' Dinner have both seen their best day.

As Assistant Press Secretary Taylor Rogers told Fox News Digital, "The legacy media's charade of inclusivity has been exposed by their resistance to allow emerging voices into the press briefing room. Americans have found new ways to digest their media—and we cater to the people, not the archaic White House press corps."

Who controls the room controls the narrative.

The room, because of President Trump and his team of strong women, like Karoline Leavitt and Taylor Rogers (are you paying attention Mark Cuban?), is once again going to represent the interests of the American people.

The briefing room belongs to the people. Not the WHCA. Not CNN. Not anyone who sacrifices the pursuit of truth for their allegiance to the Democratic Party.

As Ingrid Jacques reflects: "When it came to Biden, too many journalists tossed their curiosity out the window, accepting whatever came out of the White House as truth. Even worse, some publications actively sought to curry favor with the Biden administration, and in doing so helped hide information from the public that the president didn't want to get out—whether that related to the origins of COVID-19, his son Hunter's laptop or to his declining mental and physical health. That's the opposite of what the media should be doing. Can you imagine the outrage that would follow if journalists sought to do the same with Trump? The same standard should apply, regardless of who is president."

Kerry Picket of the *Washington Times* had a great piece on how the White House press operation is different in Trump 2.0. She explains: "Immediately upon his return to the White House for a second term, President Trump and his team adopted an aggressive press strategy to avoid constantly playing defense, as they had during his first term. Mr. Trump, who always had a combative relationship with the Washington press corps, assembled a communications team to shake up what he saw as an outdated media landscape. . . . One of the biggest changes between Mr. Trump's first and second terms is the increased presence of conservative news outlets in the White House Press Corps. The Trump White House restored all the press passes revoked under President Biden."

As Picket reports, it also "issued new ones to new media, such as podcasters and other alternative news sites, including *The Daily Wire*, *The Daily Signal*, Right Side Broadcasting, Real America's Voice and Lindell TV. That added nearly 500 new passes. They also added a new media seat in the briefing room, which is filled by a different new media correspondent at each briefing. That correspondent also kicks off the briefing with the first questions, a privilege once reserved for The Associated Press. . . . 'I don't think we had any indication of the level of hostility the legacy media was approaching,' Mr. Spicer said. 'This time, clearly, he has the ability to see everything through the lens of how things went the first term.'"

As Karoline Leavitt put it, "The campaign revealed that the majority of the American people receive their news outside of the legacy media bubble, which is why it is essential that we meet Americans where they are and allow media from across the ideological spectrum to cover the White House."

Importantly, Picket writes, "The second-term team also brought the hammer down on legacy media outlets and correspondents. They took control of picking the members of the handful of reporters from TV, radio, print, new media and wire services who cover the president's public events. Taking control away from the White House Correspondents' Association, the administration became the arbiter of which outlets get access to small events and travel with the president.

"What's more, AP lost its 'special access' to White House events, such as the Oval Office, after refusing to adopt Mr. Trump's renaming of the Gulf of Mexico to the Gulf of America." Finally, "The White House launched a 'media offenders' website to highlight what it sees as biased or inaccurate reporting by journalists and news outlets."

As I wrote in my newsletter, seanspicer.com, back on June 18, 2025, "We watched right before our eyes Biden's physical and cognitive decline. From Biden's doctor clearing Biden as fit for office in his yearly physical to Karine Jean-Pierre behind the podium saying he 'runs circles around me.' It was a blatant and egregious lie that led to some of the most disastrous policies and decisions a president has ever made." I mean, seriously, if Karine is being honest, she needs to be put into urgent care immediately.

Yet, no one called her out on this—or even questioned the plausibility of that ridiculous assertion.

The fact that the liberal media are now profiting from their own inability to do journalism during Biden's administration shows just how spineless American journalism on the Left has become.

Jake Tapper—the same guy who coined the Big Lie—wrote *Original Sin: President Biden's Decline, Its Cover-up, and His Disastrous Choice to Run Again*. This number one *New York Times* bestseller wasn't published until May 20, 2025, provoking the obvious question: Where was Jake Tapper from 2020 through 2024 when the Left was pushing the narrative that Biden was running circles around people like Karine Jean-Pierre?

The warnings that were dismissed back then have now been vindicated—no thanks to this former representative for Hooters.

Megyn Kelly was clear when Tapper appeared on her show. "Over here in my ecosphere, we were covering all of these. It wasn't just falling down. It was getting lost. It was some of the stuff you report in your book—we knew and we were reporting on." As she told Tapper, "There was an attempted cover-up. It could only ever work if you allowed it, if the press allowed it."

She was absolutely right when she told Tapper: "One of us didn't miss the biggest story of the century when it comes to presidential politics and one of us did."

I said it under oath: Biden wasn't in charge. The country deserves the truth.

In my testimony to the US Senate Committee on the Judiciary, detailing what it was like to serve under President Trump, I was clear: "During my tenure as press secretary, I interacted with the President multiple times every day. Most days, I would talk to him by phone or in person in the morning and then multiple times throughout the day, including weekends. . . . In my position, I was very well acquainted with President Trump's work, his day-to-day responsibilities, and his fitness for office. I watched him serve with the strength and endurance of a man half his age. As you can see on an almost daily basis through events, statements, and social media posts, he is up early and ends his days very late."

Yet, the liberal media has always questioned his physical fitness to serve.

"That brings us to the juxtaposition of how the very same media covered the Biden administration," I explained to the committee. "The scrutiny that was baselessly directed at President Trump during his first term was wholly absent from the media coverage of the Biden White House. The media lacked any sense of curiosity that would naturally stem from what the public could see with their own eyes. Even in the face of deeply concerning—and public—signs of President Biden's mental and physical decline, legacy media outlets were silent."

That's not journalism.

That's a cover-up.

And the Biden administration's decision to revoke press credentials from 440 journalists is certainly part of that story.

Reporter Marco Caputo, who had previously worked at *Politico*, remembers those days well. "I was covering Biden at the time, and I remember coming to my editor and saying, 'Hey, we need to write about the Hunter Biden laptop.' And I was told this came from on high at *Politico*: Don't write about the laptop, don't talk about the laptop, don't tweet about the laptop. And the only thing *Politico* wound up writing was that piece that called it disinformation, which charitably could be called misinformation, at the least."

Glenn Greenwald, a far-left journalist who co-founded *The Intercept*, left his own publication because of the censorship. Fortunately for him, he found a voice—as many others, including myself, have—on Substack, a newsletter platform that welcomes and promotes free speech. As he explained in his column: "The final, precipitating cause is that *The Intercept*'s editors, in violation of my contractual right of editorial freedom, censored an article I wrote this week, refusing to publish it unless I remove all sections critical of Democratic presidential candidate Joe Biden, the candidate vehemently supported by all New-York–based *Intercept* editors involved in this effort at suppression. The censored article, based on recently revealed emails and witness testimony, raised critical questions about Biden's conduct. Not content to simply prevent publication of this article at the media outlet I co-founded, these *Intercept* editors also demanded that I refrain from exercising a separate contractual right to publish this article with any other publication."

He concludes: "The same trends of repression, censorship and ideological homogeneity plaguing the national press generally have engulfed the media outlet I co-founded, culminating in censorship of my own articles."

Journalists like Greenwald, who are committed to the truth—wherever it may take them, even if it takes them away from their own party—they are the ones who deserve White House press credentials.

Media privileges are earned in Trump 2.0—not guaranteed.

Brendan Carr, chairman of the Federal Communications Commission, sent a message to all media stakeholders on July 24, 2025: "The FCC has approved Skydance's purchase of CBS after the company made significant new commitments on: Addressing bias & restoring fact-based reporting, Ending discriminatory DEI, Investing in trusted local news. These changes would represent an important step towards earning back Americans' trust. Will be watching."

Of course, there will always be critics.

CNN's Brian Stelter tweeted, "Last night's Truth Social post urging his FCC chairman Brendan Carr to punish CBS is the latest example of Trump encouraging his appointees to apply government pressure against his critics. To be clear, there is no evidence of illegal behavior by CBS. And there is relatively little that Carr can do to impose 'punishment.'"

But Carr's actions weren't "punishment."

They were a decision to finally hold CBS accountable to the American people.

Broadcast outlets—ABC, CBS, and NBC—unlike cable outlets, use the public airwaves and have a legal obligation to be fair.

Trump 2.0 is making media institutions pay for their bad behavior.

As the *Los Angeles Times* has lamented, "To settle Trump's lawsuit over edits to a CBS '60 Minutes' broadcast, Paramount Global agreed to pay $16 million to help finance the future library and cover the president's legal fees. Walt Disney Co. earlier pledged $15 million to Trump's library to resolve a defamation lawsuit over inaccurate statements about Trump by ABC News anchor George Stephanopoulos."

These institutions will continue to pay the price—until they begin to tell the truth.

America First isn't a brand; it's a doctrine.

That doctrine is reshaping our country for the better.

Going forward, the media landscape will be forever changed because of Donald Trump's 2024 campaign and his second term in office.

We're not only making America great again.

We're making the American media great again.

What the president has described as "the enemy of the people" will, once again, protect the American people from falsehoods, distortions, and divisive lies—instead of a force actively manufacturing and promoting them because of new, independent voices using the technology and platforms that have spawned an entire new industry.

The media will no longer be a force eroding the United States from the inside.

In the Declaration of Independence, the Founding Fathers forecasted the changes we're seeing today:

"Governments are instituted among Men, deriving their just powers from the consent of the governed,—That whenever any Form of Government becomes destructive of these ends, it is the Right of the People to alter or to abolish it, and to institute new Government, laying its foundation on such principles and organizing its powers in such form, as to them shall seem most likely to effect their Safety and Happiness. Prudence, indeed, will dictate that Governments long established should not be changed for light and transient causes; and accordingly all experience hath shewn, that mankind are more disposed to suffer, while evils are sufferable, than to right themselves by abolishing the forms to which they are accustomed. But when a long train of abuses and usurpations, pursuing invariably the same Object evinces a design to reduce them under absolute Despotism, it is their right, it is their duty, to throw off such Government, and to provide new Guards for their future security."

Trump 2.0 is the revolution they envisioned.

It's the revolution that is making America great again.

Chapter 10

The Kirk Assassination

On September 10, 2025, the American political landscape was forever changed.

That's the day that a deranged gunman took the life of Charlie Kirk.

I'll never pretend to be able to articulate what a blow that was to America, and to the conservative MAGA movement.

It shows the darkness that's facing Trump 2.0.

It's a new dynamic that is still being ironed out, and it's integral to what makes this second term so important.

But before I talk about Charlie's assassination, I want to take a step back and look at what got us here in the first place.

We've been dealing with heightened political rhetoric for around the last twenty years. Wokeness, cancel culture, and similar leftist developments have increasingly polarized the country. We all watched as drag queen story hours replaced prayer in school, and during the COVID lockdowns when churches were shuttered while strip clubs remained open.

The Left has been at war with the Right for some time—often using American institutions to do the fighting.

But this is something different.

His first time around, Trump dealt with plenty of enemies. Mainstream media tried to silence him, the deep state tried to imprison him, even his own cabinet worked against him to hold back the America-first agenda.

It wasn't pretty.

Fast forward to the 2024 election: the Left still hates him. But this time, instead of bullies, they're using bullets.

Butler, Pennsylvania, July 13, 2024.

A matter of inches made the difference between Trump's second term and civil war.

The fact that such an act was possible, that it even got that close, is unthinkable.

You'd think that the Left (and the media) would have been jumping all over themselves to condemn it. But in the minutes and hours following the attempt, the media downplayed it.

A CNN headline from that day read "Secret Service Rushes Trump Off Stage After He Falls at Rally."

Falls? Really?

In the aftermath, mainstream pundits publicly worried that the assassination attempt would radicalize the Right.

Call me crazy, but I think the bigger thing to worry about is how and why a person was motivated and able to take a clean shot at President Trump. But this is the political environment we find ourselves in.

It didn't just happen once.

Just months later, another would-be assassin was somehow able to make his way onto the Mar-a-Lago grounds with a firearm.

That's two assassination attempts within seventy days of each other, and still, crickets from the media.

The media's inability (or just plain unwillingness) to unequivocally condemn left-wing violence is damning enough, yet it's not even the extent of it. Throughout this second term, Democrats have actively celebrated violence against the Right.

Case in point: the assassination of UnitedHealthcare CEO Brian Thompson.

On December 4, 2024, Thompson was gunned down in cold blood at point blank range, allegedly by young activist Luigi Mangione. The senseless murder of a husband and father should only warrant horror and sadness.

Instead, Mangione became a cult figure on the Left. Women fangirled over him, and men idolized him. A massive legal fund was established on his behalf. The outpouring of support for a murderer was, put simply, despicable.

One example that stands out is Taylor Lorenz: journalist and political influencer.

In the wake of Thompson's murder, she commented in an interview:

"It's hilarious to see these millionaire media pundits on TV clutching their pearls about someone stanning a murderer when this is the United States of America—as if we don't lionize criminals . . . you're gonna see women especially that feel like, 'oh my God, here's this man who's a revolutionary, who's famous, who's handsome, who's young, who's smart, he's a person that seems like this morally good man,' which is hard to find."

In another appearance, she said that when she heard of the killing, "I felt, along with so many other Americans, joy, unfortunately . . . maybe not joy, but certainly not empathy."

Remember, she's talking about a man who murdered a husband and father in cold blood.

This is the Left we are dealing with.

It's a completely new political dynamic that Trump 2.0 is having to both understand and navigate.

Which brings me to Charlie.

We've established the lead-up to Charlie's death: the rhetoric, the assassination attempts, the actual violence committed and excused by the Left.

But something about Charlie's murder feels different.

There are passionate pundits and influencers in both parties, but Charlie was unique—he made his living visiting college campuses and inviting dissenting voices to have a conversation.

With his talent, he could easily have been a divisive and radical figure and would have gained a significant following from it. But he looked beyond left and right—he pursued the truth.

He pursued it through honest conversations, primarily with those who disagreed with him. He went into places where he was hated.

Why? Because he was that passionate about bringing truth to those who otherwise may never hear it.

I think that's what makes his assassination so jarring.

He was trying to have a conversation with the Left, and they killed him for it.

To understand the gravity of Charlie's assassination you have to understand why he was on that college campus. For decades, those of us on the Right have not been permitted to speak on campuses—and all sorts of other groups and events. We have been cancelled, censored, and attacked.

After I left the White House, I spoke on several campuses, mostly through the funding and support of the Young America's Foundation. Whether it was University of California, Berkeley, Harvard, or University of Pennsylvania, I was always greeted by armed officers who would brief me on the security plan. Then it would usually be followed by an explanation of what the students were permitted to do to come at me *before* action would be taken. Often, behavior to heckle or even threaten the speaker (in this case me) was supported if not encouraged by faculty, staff, and senior administrators.

That's just not the case for liberal speakers.

It's not just colleges—many employers around the country are equally guilty of this. Merely expressing a conservative view or failure to abide by the woke agenda (like including one's pronouns) are cause for dismissal.

For years, the Left has insisted that Trump and MAGA are a threat to democracy. Chuck Schumer claimed we're coming to get a Supreme

Court justice. Representative Maxine Waters encouraged supporters to accost Trump staff in public places.

For the past decade the Left, through mainstream and social media, has led an entire generation to only hear one perspective. They rejected smart discourse, instead insisting that the other side posed an extensional threat to our existence.

Now they're surprised that their followers are killing their fellow Americans?

Calling someone Hitler, calling an entire subset of Americans Nazis, has taken its toll.

The problem of political violence isn't a "both sides" problem—something Democrats love to claim.

They used the assassination of Charlie Kirk to talk about political (translation: both sides) issues.

They cited the Paul Pelosi incident, the Whitmer kidnapping plot, and the Minnesota legislators shooting.

You know the talking points: "Radicalism on *both sides* stoked this fire."

"We need to condemn violent rhetoric on *both sides*."

"There is political violence on *both sides.*"

In their minds it works like this—I want to go lunch, you want to go to lunch—so both sides want to have lunch. It's equal. Except you want to go to a five-star restaurant and I want to go to Wendy's.

Yes, there is violence and extreme rhetoric on both ends of the spectrum. But look at what the Right is facing: the scale isn't even close to comparable.

The more I've thought about it, the more it's become clear.

There are two aspects they don't discuss: the lead-up and the response.

Poll after poll, survey after survey reveals the Left believes it's acceptable to use violence—and yes, even to assassinate your opponents.

And let's be clear: their so-called leaders do nothing to tamp it down. In fact, if you listen to Joe Biden, Chuck Schumer, or Maxine Waters, they incite and condone it. Then there is the response—whether at a Catholic school, against a young Ukrainian woman, or Charlie—our side is called to prayer and tributes—the Left, riots and vandalism.

The violent rhetoric has been one-sided for years.

In the aftermath of the killing of George Floyd the Left excused vandalism, violence, and widespread destruction.

They censored voices, they weaponized the judicial system . . . they've even attempted to kick their opposition off the ballot.

Their rhetoric is extreme—and violence is the natural result. It is not, as the media claims, mostly peaceful.

The truly despicable thing about it is that they aren't sorry for it.

Throughout all the fallout from recent political violence, I haven't heard Democratic Party leaders condemn this. The media also refuses to hold them to account—because the media doesn't believe they are part of the problem.

In the wake of Charlie's assassination, the response of many on the Left was to take to social media and support his killing—much like they did after the CEO of UnitedHealthcare was murdered in cold blood.

Polling shows that Democrats support violence as a means to silence their opponents. A report from the Network Contagion Research Institute showed that 55 percent of those left of center believe that assassinating President Trump would be at least somewhat justified. Almost 60 percent of those left of center agreed that destroying Tesla dealerships was "at least partially acceptable."

This report, "also discovered an online 'assassination culture,' found in predominantly left-leaning digital spaces, such as Bluesky and Reddit. This subculture justifies and glorifies political violence. Some of these networks' users wield the name 'Luigi' or use the Luigi video game character as coded endorsements of Brian Thompson's alleged assassin, Luigi Mangione. These users cloak explicit calls for violence in stylized memes. Many believe that political murder and sabotage are acceptable forms of protest."

They know that when we meet with them in open conversation, we win.

It's not subtle anymore.

A movement that cheers the assassination of an innocent man—that mocks his widow and calls for more murders before his blood is cold—that's not a movement that can be reasoned with.

This is the modern American Left.

Let's take a look at the other side, and what it means going forward for Trump 2.0 and the MAGA movement.

In the wake of Charlie's murder, his supporters and movement prayed, gathered peacefully, and held vigils in his honor.

The first Sunday after his assassination, thousands of people—many for the first time—attended church in his honor. Social media was flooded with calls for prayer and reflection on the faith that drove Charlie.

The best example of his legacy, however, is his memorial service.

It went by a lot of names: tribute, memorial, funeral—I think the best description for it is a revival.

I've never seen anything like it.

Hundreds of thousands of Americans coming together to worship, to hear the gospel, and to reflect on the life and legacy of Charlie.

You had the president and vice president of the United States, along with several cabinet members, coming together across denominations to share the gospel message.

If that isn't a turning point for this country, I don't know what is.

It also puts the final nail in the coffin of the "two sides" position when you compare it to the George Floyd BLM riots. Entire neighborhoods were destroyed for the sake of a drug addict with a criminal record. Meanwhile, mass prayer and churchgoing follows the senseless murder of a good man.

Still think there's not a clear good and bad side here?

If you ask me, the incredible response to Charlie's death is a preview of the future of MAGA.

Just take Turning Point USA.

In the aftermath of the assassination, TPUSA was flooded with requests for new chapters, as young Americans rallied around Charlie's organization and legacy.

The interest is clearly there—Trump 2.0 is dealing with a young generation of Americans who are serious about fighting for conservative principles and values.

Now we're confronting a new chapter in American politics: how does this momentum manifest itself into a movement?

It's an open question.

I think it goes without saying that whatever the answer is, it will be shaped in large part by Charlie's legacy.

He was a giant; the response to his death just reinforced what we all knew.

What other figure's memorial could draw award-winning worship artists, high-ranking journalists, cabinet members, and heads of state?

That's to say nothing of the millions of people he impacted, both in person and through his self-made platform.

In this way, we can see Charlie's death both as a magnifying glass and an alarm.

A magnifying glass because it highlighted the reality of leftist violence in America.

An alarm because it roused so many Americans from their political complacency.

Now, in Trump 2.0, we have a base of young people, tired of empty promises, who are ready to enact real change and fight the mind viruses that have caused senseless violence.

Harnessing this energy will be the great task of the remainder of Trump's term, and beyond.

Charlie's mission will endure and grow stronger—that's never been clearer.

The path forward isn't weak calls for unity with the side that's shooting. It's standing tall for the truth in a world full of lies.

That's what Charlie lived—and died—for.

Conclusion

The difference between President Trump's first term in office and his second term in office revolves around three pillars: *people*, *process*, and *policies*.

By people, I mean the super team that Donald Trump has assembled to carry out his second-term agenda. Vice President JD Vance. Secretary of State Marco Rubio. Secretary of War Pete Hegseth. Attorney General Pam Bondi. Secretary of Interior Doug Burgum. Commissioner of Food and Drugs Marty Makary. Secretary of Veterans Affairs Doug Collins. Secretary of Transportation Sean Duffy. Secretary of Energy Chris Wright. Secretary of Commerce Howard Lutnick. Secretary of Education Linda McMahon. Secretary of Treasury Scott Bessent. Secretary of Labor Lori Chavez-DeRemer. Secretary of Housing and Urban Development Scott Turner. Secretary of Agriculture Brooke Rollins. Secretary of Health and Human Services Robert F. Kennedy Jr. Administrator of the Environmental Protection Agency Lee Zeldin. Director of the Office of Management and Budget Russell Vought. Director of National Intelligence Tulsi Gabbard. Director of the Central Intelligence Agency John Ratcliffe. Trade Representative Jamieson Greer. Ambassador to the United Nations Mike Waltz. Administrator of the Small Business Administration Kelly Loeffler. Chief of Staff Susie Wiles.

Collectively, it's the most effective group of people we have ever seen in an administration.

His senior staff is equally critical to the success of the agenda. White House Communications Director Steven Cheung, Deputy Chief of Staff and political director James Blair, longtime communications aide Margo Martin, Staff Secretary Will Scharf, and National Security counterterrorism director Sebastian Gorka have all been by his side for years.

These leaders bring an incredible wealth of experience to the Trump administration. Hardened by the battles in their respective areas, they have the know-how to get the job done. They aren't career politicians who are content to just sit around and collect a check. They know that the president wants radical change. They know that the American people voted for radical change. And these leaders, they are absolute changemakers in their areas.

The left-wing legacy media loves to describe them as "loyal," but that misses the point. A dog can be loyal. Sure, they are loyal; but more importantly, they are disruptors who know how to enact the America First agenda. From trade to public health and education, they are getting results.

It's one thing to have the willpower. These leaders also share the president's vision for America. They are in office to enact it. They are in office to put America first.

But equally important, they understand the process. Even if you are committed to the agenda, how to get the job done matters. The bureaucracy and the Left know how to fight back, the levers to pull, and the forces against them—so understanding how to plow through it matters almost as much.

Robert F. Kennedy Jr. understands what needs to be done inside the Department of Health and Human Services to make America healthy again. Tom Homan understands what needs to be done to keep our borders closed again. Pete Hegseth understands what our sailors, soldiers, airmen, and Marines need to do to keep Americans safe.

The cabinet, sub-cabinet, and senior staff all understand what they need to do to make America great again.

It's not about résumés. It's about results. Trump 2.0 has brought in people who know how to fight and win.

There were people in the first Trump administration who didn't understand this process. They came in and had to figure it out on the job. That's not easy; and by the time Trump had left office, not everyone on his team had mastered it.

Worse, we learned that there were people in his first administration who weren't there to put America first. They were in it for themselves. They were there for corporate interests. In some cases, they were there to stop Trump's agenda. They were there to preserve the status quo.

Part of the reason these people made it into the administration is because the president didn't have a cadre of former government staffers. He was not a governor, a senator, a congressman, or a politician of any sort. He was an outsider in the truest sense.

It was his first time in office. People would walk up to him and say, "You know who would be good in this position?" "You know who would make a great Ambassador?" "You know who should be leading this agency?" The president was largely going off the recommendations of people who he thought had his best interests—and the interests of the American people—at heart.

To be sure, some these recommendations came through. In fact, some of those people are still with us today. They're working hard in the president's second administration. But many people who ended up with power in Trump's first administration should never have even been there in the first place. While the president and his closest allies were trying to drain the swamp, these people were working behind our backs to fill it.

Mistakes are bound to happen. But what separates winners from losers is the ability to learn from those mistakes.

Think about our team like the 1990s Chicago Bulls. I'm not making that comparison just because that was arguably the best team in the history of the NBA (and I say this as a Celtics fan). Rather, it is because the Bulls won the championship in 1991, 1992, and 1993. In 1994 and

1995, they sat on the sidelines and watched as other teams made it to the finals. Then they returned to the top—with what many NBA analysts consider the best basketball team of all time—to reclaim the title in 1996, 1997, and 1998.

Why this example is so apt is because of what they did between the wins. They were rebuilding their team, developing new strategies, and preparing for their next win.

That's what Trump and his team did during the Biden administration.

It's difficult to build a super team; we're lucky we had four years in between these two administrations to do it. They could look back at the people, the policies, and the process. They could reassess and think about how things could be different and how they could be better.

From what Ric Grenell and his team have done at the Kennedy Center, to the Department of the Treasury, to the Department of Education, to the Centers for Disease Control and Prevention, to the Department of Justice, to the renamed Department of War, President Trump has assembled an all-star team.

These leaders, who are ready to go with a list of America First policies, and who have proven their loyalty to the movement, are the leaders who will help President Trump realize his ambitious vision for the future of our country.

As I set out to write *Trump 2.0*, there were a few key questions that I wanted to answer for the American people. How is this presidency different from the last time President Trump was in office? Why is this presidency far more likely to succeed? How will this presidency create lasting change that can't be undone by the next administration?

If Trump 1.0 gave us a glimpse of what is possible, Trump 2.0 capitalizes on every one of those possibilities.

We have great challenges in front of us:

More government reforms, artificial intelligence, military dominance, ending our dependence on China (critical minerals, manufacturing, PPE, and pharmaceuticals) by creating policies that support production in the US, and finding a cure for cancer—among many other challenges right in front of us, to say nothing of the unexpected challenges that are no doubt on the horizon.

From the border to genetically modified organisms in our food, there is no problem that is too big, too small, or too far removed from the realm of usual politics for this administration to tackle. On the contrary, this second administration is the end of politics as usual. It's the beginning of real solutions—and real changes—that last.

We were battle hardened not just by our first four years in office, but by what came after we left office. To be sure, we made enormous progress over those four years.

The economy was thriving.

The border was more secure than ever.

And other countries—from Russia to China and Iran—knew the American president meant business.

It was a historic time in American history, and I'm grateful to have been a part of it as the thirtieth White House Press Secretary and Acting White House Communications Director.

However, much of the progress we had made was undone by President Joe Biden and his administration. The economy took a nosedive. The border had basically ceased to exist. Russia invaded Ukraine. China was emerging as a greater military and economic threat. And Iran looked like it was on its way to becoming a real nuclear threat.

If America was the international leader during Trump's first term in office, it was the international loser with President Biden at the helm.

While Biden was (literally) asleep during his four years in office, his administration vigorously worked to undo everything that President Trump had achieved.

That will not happen a second time.

Believe me, I would have loved to see Donald Trump remain in office for a second consecutive term. The commander in chief had put

America on the path back to greatness and it would have been thrilling to see what he would have accomplished next.

This president, he has no shortage of ambition. I've spent a good amount of time around the highest level of achievers in the world. The president is right there at the top. He is someone who is never satisfied, never content to just pack it up and call it a day.

From business to media—and now politics—Donald Trump isn't someone who follows a path created by anyone else. He is the trailblazer. And he blazes trails not only for himself, but for all the people who look to him for leadership.

If we had stayed in office in 2020, there really is no telling what he and his administration would have accomplished.

That is why Biden being sworn in as president in 2020 was so disappointing.

But the break has created incredible opportunities. There would be no America 250 celebrations had we won that 2020 election. There would be no FIFA World Cup or Summer Olympics on American soil. The USMCA review. The renewing of tax cuts. Even the new Air Force 1. None of it was supposed to happen during his second term, but now it is.

"Starting with America's 250th birthday celebration, President Trump is planning a years-long mega-celebration that puts him at the center of the world's biggest events," writes *Axios*. Why does this matter? "Trump's vision for the semiquincentennial goes beyond purely American fare to showcase the country's military, economic and cultural power on a global stage."

And there's no telling what other surprises for the American people are on the horizon.

As *Axios* reports, "Trump is floating additional programming like a 'Great American State Fair,' 'Patriot Games' and a 'Freedom Plane' inspired by the Bicentennial-era 'Freedom Train.'"

Unlike many of the Democrats—who would rather trash America than celebrate it—our president is proud to be an American. And that pride can be felt in everything he is doing for this country.

It's not just events.

It's not just policy.

It's the new Department of War.

It's the Gulf of America.

Trump is even leaving his imprint on the actual White House, in the freshly paved Rose Garden (where women used to get their heels stuck in the grass), in the Oval Office, in the Palm Room, and in the new ballroom (that is being paid for entirely with private funds), which will have a far larger capacity to host world leaders than the East Room of the White House. None of that could have happened had the president not had time to plan. These are the kinds of changes that you simply do not have time to think about during sequential terms in office. Whether you are the most diehard fan or biggest hater, you have to admit that having four years out of office to reflect on your return is making Trump the most consequential president in history. He is getting the job done.

As Susie Wiles commented to *Vanity Fair,* "Trump has been clear-eyed about what he wanted to do, 'having not been there for four years and [having] had time to think about it.'"

The *Washington Post* has written about many of the changes. "Construction of a triumphal arch to mark the nation's 250th anniversary, which was first publicly suggested by art critic Catesby Leigh in an article last year, would represent the president's most audacious effort to remake the landscape of D.C." In August, the president "also signed an executive order titled 'Making Federal Architecture Beautiful Again,' which called for new federal buildings to be constructed in a 'classical and traditional' style, in the spirit of the Capitol building or the White House, rather than the Brutalist or modern styles that became widely used over the past half century." He even announced a two year renovation of the Trump Kennedy Center beginning in July 2026.

Politico, for its part, focused on the "24-karat gilded ornamentation in the Cabinet Room, two massive flagpoles on the North and South Lawns, a paved patio over what had long been the Rose Garden's grass lawn and plans to break ground this fall on a massive new $200 million ballroom that will completely alter the scale of the White House's East Wing."

As this publication summarized it, "In a second term defined by the scope of Trump's unrestrained ambition, America's first property developer-turned-president is at times approaching the job like a modern day Howard Roark or Baron Haussmann, determined to leave his distinctive mark on the physical spaces that define the presidency and the nation's capital."

"Distinctive mark": that sums it up perfectly.

That new design vision extends to the digital world, too.

In this venture, President Trump has been aided by the first Chief Design Officer of the United States of America, Joe Gebbia. As Joe put it in a X post, "My directive is to update today's government services to be as satisfying to use as the Apple Store: beautifully designed, great user experience, run on modern software. An experience that projects a level of excellence for our nation, and makes life less complicated for everyday Americans."

To again quote the great philosopher Charlie Sheen: "winning."

And this time around, Trump is taking on culture as well. *Breitbart* founder Andrew Breitbart famously said that "politics is downstream of culture." In Trump 1.0 we largely ceded that ground, but not this time. During his first four years Trump did not attend a White House Correspondents' Dinner nor any of the Kennedy Center Honors events. This go-round, not only did he attend the Kennedy Center Honors, he helped choose the recipients and he emceed the event, which was broadcast on CBS. Oh, and then the board of the Center announced it would be renamed the Donald J. Trump and John F. Kennedy Center.

While what President Trump accomplished during his first term in office was, to be completely frank, monumental and historically unprecedented, he felt that it was just the beginning—really just the preamble to a brighter future for the United States of America.

That said, there were real problems with his first administration.

There were people in that administration who didn't have the willingness or courage to enact the policy changes we needed. To be honest, some of these people did not share the president's vision for America. They did not put the American people first. It was President Trump who was elected by the American people; yet, they stood in the way of his agenda.

The beautiful thing about nonconsecutive terms is that it forces you to take a step back. It forces you to take a long, deep breath. It forces you to look around. Who got the job done during that first administration? Who didn't? Who deserves to remain on the team and who should be let go? Who can we add to our team? Who are the very best people for the job?

These are the kinds of questions that great leaders ask.

These are the questions that President Trump asked.

In the end, this downtime forced us to reevaluate where we went wrong, where we went right, and what we would do better when we were back in office.

Now, he's back in office.

And he is more successful than ever.

As Frank Luntz said on CNN, "If you voted for Donald Trump, this is exactly—almost to the letter—what you wanted."

"Element after element," Luntz went on, "he delivered exactly what he said he was going to do."

We've all spent the past four years not only watching the decline of the United States, but also during that time planning what we would do to make our country great again. This time around, we have the people, the policies, and the understanding of the process to make America greater than it has ever been.

This isn't hyperbole.

This is Trump 2.0.

And the effects of this administration are going to be long-lasting.

We're showing the American people that the change that was once thought to be impossible is absolutely possible, with the right leaders in charge. All the talk in Washington—"this can't be done" and "this is the way things have always been"—has proven to be little more than swamp talk. When you have leaders who are not only willing, but prepared to overturn the status quo, the status quo will be overturned.

Just look at what President Trump has already accomplished during his first two hundred days in office. From the White House report published on August 7, 2025 titled "200 Days of Winning: President Trump Is Keeping His Promises":

"As President Donald J. Trump celebrates 200 days in office, the winning is never-ending—and if his first 100 days were historic, his second set was equally as impressive. From securing unprecedented trade deals and locking in massive investments to unleashing American energy dominance and ending woke culture, President Trump has accomplished more in his first 200 days than most administrations do over an entire term—and the best is yet to come.

President Trump made good on even more of his promises between Day 100 and Day 200:

PROMISE MADE: 'We're going to have very large tax cuts for workers and . . . No Tax on Tips, No Tax on Overtime.' (10/12/2024)

PROMISE KEPT: President Trump signed the One Big Beautiful Bill into law, delivering the largest tax cut in history for working- and middle-class Americans—including No Tax on Tips, No Tax on Overtime, and No Tax on Social Security—along with unprecedented tax relief for small businesses, farmers, workers, and families.

PROMISE MADE: 'We will close the border. We will stop the invasion of illegals into our country.' (10/12/24)

PROMISE KEPT: The US reached a new monthly immigration low for illegal crossings at the southern border—including multiple months in a row with ZERO illegal immigrants released into the country's interior. Border wall construction has resumed, with new border barrier projects underway in El Paso and the Rio Grande Valley.

PROMISE MADE: 'We get all these bad deals. We changed a lot of them . . . but still plenty of them out there—a lot of unfair deals. If China or any other country makes us pay a tariff . . . we will make them pay a reciprocal tariff.' (3/9/24)

PROMISE KEPT: President Trump reached eight historic trade deals with major US trading partners covering more than half of global GDP and tariff revenues have totaled $150+ billion—keeping his promise to liberate the country from decades of failed, anti-American trade policy.

PROMISE MADE: 'A vote for President Donald J. Trump is a vote for prosperity.' (9/13/24)

PROMISE KEPT: President Trump's America First economic policy has created a windfall in the stock market, with the S&P 500 and Nasdaq reaching new record highs several times over the course of the second hundred days—while inflation has moderated, business is booming, the economy is growing, and egg prices fell 67% from their peak.

PROMISE MADE: 'I'll insist that every NATO nation must spend at least 3%.' (8/26/24)

PROMISE KEPT: President Trump secured an agreement from NATO member nations to raise their defense spending to 5% of their GDP—a remarkable foreign policy feat long thought impossible.

PROMISE MADE: 'To reduce costs for both manufacturers and consumers, I will remove ten old regulations for every new regulation.' (10/10/24)

PROMISE KEPT: *The Washington Examiner*: 'Trump killing federal regulations at 10-1 rate, tops first term's 4–1 cut'

PROMISE MADE: 'I will defend religious liberty.' (1/19/25)

PROMISE KEPT: The Trump Administration directed all federal agencies to protect religious expression in the workplace.

PROMISE MADE: 'We are not going to allow child sexual mutilation.' (11/18/23)

PROMISE KEPT: Stanford Medicine ended sex-change surgeries for minors, Children's Hospital Los Angeles closed its 'Center for Transyouth Health and Development and Gender-Affirming Care,' UChicago suspended so-called 'gender-affirming care' for minors, Rush Medical Center halted so-called 'gender-affirming care' for new patients under 18, the University of Pennsylvania Health System all stopped so-called 'gender-affirming care' for patients under 19, Kaiser Permanente paused sex-change surgeries for patients under 19 across all its hospitals and surgical centers, and Yale New Haven Health and Connecticut Children's Medical Center announced they are ending their so-called 'gender-affirming care services.'

PROMISE MADE: 'We will keep men out of women's sports.' (5/26/24)

PROMISE KEPT: The US Olympic and Paralympic Committee banned men from competing in women's sports.

PROMISE MADE: 'We will make America safe again.' (11/4/24)

PROMISE KEPT: After deporting tens of thousands of criminal illegal immigrants, the US is on track to see the lowest murder rate on record.

PROMISE MADE: 'We will stop the Biden-Harris war on American energy . . . American energy is such a big deal. We will drill, baby, drill.' (8/3/24)

PROMISE KEPT: The Trump administration announced it is opening 13 million acres in Alaska to mining and drilling and terminated Biden-era preferential treatment for unreliable, foreign-controlled wind energy.

PROMISE MADE: 'We're going to go back to a merit system.' (8/29/24)

PROMISE KEPT: The Trump Administration rolled out new merit-based federal hiring plans.

PROMISE MADE: 'We're going to get your gas prices down.' (1/16/24)

PROMISE KEPT: *Breitbart*: 'Promises Made, Promises Kept: Memorial Day Set For Lowest Gas Prices in Over 20 Years'

PROMISE MADE: 'We will build a great Iron Dome over our country . . . a state-of-the-art missile defense shield that will be entirely built in America and create jobs, jobs, jobs.' (6/15/24)

PROMISE KEPT: President Trump announced a draft architecture and implementation plan for a Golden Dome missile defense system to protect our homeland from 21st Century threats—and secured funding for it in the One Big Beautiful Bill.

PROMISE MADE: '325,000 children are missing or dead. They came through the border . . . 325,000 children went through her stupid open border, and now they're either missing, dead, or slaves. If you want to end this disaster, you must get out and vote.' (11/1/24)

PROMISE KEPT: After the Biden Administration lost track of 325,000 migrant children, the Trump Administration has already located more than 13,000 of them—fulfilling President Trump's promise to do everything possible to save child victims of human trafficking.

PROMISE MADE: 'We're going to be way ahead on AI.' (12/12/24)

PROMISE KEPT: The White House unveiled America's AI Action Plan in order to secure US AI dominance and usher in a new golden age of human flourishing, economic competitiveness, and national security for the American people.

PROMISE MADE: 'I will also stop Joe Biden's crusade to crush crypto. We're going to stop it. I will ensure that the future of crypto and the future of Bitcoin will be made in the USA.' (5/26/24)

PROMISE KEPT: President Trump signed the GENIUS Act into law, establishing a regulatory framework for stablecoins and helping to ensure the US remains the global leader in cryptocurrency, and unveiled a framework for achieving US digital asset dominance—keeping President Trump's promise to ensure the future of crypto is American."

Having spent most of my adult life in American politics, I can't even begin to explain how significant these accomplishments are, especially when executed in such a short amount of time. As I've said before, an American president would be lucky to get one big win during their term in office. Winning has become the de facto state of this second Trump administration.

The winning isn't going to stop when President Trump leaves office.

Trump 2.0 is about building something that endures. Not tweets. Not headlines. Real change.

All of these interventions—from tariffs to the revocation of student visas—are like pilot programs. They are showing what the smart way and the right way forward for this country looks like. The success of this administration is bringing the American people on board. That is going to make it harder for the next administration to reverse course.

Just think about it for a second: Is the next administration going to bring back red dye No. 3? Are they going to let caravans of criminal illegal aliens back into our country? Are they going to let Iran go back to building a nuclear bomb?

Right now, even some of the Democrats are wising up to what the American people voted for. This kind of headline, published in *The Telegraph* on October 14, 2025, was once unimaginable: "California to ban ultra processed foods from school meals. The legislation is seen as a move by California's Democrats to outflank the Trump administration's efforts to reform American health."

The changes that we have been seeing are going to endure.

Do you think the American people are going to delete their X accounts and Substack subscriptions so they can go back to listening to fake news? Independent media was central to Trump's second election win and, fortunately for the America First movement, it isn't going anywhere.

But this is not the time to take our foot off the gas.

The Left still has its own agenda.

Democrats want DC to be a state not because of their concern for voting rights, but because it would give them one more vote in the US House and an additional two seats in the US Senate. In an age of close majorities, two additional Senate seats for them would be a massive hurdle to overcome. Think about the nominations. Historically, the odds of Democrats controlling the one chamber of Congress is high.

We cannot let that happen.

It would be nonstop investigations and weekly impeachment votes.

We also know why the Democrats love open borders. It isn't just about cultivating future voters (giving them a pathway to citizenship); it's also about affecting the census. It's about bodies in the country, not just citizens. Joe Biden, the president of the United States, claimed he could not do anything about the border—so let's clarify asylum laws, immigration based on merit. Let's keep playing offense, not defense.

And we cannot let the liberal tech wizards in Silicon Valley, the DEI indoctrinators still engrained inside our K-12 schools and colleges, woke judges and district attorneys, and other anti-MAGA forces shift the tide of elections, court decisions, and public opinion. After losing the presidential election by millions of votes, they are on the defense. And we need to continue fighting to keep them on the defense.

Trump 2.0 isn't the destination; it's the roadmap to a better future.

For those of us who are in the trenches, we need to continue to produce truthful coverage of the MAGA movement, we need to continue to secure Republican majorities, and we need to continue to pressure our federal, state, and local legislators to stick to the MAGA agenda.

Even within the Grand Old Party, there are people who don't share President Trump's vision for the country. We saw this when we were trying to pass the Big Beautiful Bill and our own members were the ones who were trying to keep funding PBS and NPR. Suddenly, it was our own people from within the party who were holding us back. It's our own people, in many cases, who are fighting the DOGE agenda, or who are siding with Big Food and Big Pharma when it comes to implementing the MAHA agenda.

While it's easier sometimes for us to look at the threats that we face externally, and they're obviously very real, we equally need to pay attention to the internal threats within the party, from people who claim to be on board with the agenda, but who are maybe just doing it to buy time—to wait out Trump, if you will. The politicians who aren't really committed to the America First agenda should not escape criticism and even the threat of being primaried by new politicians who are committed to our agenda.

Above all, we need to continue to remind our fellow Americans what winning feels like.

Winning feels good—and we are all learning what it feels like to be winners.

After four years of winning, the American people are not going to go back to losing in trade, in public health, on the border, and in the other areas that President Trump and his team have made great again.

Millions of Americans have already decided: The greatest country on planet earth will never be last again.

Afterword

What's Next—JD Vance

Trump 2.0 won't last forever.

The end of his historic second term is less than three years away.

Which brings me to the key question.

Does the MAGA movement end with Donald Trump?

Does the America First crusade that started on that golden escalator end with Trump's time in office?

Not by a long shot.

Trump chose well when he picked JD Vance to be his running mate, and if you ask me, Vance is showing that he's got what it takes to lead the next generation of MAGA.

He might be vice president, but Vance's role in Trump 2.0 has clearly showcased his ability to lead.

And it makes me optimistic about where MAGA goes after Trump.

The vice presidency isn't usually a very flashy job, yet Vance is taking a leading role in this administration.

We've seen it in foreign policy and domestic issues—it's clear that he's got what it takes to lead the next generation of conservatives.

Vance knows the people, he knows the policies, and maybe most importantly, he knows the process of president.

He knows what it takes to make America great.

Looking ahead to 2028, this is great news for the Right.

I want to start by talking about Vance and foreign policy.

Coming into the White House, he was untested on the global stage, yet he showed that he's got the negotiating chops to hold his own with world leaders.

Take his meeting with President Trump and President Zelenskyy of Ukraine—which occurred just over a month into his time in office.

Vance held his own in a publicly contentious discussion with Zelenskyy, showing both diplomatic savvy and cool under pressure.

This interaction set the tone for the critical role that Vance would play in American foreign relations.

He has been a key figure in US diplomacy throughout Trump's second administration, negotiating trade deals and traveling the globe to secure America's best interests abroad.

At the Munich Security Conference he delivered a strong message to the European powers. In it, he defended our shared values and goals while also calling out Europe's failed policies.

The remarks were an incredible showing of strength and diplomacy on a high-stakes stage, giving a preview of what we could expect in 2028.

It would have been easy for Vance to spend his time as vice president coasting on Trump's coattails.

And sure, he's got Trump's back when he needs him.

But he also plays an active role in negotiations, proving he can handle high-stakes decisions.

Vance has met the challenges facing Trump's administration as a champion for America.

Quite a step up from Kamala's time as border czar.

That's exactly what we want—and need—in our leader.

We've seen that Vance has what it takes to be presidential on the world stage, what about domestically?

On the policy front, he's a powerhouse.

Since day one, Vance has been huge in promoting the work of Trump's administration.

He's relentless in his role as president of the Senate, pushing bills like the Laken Riley Act and the One Big Beautiful Bill over the finish line.

He's voted to confirm Trump's nominees, ensuring the agenda moves forward.

He's also been a great partner to members of the cabinet, appearing at events and coordinating key policy initiatives.

And he's proved he can handle the domestic battle of calling out dishonesty in media—he's a strong voice for truth against the Left's deception.

Trump started a tradition of bypassing traditional mainstream media, and Vance has taken that example and run with it.

He's appeared on many alternative media shows, during both the Trump campaign and presidency.

His conversations with figures like Theo Von reached millions of young Americans, resonating with them in a relevant medium.

And that's to say nothing of his work with organizations such as Turning Point USA, which has done wonders to galvanize the conservative movement.

I could give countless examples of Vance's domestic accomplishments, but I think the best examples of his domestic leadership have come in the wake of the Kirk assassination.

Weeks after Charlie's murder, Vance appeared at a TPUSA event, both speaking and taking questions from an audience at Ole Miss.

It was a glimpse into how well he can lead.

Vance didn't dodge tough questions; he sparred with them, covering tough topics like immigration, Israel, Big Tech, and religion, among many others.

He defended conservative values on everything from border security to economic fairness.

One student pressed him on Trump's tariffs; Vance fired back, explaining how they've added fifty thousand steel jobs and forced the EU to buy $750 billion in US energy by 2028.

It was a masterclass in connecting with young people.

It showed both Vance's command of issues and relatability.

You don't see that often.

One of the most powerful men in the world, willing to engage with college students—many of whom disagree with him.

This wasn't one of the scripted, teleprompter-led appearances that we're used to seeing from presidents.

Vance took questions in real time from young Americans who wanted to engage with him.

And as we've seen through his actions, he isn't just good at explaining talking points; he can actually get the job done.

That's the kind of hands-on leadership that we need.

And it's exactly what will resonate with the younger generation

During his appearance at Ole Miss, Vance commented on his role in Trump's second administration:

"I believe that I have been placed in this position for a brief period of time to do the most amount of good for God and for the country that I love so much."

Right on, Mr. Vice President.

It's just the latest proof that Vance has got what it takes to guide the next generation.

He speaks to the heart of the movement—young and working-class Americans tired of elites and empty promises.

He's not afraid to call out the media's bias or the Democrats' open border chaos.

If you ask me, that's leadership.

The GOP needs someone who can rally the base and win the middle, and Vance is showing he's that guy.

I'm excited to see him step into his own as the administration continues its work.

His TPUSA performance, Senate work, and foreign policy chops prove it.

The Left's been steadily losing ground because they can't cater to the next generation; meanwhile, Vance is embracing it.

In 2028, there is only one person who is currently in a position to carry the torch of the Make America Great Again movement: JD Vance.

Since day one of Trump 2.0, JD has been critical to the success of President Trump's second term in office. Aside from the president, there is no one who better understands the *people*, the *policies*, and the *process* needed to make this country great again.

When JD Vance accepted the vice-presidential nomination at the Republican National Convention in Milwaukee, Wisconsin, on July 17, 2024, he was clear: "Tonight is a night of hope. A celebration of what America once was, and with God's grace, what it will soon be again. And it is a reminder of the sacred duty we have to preserve the American experiment, to choose a new path for our children and grandchildren."

Since he took office on January 21, 2025, Vice President Vance has honored his promise to the American people. Along with President Trump, he has been tirelessly working to secure the American border, to make our country once again the world leader in trade, and to make sure our NATO allies are finally paying their dues.

Moreover, he understands the need for smarter defense and cleaner intelligence, the critical importance of DOGE, and where our media has gone astray. Whether he is walking through Union Station in Washington, DC, visiting our National Guard troops, or speaking to our Marines at Camp Pendleton in Southern California, JD Vance also understands the need to protect the United States from our many enemies—both foreign and domestic.

JD Vance has served our country courageously as a US Marine.

He has served our country honorably as a US Senator.

And he is now serving our country boldly as the fiftieth vice president of the United States of America.

If President Trump is the architect of the America First movement, then Vice President JD Vance is its natural successor.

He has proven time again that he is not only loyal to the MAGA movement, he also understands the people, the policies, and the process needed to continue realizing our president's bold vision for the future of the United States of America—and the world.

Trump 2.0 won't fizzle—Vance can carry it to the next generation of Americans, ushering in a new era of conservative greatness.

In 2028, there is no question.

JD Vance is our man.

Acknowledgments

I owe a huge thank you to President Donald J. Trump.

He has worked tirelessly to ensure that his second administration has the people, the policies, and the processes in place to make America great again.

I also owe a big thank you to the Democrats: Joe Biden, Kamala Harris, Alexandria Ocasio-Cortez, Chuck Schumer, Nancy Pelosi, Elizabeth Warren, Corey Booker, Hakeem Jeffries, and Democratic National Committee Chair Ken Martin.

Your failed leadership, sense of direction, and broken moral compass have paved the road for the MAGA movement.

I also want to thank the liberal media.

If you had done the job you were paid to do, so many Americans would not have turned to X, Substack, Truth Social, and other platforms where the truth still lives.

Finally, I want to thank the 77,302,580 Americans who voted the forty-fifth president back into the Oval Office in a landslide victory.

Your demand for radical change was heard.

Trump 2.0 will not let you down.

Please stay in touch at seanspicer.com.